THE CULTURAL FOUNDATIONS OF ECONOMIC DEVELOPMENT

One of the principal reasons why international aid programs have often been unsuccessful is that imported solutions are not based upon the indigenous institutions in African countries. In *The Cultural Foundations of Economic Development*, Emily Chamlee-Wright argues that connections between these institutions and the cultural context which produces and sustains them has been misunderstood by mainstream economic theory which is fundamentally acultural.

Instead, Chamlee-Wright argues, the economics of the Austrian school provide a far stronger theoretical framework which can introduce cultural analysis into questions of economic development and other market processes.

The author draws on extensive ethnographic field research as well as a challenging and original critique of mainstream neoclassical analysis in a detailed case study of women entrepreneurs in Ghana.

Emily Chamlee-Wright is Assistant Professor of Economics at Beloit College, Wisconsin, USA.

FOUNDATIONS OF THE MARKET ECONOMY
Edited by Mario J. Rizzo,
New York University
and
Lawrence H. White
University of Georgia

A central theme of this series is the importance of understanding and assessing the market economy from a perspective broader than the static economics of perfect competition and Pareto optimality. Such a perspective sees markets as causal processes generated by the preferences, expectations, and beliefs of economic agents. The creative acts of entrepreneurship that uncover new information about preferences, prices, and technology are central to these processes with respect to their ability to promote the discovery and use of knowledge in society.

The market economy consists of a set of institutions that facilitate voluntary cooperation and exchange among individuals. These institutions include the legal and ethical framework as well as more narrowly "economic" patterns of social interaction. Thus the law, legal institutions, and cultural or ethical norms, as well as ordinary business practices and monetary phenomena, fall within the analytical domain of the economist.

THE CULTURAL FOUNDATIONS OF ECONOMIC DEVELOPMENT

Urban Female Entrepreneurship in Ghana

Emily Chamlee-Wright

London and New York

First published 1997
by Routledge
11 New Fetter Lane, London EC4P 4EE

Simultaneously published in the USA and Canada
by Routledge
29 West 35th Street, New York, NY 10001

© 1997 Emily Chamlee-Wright
Typeset in Garamond by Routledge

Printed and bound in Great Britain by Creative Print and
Design (Wales) Ebbw Vale

British Library Cataloguing in Publication Data
A catalogue record for this book is available from
the British Library

Library of Congress Cataloguing in Publication Data
A catalogue record for this book has been requested

ISBN 0–415–16994–1

To Mom and Dad,
who taught me all the important things:
how to love, how to laugh, and how to sail.

CONTENTS

ACKNOWLEDGMENTS

I owe many thanks to those who provided helpful comments and direction in the course of writing this book, including: George Ayittey, Michael Alexeev, John Paden, Jack High, Peter Boettke, Deirdre McCloskey, Mark Addleson, Roger Koppl, and two anonymous referees. Their guidance and suggestions were invaluable in completing this project.

To my mentor and dear friend Don Lavoie, I owe a debt which can never be repaid. He was instrumental in carving out the vision to which this project aspires. Through his example, a student learns that there may be no higher calling than that of scholar, as the only true weapon against tyranny is knowledge.

Equally important to the completion of this project are the organizations which provided financial support for research and travel, including: The Center for the Study of Market Processes, The Gilder Foundation, The Earhart Foundation, The Institute for Humane Studies, and The Atlas Foundation.

I also want to thank the entrepreneurs of Ghana who participated in this study, and my interpreters. It is my sincerest hope that they will some day benefit from what is written upon these pages.

I wish to thank my colleagues in the Department of Economics and Management at Beloit College for their encouragement and support. For helping me to maintain a sense of humor and perspective, special thanks go to my best friend and greatest love Brian Andrew Wright. Last, but not least, thanks go to a Labrador retriever named "Barley," a most diligent co-author. Any mistakes which remain are solely my own and Barley's.

INTRODUCTION

> For any reform to be permanent and enduring, it must be based
> on and rooted in the principles of the aboriginal institutions.
> (John Mensah Sarbah 1901, cited in Langley 1979: 98)

> The needle you are looking for in the haystack may be right
> there at your feet.
> (Ga proverb, cited in Ayittey 1991: xxxviii)

In his study of indigenous African institutions, George Ayittey
(1991) proposes a radical notion. He argues that the principal
reason why international aid programs have not met with an acceptable record of success is that imported solutions do not rest upon
the indigenous institutions which have emerged over the course of
African history. Only solutions based upon indigenous institutions,
he argues, will have a lasting positive impact. By disrupting the
social and economic fabric of developing economies, international
lending institutions may be doing more harm than good. The best
way to foster economic development, Ayittey states, is dramatically
to reduce rather than increase international aid assistance. A radical
proposition, indeed.

If Ayittey is correct, the ramifications for the development disciplines and the international organizations set up to promote
economic development are immense. It would require us not only to
rethink our strategies for promoting economic development, but
also to reconsider what the crucial elements of economic development actually are. Society's particular institutions and their cultural
context become focal points for development analysts. The introduction of the new institutional economics into development theory
has contributed a great deal to our understanding of how and why
social institutions, such as property rights, credit institutions, law,

1

and rules of contract are instrumental in the development process. Yet the connections between these institutions and the cultural context which gives rise to and supports them is far less understood. Much more work needs to be accomplished in this area if we are to understand fully the role particular institutions play in the economic development of particular societies.

The social institutions necessary for economic development emerge from and reflect a particular cultural context. Successful strategies for enhancing development must be similarly rooted. In the West African context, the role of women in indigenous market trading is one such example. The female-specific networks of kinship, friendship, and business relationships have produced culturally specific ways of acquiring capital, and securing mutual assistance. If we are to find useful solutions to under-development, as Ayittey suggests, economic analysis will have to turn to the cultural realm. The mainstream of economic inquiry unfortunately offers little opportunity to explore the connections between cultural processes and economic development.

As will be argued, the Austrian school of economics offers an alternative to mainstream theory by which the study of culture and the study of economic development can be brought together. Three themes within the Austrian school are particularly relevant in this endeavor. First, the Austrian emphasis on how knowledge is generated, transmitted, and used in the market process extends to all social processes, including cultural evolution and the ways in which culture establishes the foundations for economic development. Second, Austrian theories of entrepreneurship focus our attention squarely on the source of economic development—individual entrepreneurs in the market context—which, surprisingly, is missed in mainstream economic thought. Third, the tradition of radical subjectivism within the Austrian school offers a direct path by which culture can be imported into economic analysis. This tradition allows us to recognize the perspectival nature of knowledge: how market perceptions and decisions, and thus economic development itself, are shaped by the cultural context.

It will be argued that indigenous solutions to overcoming economic development do indeed exist in the Ghanaian context. The arguments made here are informed by field research conducted in 1991 and 1992, mainly in Accra, the capital city of Ghana, to a lesser extent in Kumasi, Ghana's next largest city, and in a smaller market area outside of Accra known as Madina. Participant observation in the market areas and in-depth interviews with market women were the principal empirical methods employed. While a set survey approach might have afforded more quantifiable generalizations, the interviews allowed the perspective of the market traders themselves to emerge. Given the thesis that cultural perspective shapes market decisions and the development process, the interview approach seemed more appropriate.

Before turning to the theoretical arguments made in Chapter 1, a historical and economic background is offered to introduce the reader to the Ghanaian context. Besides some basic geographic and demographic information, a brief historical summary is provided, as well as an overview of Ghana's economic structure and the urban market context. In this brief introduction, no attempt is made at original scholarship. Rather the point is to acquaint the reader with the rich texture that is Ghana's history and society. Following the overview of the urban context, chapter summaries are also provided.

THE GHANAIAN CONTEXT

Geographical features

Physically, Ghana's roughly rectangular shape covers an area of 238,537 square kilometers in the tropical zone. Ghana shares a western border with the Ivory Coast, a northern border with Burkina Faso, and an eastern border with Togo. The coastline rests along the fifth latitude and runs 554 kilometers along the Gulf of Guinea. Ghana reaches approximately 850 kilometers north. The flat area along the Atlantic is called the Accra Plains. The hills and dense vegetation of the tropical rain forest begin approximately 75 kilometers northward. The annual rainfall in the southern plains is 750 millimeters, and the annual rainfall in the forested areas can reach averages of 2,000 millimeters. Beyond the rain forest belt lies the savanna region where annual rainfall falls back to about 1,000 millimeters per year. Temperatures range from 22–27° Celsius in the coldest month of August, to 24–31° Celsius in the hottest months of March and April.

Population and ethnic composition

Ghana is home to approximately sixteen million people. The largest urban area is the capital city Accra. Accra lies on the coast, with a population of approximately one million people. Kumasi, with a population of about 440,000, lies 270 kilometers inland. The next largest city, Tema, with a population of approximately 206,000, lies just to the east of Accra along the coast. The largest city in far northern Ghana is Tamale, with a population of just over 100,000.

Ghana's population is a mosaic of ethnic diversity. While the official language of Ghana is English, approximately seventy-five languages and dialects are actually spoken, each associated with a different ethnic group. The largest tribal group are the Akan, which include the Ashanti, primarily in the central region, the Fanti along the coast, the Nzima in the southwest, the Brong in the western region of the country, and the Akim and Akwapim in the northern hills. Taken together, the Akan constitute over 44 percent of the population. The other principal groups of the southern region are the Ewe, accounting for 13 percent of the population, and the Ga-Adangme who constitute 8.3 percent of the population. The mainly northern Mole-Dagbani tribal group, which includes the Dagomba, Frafra, Dagarti, Kusasi, Moshi, and Mamprussi peoples, accounts for 15.9 percent of the population (Pellow and Chazen 1986).

GHANAIAN POLITICAL ECONOMY: A BACKGROUND

Trade and urbanization extend far into West Africa's past. The archeological mound-site of Jenne-jeno in the flood plain of the inland Niger delta provides the latest evidence of early West African trade and urbanization (McIntosh and McIntosh 1984, 1993; Phillipson 1993). Founded in the first century BC as an agricultural village, Jenne-jeno had emerged as an urban center by the first century AD. McIntosh and McIntosh (1984) found that the inhabitants exported food, including millet, sorghum, and rice, in exchange for iron, copper, and stone that the inland delta lacked. By the seventh or eighth century, gold was also accepted and circulated within Jenne-jeno.

Between the tenth and fourteenth centuries, the great trading states of the Western Sudan flourished as mediators in long-distance trade between black Africa and the Mediterranean populations to the north. The ancient trading state of Ghana constituted one such political and economic center. Though the center of ancient Ghana was located far to the north of the modern state which now bears its name, the two are indirectly related, in that the main trade routes of ancient Ghana connected the Arab populations in the north with the northern region of the modern Ghanaian state (Pellow and Chazen 1986). Though the long distances kept most northern goods from reaching the coastal areas to the far south, the coast eventually

4

came to play an important role in long-distance inland trade as the source of salt and fish (Daaku 1971).

As inter-regional markets developed, so did local markets, many operating on a daily basis. Markets supplied not only essential goods and services, but provided a central point of communication for the dissemination of information concerning commerce and news of interest to the community. Further, marketplaces served as cultural, political, and religious centers. The marketplace was not separate from spiritual or community life, but rather, was intricately tied to every aspect of life. In short, the marketplace was the heartbeat of African society. Or as Ayittey (1991: 329) puts it, "Perhaps the most pernicious punishment that could be inflicted on an African society was to destroy its market, as this would assail its inner sanctum."

By the fifteenth century, Europeans had arrived on the West African coast, the Portuguese arriving first in 1471. Principally, the Portuguese were in search of gold, as suggested in the name they imparted to the area—the "Gold Coast." In 1482, the Portuguese built a castle at Elmina, establishing a trading headquarters that attracted African traders from the inland areas. The European presence did not so much establish a new trade network, however, as extend the existing trade networks (Daaku 1971). Trading became so active that by the late sixteenth century, the Gold Coast was the source of one-tenth of the world's gold supply. In 1553, the British arrived, followed by the Dutch in 1595, the Swedes and Danes in 1640, and the Germans in 1683. In the early seventeenth century, the dominance of the Portuguese was replaced by British, Dutch, and Danish merchants.

Though gold remained a principal European interest, the emergence of plantation agriculture in the New World fueled the slave trade in the late seventeenth and throughout the eighteenth centuries. In all, Europeans eventually took over one million slaves from the Gold Coast. Slaves were captured by enemy tribesmen and exchanged for European manufactured goods. Slave traders then took them to America to exchange for minerals and agricultural crops. In turn, the European traders sold the American agricultural goods in their home countries (Pellow and Chazen 1986).

During this period, the Europeans restricted their trading to the coastal areas, leaving control over the inland trade routes to the native populations. In the late seventeenth century, a collection of Akan chiefs known as the Ashanti Union (centered in Kumasi) established political and economic control over the supply of both gold and slaves. Their principal trading partners were the Dutch who had taken over the trading castle at Elmina. The Ashanti Union also controlled much of the local trade in imported European goods. Their principal adversary was a similar coalition of Fanti, which had established control over the coastal trading area in and around Accra and Cape Coast, mainly trading with the British. Both the Ashanti and the Fanti sought to control coastal trade with the Europeans, leading to periodic conflicts between the two states.

Through the eighteenth century, the British had refrained, for the most part, from intervening in Ashanti–Fanti conflicts. But the nineteenth century brought with it increasing pressure from economic and political interests to take a more proactive role. In 1807, political, economic, and humanitarian considerations inspired Britain to abolish the slave trade. Enforcing the ban proved more difficult than had been anticipated. The Ashanti ignored the British prohibition on slave trading, continuing to supply slaves to other Europeans. It was apparent to the British government that the merchants were incapable of enforcing the ban, and thus more direct intervention was necessary. In 1821, the British government assumed political dominion over coastal forts in an effort to rein in the resistant Ashanti. The British forged an alliance with the Fanti who sought protection from the Ashanti Union. In a final move, the governor of British West Africa led a failed military attack against the Ashanti, only to be killed in the conflict.

The British government saw this episode as reason for avoiding political alliances with native interests and further imperial expansion. Yet the Fanti and the British merchants still sought protection for their interests (Pellow and Chazen 1986). Administrative control was thus returned to the merchants, under the leadership of George Maclean. During Maclean's tenure, the tensions between the Fanti and Ashanti eased, substitute commodities for the slave trade were found, and the volume of trade expanded dramatically.

From 1820 to 1850, West African trade with Britain and France alone increased by a factor of six or seven. In 1817, Britain imported 297 loads (50 cubic feet) of West African teak, but in 1837, imports had increased to 23,251 loads. The imports of other hardwoods, such as ebony and mahogany, tripled in the same period (Newbury 1971). West African exports of palm oil increased by a factor of 24.9 from 1820 to 1850. British exports to West Africa, principally cotton, salt, iron, and woolens, correspondingly increased. Between 1820 and 1850, cotton exports to West Africa increase by a factor of 47.7. Between 1827 and 1850, iron exports to West Africa increased by a factor of 5.6, and woolens by a factor of 13.8 (Newbury 1971).

Beside an increase in trade, Maclean also facilitated increased political control by issuing a series of bonds with local chiefs. Beginning with the Fanti Bond in 1844, these agreements gave the British limited authority to administer justice in the region. At this point, there was no direct attempt to govern. Over the next thirty years, however, the traditional states which had entered into the bond agreements—referred to as the "British protectorate"—gradually found their political autonomy threatened by British control. Even the Fanti who had sought alliance with the British were beginning to resist their authority (Pellow and Chazen 1986).

In 1868, the British purchased the Elmina fort from the Dutch, and the Ashanti, who had long resisted the British, attempted to drive them out by taking control of Cape Coast and Elmina. The British responded by invading and destroying the city of Kumasi. In 1874, the Ashanti reluctantly entered into a treaty with the British, relinquishing all claims to the coastal forts, and the Gold Coast was declared a British colony. But neither the geographical area, nor the nature of the relationship between the British and native peoples were precisely defined at this point (Rimmer 1992). Ashanti resistance did not end with the treaty, and the British responded with another invasion of Kumasi in 1895, exiling the *Asantehene* (the Ashanti king) to the Seychelles Islands. By 1900, Ashanti power had been effectively demolished, and in 1902, the colonies and Ashanti protectorate which constituted the Gold Coast were formally defined.

Between 1890 and 1910, the structure of the Gold Coast economy was again transformed. Cocoa had been introduced to the Gold Coast by missionaries in the 1860s, but exporting did not begin until the 1890s. In 1891, 80 pounds of cocoa were exported. By 1911, cocoa exports had increased exponentially to 89 million pounds, and the Gold Coast had become the world's largest cocoa supplier. During this period, gold exports were also on the rise. In 1891, gold exports were less than 25,000 ounces. By 1911, gold exports had increased to 280,000 ounces (Rimmer 1992; Szereszewski 1965). Up until World War II, these two commodities dominated the colonial economy, though the mining of manganese, bauxite, and industrial grade diamonds was also initiated in the early twentieth century. Infrastructural improvements made by the colonial government, particularly in rail transport and harbors, dramatically lowered costs in mining and cash-crop industries.

Politically, the colonialist government became increasingly interventionist. In 1904, the British governor was given the authority to confirm local chiefs. Interventionist policies were stepped up further after the 1919 appointment of Gordon Guggisberg as Governor, who sought to improve the prospects for economic development through Western education and infrastructural improvements.

As Rimmer (1992) argues, the influx of wealth and the introduction of Western education into indigenous society gave rise to a new African elite—elite status being determined by education and European life-styles rather than traditional concepts of status and authority. Though they were small in numbers, the new intelligentsia represented the seeds of what would grow into a nationalist movement, eventually bringing colonial rule to an end. The Aboriginal Rights Protection Society (ARPS) was formed in the 1890s to impede the British in further expropriation of uncultivated land. The ARPS provided a forum by which educated Africans would challenge British political control, calling for African representation on the Governor's Legislative Council.

The seeds of anti-colonialism planted by the ARPS and other voluntary organizations both before and after World War I, had firmly taken root by the end of World War II. The United Gold Coast Convention (UGCC), headed by the prominent lawyer J.B. Danquah and others among the "new African elite," called for the transfer of British control in the "shortest possible time." Kwame Nkrumah's entrance into Gold Coast politics began here, as the executive secretary of the UGCC. Yet Nkrumah's pan-Africanist vision was far more radical than that of the UGCC leadership. In 1949, Nkrumah established his own organization called the Convention People's Party (CPP). The CPP called for the immediate transfer of power from colonialist rule. The CPP had a much wider populist appeal among the poor and middle classes than the elite members of the UGCC could capture.

Attempting to crush the growing political dissent, the colonialist government imprisoned members of the UGCC in 1948 and Nkrumah in 1950. In both cases, mass protests led to their release. The inability of Britain to maintain control was becoming evident and in 1951, the British agreed, in principal, to eventual Gold Coast independence. A new constitution was adopted and local elections were held, though Britain still retained colonial control. Despite the fact that considerable political tensions divided the African leadership, Nkrumah's Convention People's Party won handily in the 1951 elections, and later in 1954 and 1956. Nkrumah continued to press for full independence. On 6 March 1957, full independence was granted and the Gold Coast was renamed "Ghana" in homage to the ancient African empire.

Under Nkrumah's leadership, Ghana's economic structure would once again be transformed. Armed with the advice of leading Western development economists, Nkrumah launched a "big push" development planning strategy in which the state would take the lead in industrializing the Ghanaian economy. In Chapter 2, much more will be said regarding this period of Ghana's economic history, but suffice it to say that the economic policies instituted under Nkrumah were a resounding failure. Rapid and severe economic decline resulted in a military coup in 1966, toppling Nkrumah and the CPP from power. The country was returned to civilian rule in 1969 under the leadership of Dr. Kofi Busia, only to be terminated by another military coup led by Colonel Ignatius Acheampong. The corrupt military dictatorship continued until 1979, when yet another military coup threw the old guard from power. Flight-Lieutenant Jerry Rawlings and a handful of other junior military officers returned the country to civilian rule for a short time, only to recapture control through another military coup in 1981. Throughout the period following Nkrumah, the economy only worsened. The heavy interventionist policies instituted by Nkrumah continued up into the 1980s. Only since Rawlings reluctantly adopted the IMF Economic Recovery Program (ERP) in 1983 — designed to reduce government intervention in the economy—has the Ghanaian economy shown any signs of economic improvement.

PRESENT ECONOMIC STRUCTURE

Economic performance and the regulatory environment

Since 1983, ERP reform measures have improved Ghana's economic performance considerably. The negative growth rates which were characteristic of the 1960s and 1970s have turned positive, with an annual average of just under 5 percent since 1983. However, considerable hurdles remain. The 5 percent growth rates have only served to help Ghana regain the ground lost in the post-colonial era. A per capita GDP of $430 in 1993 still lags behind the average of $520 for other sub-Saharan countries (Armstrong 1996: 38). An average

9

inflation rate of 25.2 percent in 1993 represents an improvement over previous years, but is high nonetheless (Armstrong 1996: Table 5.3). Private investment has been slow to improve and only represented 4 percent of GDP in 1993 (Armstrong 1996: Table 5.8). Though the regulatory environment has improved overall, high taxes, a heavy bureaucratic sector, and remaining regulatory controls continue to hinder economic performance (Steel and Webster 1991).

Structurally, the Ghanaian economy is almost evenly divided between agriculture (including food crops, cash crops, and timber) and services (including wholesale and retail trade, communications, transportation, finance and insurance, and government social services) as the dominant sectors of the economy, but this represents a decline in the clear dominance agriculture once represented. Since the beginning of the ERP, agriculture's share in GDP has fallen from 52.5 percent in 1984 to 41 percent in 1993. The political and economic uncertainty of the post-colonial era gave farmers little incentive to maintain or expand their crops. In particular, the long maturation process needed for cocoa production has meant a rocky recovery in this industry. Poor growing conditions in 1984, 1988, and 1991 resulted in falling levels of cocoa production, but modest gains have been made in more recent years (Armstrong 1996: Table 5.5). In 1984, industry (including mining and manufacturing) represented 11.3 percent of GDP, growing to 14.1 percent in 1993. But the significant increase has been in the service sector. In 1984, services accounted for 36.2 percent of GDP, rising to 44.9 percent in 1993 (Armstrong 1996: Table 5.5).

Agriculture

The principal food crops are maize, yams, cassava, cocoyams, plantains, groundnuts (peanuts), sorghum, and millet. Secondary food crops include bananas, tomatoes, rice, onions, and oranges. Cocoa is the principal cash crop, accounting for 40 to 60 percent of total foreign trade earnings between 1987 and 1990 (EIU 1995). The major industrial crops are oil palms, cotton, rubber, sugar cane, and tobacco, yet none of these represent a substantial portion of GDP.

One-third of Ghana's land area is covered by forest, (though not all of the area is suited to commercial purposes). In 1991, timber, which represented 3.9 percent of GDP, was the third largest foreign exchange earner behind cocoa and gold. Yet concerns over deforestation—an estimated 2 percent annual loss of total forest cover between 1981 and 1990—place the sustainability of this industry in doubt.

Mining

As noted earlier, gold is one of Ghana's oldest export industries. Ninety percent of the gold is found in underground mines in western Ashanti, and the rest in riverbeds in the Ashanti and Central regions. In 1938, eighty gold mines were in operation. The economic decline from the 1960s to the 1980s reduced investment and forced the closing of most of the gold mines, leaving only four operating mines in 1987. However, economic liberalization has inspired increased investment in gold mining, and in 1993, foreign exchange earnings from gold surpassed those of cocoa. Ghana has also improved its production in manganese, bauxite, and industrial grade diamonds, but production levels have not returned to full capacity since the economic decay following independence. The annihilation of rail transport and general infrastructural decline made large-scale mining of bauxite and manganese prohibitively costly. Even with infrastructural improvements, the lack of investment has inhibited recovery in these industries.

Manufacturing

With the big push industrialization policies of Nkrumah and subsequent governments, manufacturing claimed a 10 percent share of GDP in the 1960s. By 1970, manufacturing had increased to 14 percent of GDP. Through protection, subsidization, or outright government ownership, the state supported aluminum smelters, timber processing plants, cocoa processing plants, breweries, cement factories, oil refineries, textile factories, and vehicle assembly plants. Yet on average, such firms were only running at one-quarter capacity, even as late as 1981 (EIU 1995). The only reason any of the firms survived at all was the protectionist measures which kept foreign firms from competing. The liberalization policies instituted under ERP have meant the demise of many white elephant projects. Foreign competitors offering superior quality and lower costs resulted in the closing of 120 factories between 1988 and 1992 (EIU 1995). Yet liberalization has also meant an increase in the emergence of private enterprises. Between 1986 and 1990, the Ghana Investment Centre reported that 444 manufacturing projects had been approved (though even more remain caught in the bureaucratic morass).

Foreign trade

Significant exchange rate devaluation measures instituted with the ERP have made it difficult to discern a general pattern in foreign trade. The removal of restrictive trade policies has improved the availability of imported inputs, and devaluation has made Ghanaian exports more attractive on the world market. Yet balance of payments deficits have been the norm in the 1980s and into the 1990s.

Gold, cocoa, and timber account for the lion's share of export income. In 1993, total foreign exchange earnings were roughly $1.08 billion, of which gold earned $416 million, cocoa earned $280 million, and timber earned $140 million. These leading industries were followed by electricity, diamonds, and bauxite. Ghana's principal export markets are Germany, followed by the United Kingdom, the United States, and Japan. Capital goods represent 43 percent of Ghana's total imports, intermediate goods represent 28 percent of total imports, fuel and energy (mostly oil) represent 10 percent of total imports, and consumer goods represent 10 percent of total imports (EIU 1995). Ghana principally imports from the United Kingdom, followed by Nigeria, the United States, and Germany.

The legal status of the informal sector

According to the International Labor Organization, 60 percent of the work force in sub-Saharan Africa is employed in the informal sector. In Ghana, 80 percent of all food is marketed in the informal sector. As food accounts for the largest proportion of the average Ghanaian's income, informal sector conditions play a central role in determining nutrition standards, particularly in the urban context (Armstrong 1996). Formal supermarkets exist in Ghana, but they cater generally to foreign business people and diplomats (Lawson 1971). Cloth for clothes, tailoring and seamstress services, dry goods provisions, as well as fresh produce, are all purchased in the informal sector. Thus, for most Ghanaians, the "informal market" is the only market and to the extent that it is hindered by government restrictions, the average person's standard of living can be greatly affected.

The legal status of informal market trading is generally a matter of degree. In the 1960s and 1970s, trading in the informal market itself was considered legal in Ghana. Yet most traders sold their goods well above the state-controlled prices, making their economic activities illegal. Today, much of the informal economic activity has a quasi-legal status. Trading on the street in large urban areas is officially illegal, but unofficially tolerated by city officials who collect fines from thousands of hawkers who come to market each day. Fines and the confiscation of goods can interrupt trading for days, destroy credit relationships with suppliers, and even force traders to leave the urban market and return to their villages.

Traders who have access to designated market stalls enjoy a better legal status and have an easier time avoiding fines, as long as they pay their stall taxes to the municipal authority. However, their legal status remains ambiguous if they are not the officially designated occupant, which is often the case. Most traders have gained access to market stall space by "inheriting" it from a relative or by making side payments to a former occupant. As the market stalls are officially owned by the municipal authority, such arrangements give the traders no legal claim in a dispute involving the city council.

THE URBAN MARKET CONTEXT

The most striking demographic shift in late twentieth century Ghana has been the dramatic increase in urbanization. In 1948, Ghana's population was approximately 4.4 million (the Census figure having been adjusted by 7.5 percent in later estimates), and the population had been growing by about 1.6 percent per year since 1931 (Rimmer 1992). In 1948, only 13 percent of the population lived in urban areas. By 1960, the Census recorded a total population of 6.727 million people, an (adjusted) increase of 3.5 percent per year. The proportion of people living in urban areas had jumped to 23 percent of the population by 1960. Today, over a third of Ghana's sixteen million people live in urban areas. While the total population has increased by a factor of 3.67 since 1948, the urban population has increased by a factor of 9.23 (Rimmer 1992).

The development of Accra is representative. From 1921 to 1931, the population of Accra increased from 38,000 to 60,000. It rose to 135,000 in 1948, to 388,000 in 1960, and stands at over a million today. Up until World War II, the traditionally urban Ga were the dominant ethnic group, but immigration into Central Accra and the suburban area outside of Accra soon rendered them in the

13

minority (Robertson 1984a). The increasing population was partially due to improved sanitation and health care facilities, which decreased infant mortality rates and increased life expectancy. From 1930 to 1960, average life expectancy among Gold Coast natives increased from thirty to forty-five years (Robertson 1984a). But the lion's share of the increase in the urban population has come from domestic rural and international migration.

Historical development in the urban context

Prior to the introduction of European trade, the area upon which the capital city of Accra now sits was a center for agricultural trade along the coast (Belasco 1980). Yet the arrival of the Portuguese in the fifteenth century marked a turning point in the evolution of the city, which developed as a series of settlements. By the mid-seventeenth century, Accra was a major center for European trade with West Africa. Ga and Fanti traders brought European goods, salt, and fish to the interior, in exchange for gold and slaves. The control the Ga and Fanti maintained over the coastal area brought with it pronounced increases in wealth, not only for the traders connected to the tribal leadership, but for many average traders who sold in the local and nearby markets as well (Daaku 1971).

The history of trade in Kumasi was directly connected to the developments in Accra and the conflicts which emerged between the Ashanti and Fanti. In the seventeenth century, the Ashanti had established their capital in Kumasi and controlled most of the gold mining areas and interior trade routes which extended the trans-Saharan network to the European traders at Elmina. Yet the growing dominance of the British fueled tensions with the Ashanti. In the early nineteenth century, the British and their Fanti allies threatened the Ashanti with blockades to enforce the prohibition on slave trading. When the British purchased the Elmina fort from the Dutch in 1868, this represented one of the few remaining direct links the Ashanti had with non-British European traders, and inspired the attacks by the Ashanti army in 1870 and 1874. After the British countered back by destroying Kumasi and exiling the *Asantehene*, British control over the city assured open access to the coastal Fanti and northern tribes who migrated into the Ashanti region to engage in trade. Such groups eventually migrated into Kumasi itself.

Over the centuries, Accra also emerged as an ethnically heterogeneous society. The seven segments which constitute Central Accra

14

are still identified with the ethnic groups which settled there. Though intermarriage has often blurred ethnic identity and practice, distinct cultural identities persist, and Accra remains a multi-lingual city (Robertson 1984a). The oldest settlements of Gbese, Asere, and Abola are predominantly Ga. The Akwamu and Denkyera settled Otublohum. Collectively, these four segments are referred to as Ussher Town, the area controlled by the Dutch from the seventeenth century. Sempe and Akanmadze were settled by the Akan, particularly the Fanti. Alata was settled by Nigerians who were brought to the coast to build European trading forts (Robertson 1984a). Sempe, Akanmadze. and Alata are collectively referred to as James Town, the area controlled by the British. With the sale of the Dutch forts in 1868, British dominance had been secured. Accra became not only an economic but also a political center for British control. In 1877, the British moved the administrative headquarters from Cape Coast to Accra.

The prosperity in Accra and Kumasi diminished somewhat after the British ban on slave trading was imposed at the beginning of the nineteenth century, but trade in gold dust and ivory continued, and palm oil also became an important export in the first half the nineteenth century. By the end of the nineteenth century, Accra had also become an important source of skilled labor, as missionaries trained Africans in carpentry, masonry, tailoring, and shoemaking (Szereszewski 1965). The other important trend taking place at this point was the increasing cultivation and trade in cocoa. After World War I, infrastructural improvements in roads and rail transport in and around Accra laid the foundation for the accelerated urbanization which has taken place since World War II. In 1923, the railroad line between Kumasi and Accra, financed principally by cocoa revenues, was completed. The railroad quickly became the major artery for cocoa transport, and galvanized both Kumasi and Accra's central position in the world market for cocoa. Further, it was in the inter-war period that the first major market stall areas were built. In 1924, Makola Market No. 1 was built in Accra and the local government in Kumasi issued bonds to establish a series of market stall areas. While the colonialist government argued that the market stalls would improve sanitation, it was also clear that sedentary traders (as opposed to mobile hawkers) made tax collection much easier (Clark 1994).

15

Women in the urban market

In the West African context, market trading has long been considered women's work, and this role only became more entrenched in the colonial period. Though some colonial influences might have discouraged the role of women in the market, such as Christian teachings regarding women's domestic role, other aspects of colonial rule served only to reinforce women's position in the market. As more and more men engaged in long-distance trade, the concentration of women in local market and near-distant trading increased. Some wealthier women did engage in long-distance trade, both with Africans and Europeans, but they often employed younger men or slaves to carry out their business. Further, missionary training in the skilled trades, with the exception of sewing, were offered only to men, leaving women as the dominant force in market trading (Szereszewski 1965). Lastly, Western education which had been provided to men afforded them opportunities in the civil service and clerical positions, again leaving indigenous market trading to women.

Today, anywhere from 70 to 83 percent of market trading in the southern urban areas is conducted by women (Clark 1994; Lawson 1971). Women typically sell local food staples such as yam, cocoyam, cassava, and plantain, as well as secondary food crops such as tomatoes, rice, onions, bananas, and oranges. Besides food crops, the most dominant market in Accra is the cloth trade. Cloth is also an important commodity in Kumasi, but most of the premium wax print cloth is imported from the United Kingdom or the Ivory Coast and the ports of Accra give it a privileged position in this particular industry. Women also sell dry goods and other provisions, beads and jewelry, fresh meat and dried fish, and prepared foods such as *kenkey*, small meat pies, and bakery items. These represent the major categories, but odds and ends of all sorts can also be found, such as utensils, cosmetics, locally produced soap, sandals, linens, and fashion accessories.

The market stall areas are relatively well defined, with particular areas designated by the commodity sold there, though the rules of what one can sell vary in their flexibility from one commodity to another. In the cloth market, for example, a trader might sell scarves or accessory items, but neighboring cloth sellers will not tolerate food or other goods which might stain their supplies. Yet a trader may sell cloth elsewhere in the market if she chooses. Yams, cassava, plantains, tomatoes, and other major commodities all have their designated areas, but again it is not uncommon to find onions being sold in the tomato market or vice versa.

Outside of the relatively ordered market stall areas, one can find virtually all the same commodities (with the exception of fresh meat) being sold by hawkers, either walking the streets or perched on the sidewalk. From the consumer's perspective, this represents a sort of convenience shopping. Buying from hawkers saves the time needed to navigate the maze of the covered market, but the quality, variety, and prices can be better inside the market stall area.

The market traders who represent the focus of this study are themselves connected to a much larger network of suppliers, whole-sale traders, importers, and manufacturers. Clark's (1994) description of the wholesale yards just outside of the Kumasi market area, provides a contrasting image to the bustle and concentration of traders in retail trade.

> The wholesale yard or *bode* (plural *mbode*) represents quite another type of visually distinct location specialized by commodity. Each of the local foodstuffs sold in the highest volume has a wholesale yard along the outer edge of the market, where trucks can squeeze in to unload. The small numbers of traders dwarfed by huge piles of goods there contrast sharply with the surrounding open retail areas, where swarms of small-scale retail traders dwarf the goods they display. Wholesale traders use stacks of boxes, bags, or baskets to keep squatting retailers and passing traffic from encroaching on their territory.
>
> Clark (1994: 8)

Most of the wholesale traders are based in the city itself, buying from farmers who have brought their produce in from the field, or traveling buyers who contract with farmers in the rural areas and transport the produce in. Local wholesale traders may sell most or all of their supplies in the morning, often offering goods on credit to the more trusted retail traders. Others will sell throughout the day to hawkers who only have enough to purchase small amounts and need to return frequently to replenish their supplies (Clark 1994).

Most of the traveling wholesale traders are also women, and negotiate with both male and female farmers directly for produce, such as yams and cassava, which can be harvested in large quantities. For highly perishable produce which requires more frequent harvesting, such as tomatoes or garden eggs (white eggplant), individual farmers

17

will not provide traveling traders large enough supplies. Thus, farmers will bring their produce to local village markets where traveling traders can make bulk purchases (Clark 1994).

An option frequently employed by market traders is to enter into a partnership with another trader, often a daughter, niece, or sister, such that one travels to secure goods at a low price while the other stays behind to conduct the retail business (Robertson 1984a). In the case of agricultural goods, the farmer him or herself may also be kin. Trade in cloth, jewelry, and other imported goods can also take this form among wealthy traders who can afford international travel.

The distribution of imported and locally manufactured goods follows something of a pyramid pattern in which operating capital and credit worthiness determine a trader's position within the pyramid. High-volume market traders and shop owners are able to deal directly with the import firms, securing the best price with high-volume purchases. Often such sales are provided on credit, but the perceived risk is generally small, as only established traders and shop owners will be considered for such an arrangement. Mid-level traders then purchase cloth from local high-volume traders. In turn, mid-level traders may also supply cloth to hawkers, often at or near cost, for a niece, daughter, or cousin starting out in business.

The networks of business partnership, friendship, and kinship among female market traders will be a central focus of the analysis presented in later chapters, as they provide a crucial vehicle by which women negotiate strategies for economic survival and success. In turn, such networks possess the potential to foster the development of indigenous markets.

CHAPTER SUMMARIES

The central thesis of this study is that the process of economic development relies in part on the cultural resources at hand. However, economists' understanding and appreciation of the role culture plays is, in general, rather weak. In Chapter 1, a case is made in favor of a culturally informed economics. It is argued that economic anthropology failed to deliver such a paradigm because neoclassical economic theory—a fundamentally acultural construct—was seen as the only way to describe economic processes. The new institutional economics makes important progress in recognizing the role institutions play in the development process, but again, the adherence to neoclassical constructs limits our understanding of the interconnectedness of cultural and economic processes. The tradition of radical subjectivism within the Austrian school of economic thought, on the other hand, offers a better foundation for such a project. The radical subjectivist tradition within the Austrian school starts with the understanding that most market decisions, at least those which are of any interest, are based on complex personal interpretations. The interpretations may be informed by the decision maker's past experience, the language in which he or she speaks and thinks, and his or her cultural perspective. Thus, Austrian economics offers a path by which we might introduce cultural analysis into the study of market processes.

In Chapter 2, an Austrian interpretation will be offered as to why development policy in Ghana failed so dramatically following the colonial period and why it continues to yield disappointing results in the present context. The Austrian literature on the nature of knowledge within social processes will be employed to diagnose the failure of industrialization and development planning under Nkrumah in the 1960s. Again, a culturally informed economics is relevant here as the attempt to eradicate indigenous market institutions and the cultural forces which lie at their foundation is an important aspect in understanding this era in Ghana's post-colonial history. Further, Austrian arguments will inform current policy debates regarding World Bank and state efforts to promote the indigenous private sector.

In Chapter 3, it is argued that indigenous tribal and religious structures provide the institutional requirements essential to economic development in Ghana. Indigenous sources of conflict resolution, and evolving systems of property and inheritance have laid the foundation for an emerging entrepreneurial class. Further, indigenous religious concepts and ethical standards regarding responsibility and kinship combine to establish a vibrant capitalist ethic in southern Ghana. Lastly, the traditional role women hold in the market, and the relative autonomy indigenous concepts of family and marriage afford women, suggest that Ghanaian women may indeed have the greatest potential for leading the way towards economic development.

In Chapter 4, some of the strategies market women employ to overcome obstacles and to take advantage of opportunities their position affords them will be investigated. It will be argued that indigenous networks of credit and mutual assistance which arise out of the indigenous cultural context have the potential to foster economic development. Yet, as will also be discussed, appropriate policy measures must be instituted if such ends are to be realized.

In Chapter 5, profiles of three market women are presented. Here, we take the opportunity to present the whole person in order to gain a better understanding of how entrepreneurs face constraints and forge plans within a specific cultural context. In Chapter 6, we return to the theoretical considerations of building a culturally informed economics.

1

MARKETS AS AN EXTENSION
OF CULTURE

A walk through central Accra, the capital city of Ghana, is almost a
religious experience for an economist. Ghanaian marketplaces are
the site of intense and vigorous bargaining. Although it is officially
illegal to trade outside the market area designated by the city
council, the streets teem with hawkers selling produce and fish from
their head trays. What strikes the economist most is the precision
and efficiency of these small transactions. The sidewalks are scarcely
passable as market women perch four deep on either side. Their
voices rise and fall in laughter and conversation, briefly pausing to
catch the attention of potential customers. The camaraderie and
good nature of the market should not deceive the observer into
seeing the marketplace only as a point of social contact, however.
While it undoubtedly fills this role as well, the keen alertness to the
smallest of profit opportunities is always at work. In southern
Ghana and many cities of West Africa, this is the work of women.
Some young men dot the marketplace selling frozen yogurt or
second-hand clothing, yet the majority of goods are marketed by
women and girls (Lawson 1971; Pellow 1977; Clark 1994).

A striking pattern which emerges is the hierarchical nature of
goods sold and the conditions under which women and girls trade.
Girls sell water from jugs atop their heads to bus commuters,
parched from the dusty hot car-park. Girls and young women hawk
baked goods or traditional foods that their mothers or aunts have
prepared. Women of various ages sell fish and produce either from
head trays or seated on the sidewalks. The most comfortable conditions are those within the established market stalls. Here is where
one will find more expensive items such as imported cloth for sale,
as well as staple foods, canned goods, jewelry, and a few services
such as sewing.[1] While the conditions here are cooler and cleaner,

21

access requires financial capital many market women do not have—limited access to capital being the most frequently cited problem microenterprise entrepreneurs face throughout the developing world (Kurwijila and Due 1991; Levy 1993; Lycette and White 1989; Squire 1981; Steel and Webster 1991; United Nations 1995).

In the first four decades of research on developing countries, the role of women in the market system was all but ignored by mainstream economists. The male bias of the profession in the early years of the economic development discipline, along with Western notions of women's role in economic activity, contributed to this oversight. The main mechanism for the oversight was the miscategorization of female market activity as a variant of domestic labor (Smith 1978). The habit of not counting domestic labor as real economic activity still pervades the discipline and is itself problematic (Anker 1994; Goldschmidt-Clermont 1994; Waring 1988). This mistake is compounded, however, when the public nature of female work is systematically ignored. Indeed, much of the indigenous African market is driven by women, in part as a means to fulfilling their domestic responsibilities. According to the United Nations Development Fund for Women, female labor and entrepreneurship accounts for 80 percent of all the food produced, processed, and marketed in sub-Saharan Africa. This may even be too conservative an estimate, given the hidden character of women's work in Muslim areas (P. Hill 1969; Schildkrout 1983). The tragedy is not just that women have been slighted by not receiving due recognition for their role in economic growth. The real tragedy lies in the fact that, since women were ignored, the indigenous economy was also overlooked for its role in economic development.

More recent research has significantly improved our understanding of the importance of informal market trading to economic development. For various reasons—including the questionable legal status of firms in the informal economy, the desire to avoid revealing income levels to government officials, and the ease with which entrepreneurs both enter and leave the informal market—measuring the size of the informal sector presents many practical problems. But recent attempts to establish a more accurate accounting of the informal sector relate to the significant role indigenous markets play around the world. In their extensive survey of the informal sector in Peru, for example, Hernando De Soto (1989: 61) and the Instituto Libertad y Democracia found that 83 percent of market trading in Lima was attributed to the informal sector. The International Labor Organization (ILO) estimates that 61 percent of the urban labor force in sub-Saharan Africa are employed in the informal sector (ILO 1990). Thus, if for no other reason, the role indigenous markets play in employment, production, and distribution necessitates that they capture the attention of development theorists and policy makers.

Much of the literature concentrates upon the limitations indigenous markets face, particularly their inability to take advantage of economies of scale. Yet, the small and medium-sized enterprises characteristic of the informal sector also have particular advantages in production and marketing. Relative to large-scale industry, microenterprises within the informal sector can often take advantage of low-cost labor, they can more easily fill niche markets, and have the potential to be more flexible in responding to changing market conditions (Sandesara 1991). With the advent of structural adjustment programs designed to reduce the size of the bureaucratic sector, indigenous markets often represent the best hope of avoiding widespread unemployment and deepening poverty; but this also means that those who already operate within the indigenous economy will face even greater competition (Parker *et al.* 1995; Steel and Takagi 1983).

It is clear that development analysts must now take informal or indigenous markets seriously in their search for solutions to continued economic stagnation. What is less clear, however, is what tools to employ in our attempt to better understand the potential and limitations of indigenous markets; to understand the contributions made by and the constraints faced by indigenous entrepreneurs. Further, finding such tools is essential if we expect to make wise policy recommendations.

As we study indigenous markets up close, we find that standard economic models pass over much of the context-specific detail of market and other social processes. Rules which govern credit acquisition and capital accumulation, for instance, differ dramatically from one cultural context to another. (See, for example, Timberg and Aiyar (1984) for India; Shanmugan (1991) for Malaysia; Hiebert (1993) for Vietnam; Little (1965) for West Africa.)

Corporate practices which support economic success in one cultural context, such as the Japanese use of Confucian symbolism, ceremony, and training, often meet with failure in another (Clegg and Redding 1990), as they do not fit the new cultural context (Lavoie and Chamlee-Wright forthcoming). Government institutions often meet with different records of success depending on the cultural and historical context, as Putnam *et al.* (1983; Putnam 1993) found in their studies of Italian regional governance. Patterns of economic development once assumed to be universal, are now recognized as contingent and dependent upon cultural and historical influences. Trade among the Kenyan pastoralists known as the Orma, for example, became widespread as a result of the conversion to Islam as it provided a common institutional structure by which to engage in long-distance and inter-temporal exchange (Ensminger 1992). Standard neoclassical economics cannot adequately address such issues, as it has no way of incorporating the role of culture in the market process. This chapter is an attempt to integrate cultural analysis within our economic methodology so that we might be in a position to better understand the nature of economic development itself, and to have a better guide in our search for sound economic policy.

The term "culture," as it is used here, is not simply meant as an independent force imposing itself on social institutions and individual behavior. Rather, culture is intimately connected to social institutions and individual behavior. Culture is better characterized as a context rather than an independent force. Culture is not just a list of rules constraining behavior that would otherwise maximize profit or utility. Culture is the context in which meaning is negotiated and renegotiated. Social institutions depend upon this framework of meaning, as it provides legitimation to institutional rules. Police and court systems would be incapable of enforcing property rights and contracts, for instance, if most members of a society did not accept the legitimacy of the institutional rules. Such acceptance comes not from social contracts devised in the abstract, but through an evolutionary process within the culture of a community.

Not only does culture provide the "glue" which enables social institutions to stick, it is the context in which individuals make sense of the world around them. Objects and actions have no inherent meaning in and of themselves. Individuals must interpret their meaning within a particular language community, at a particular point in history, in reference to a complex of meanings that have already been read out of previous experience. Culture provides the interpretive framework that allows us to understand objects as symbols, actions as part of an overall plan, or interaction as social relationship. The world is never experienced directly. It must be interpreted through the lens of culture. Thus, understanding complex social interaction—the sort which is most interesting to economists, anthropologists, and other social scientists—will require us to address the cultural context in which it takes place.

Introducing aspects of culture is not novel to economics, yet a full appreciation has not yet been realized. Economists usually recognize only two functions of culture within the economy—determining preferences and constraining optimizing behavior. The first approach, or what we might call "Culture as Preferences" is the most dismissive. Since economic analysis generally takes preferences as given, the forces which shape those preferences tend to be of little interest. This position assumes that once preferences are formed, they play a neutral role in the market process. Yet, if cultural influences promote distrust for one's fellows as the basis for wise business practices, we can expect that the costs of acquiring credit are higher in this case than in cultures where trust is the initial response. The Grameen Bank in Bangladesh has used the trust and shared sense of mutual obligation present among women in that culture to generate a 98 percent loan recovery rate from their practice of group-lending (Wahid 1994). The capacity of some ethnic groups, as within Jewish, Chinese, and Indian cultures, to resettle across vast distances while maintaining tight bonds of kinship, nationality, and identity have enabled them to establish successful global economic networks (Kotkin 1992). Cultural and economic processes do not neatly separate out from one another. Such "preferences" for caution, trust, and ethnic identity are not neutral. Rather, the specific cultural context shapes and directs individual economic choices and the market process.

The second approach, or what we might call "Culture as Constraints," concedes a slightly more active role to culture, as it recognizes the non-neutral role customary rules, which evolve out of the cultural context, might play in constraining optimizing behavior. For example, Akerlof (1980) describes how individuals may adhere to social customs over time, even if it is economically disadvantageous, if there is a corresponding cost in lost reputation for non-compliance. Thus, the social custom of a "fair" (but above market-clearing) wage may result in unemployment and the inefficient allocation of resources. Within development literature, customary practices or value systems are blamed for discouraging the efficient allocation of resources (Lewis 1955; McClelland 1961). Traditional allegiance to the family farm rather than expansion into alternative trade, for example, is blamed for stifling economic development.

Yet, this approach fails to recognize the *enabling* role culture plays in economic processes. By selecting out only those aspects of culture which inhibit allocative efficiency, we set culture up as a counter-rational force; as if without culture, market exchange would be a smooth frictionless process. Yet, in accepting this account of the world, we forget that in a world without culture, property rights, legal custom, and language would not emerge. We have to ask ourselves how smooth and frictionless exchange would be without the benefit of such institutions. Further, culture is the context of shared meaning that enables the entrepreneur to make sense of the economic environment. Neoclassical literature tends to treat economically efficient or "correct" decisions as separable from the cultural context. However, in the abstract, efficiency only means that certain criteria are well-balanced against other criteria. Just what those criteria are have to be interpreted. Other than at the most abstract level, any meaningful notion of efficiency will be, at least in part, culturally defined. Wise or efficient decisions will only be so with reference to a particular context—including the cultural context. Thus, rather than a counter-rational force which inhibits efficient decision making, culture provides the framework within which to interpret the best course of action.

Economic anthropologists have a much longer history than economists in attempting to bridge the gaps between culture and economic theory (see, for example, Malinowski [1922] 1961). By the late 1930s, economic anthropologists were beginning to accept the principles of neoclassical economics as their theoretical guide in what were then called "primitive societies." For the time, this was a significant move, as it suggested that all peoples—whether European or African, colonialist or native—shared the universal quality of rationality. If all individuals were essentially the same in this respect, then neoclassical tools and concepts ought to be equally applicable around the globe. Many within anthropology saw this as a radical advance, as it provided a theoretical framework within which to model and understand non-Western cultures. Similarly, such a move represented a crowning achievement for neoclassical theory, as it could generate explanations for social and economic behavior across the globe.

But the match which seemed to be made in heaven was not to survive. By the 1950s and into the 1960s, neoclassical economics faced serious challenges as to its universal applicability. Many economic anthropologists argued that a theoretical paradigm which grew out of an advanced industrialized context would ultimately distort rather than explain the realities of pre-industrial societies. Cultural anthropologists also rejected neoclassical theory as incapable of addressing the differences among cultures with regard to economic decisions and institutions. Most anthropologists accepted the validity of neoclassical theory when applied within a Western indus-trialized context. But for their own areas of interest, most were willing to leave the principles of economic theory behind.

The debate over the role neoclassical theory can play in pre-indus-trialized contexts dominated the economic anthropology literature of the 1960s. The "formalists" were those who argued in favor of the universal applicability of neoclassical theory, even in pre-industrial societies. The "substantivists" were those who saw this as an empty enterprise, given the industrialized context out of which neoclassical economics emerged. The formalist–substantivist debate has been detailed elsewhere (LeClair and Schneider 1968). The point behind revisiting the debate here is to identify the subtler shortcomings of neoclassical theory which were missed by both sides. This new perspective of the debate will open the way for an alternative route by which the connections between culture and economy can be investi-gated; yet perhaps this time, with greater success.

The "new institutionalist economics" represents an important advance in this direction, as it attempts to ground neoclassical anal-ysis within specific institutional contexts—a dimension of the market process essentially missed within standard theory. We will move a step beyond this by investigating the cultural context which gives rise to social institutions on the one hand, and shapes the perspective with which entrepreneurs carve out opportunities for profit on the other. In order to make this next step, Austrian economics offers an alternative to the institutionless, cultureless neoclassical paradigm. In particular, the interpretive tradition within Austrian economics and cultural anthropology makes it possible to address the role culture plays in shaping entrepreneurship and the social institutions necessary for economic development. Such an approach may convince social scientists outside of economics to consider once again the value of economic theory in their own inves-tigations. Further, cultural analysis will allow economists to address questions that are systematically pushed aside by neoclassical theory, but which are fundamental to the development process.

ECONOMIC THEORY AND ECONOMIC ANTHROPOLOGY

Considered by many to be the father of economic anthropology, Bronislaw Malinowski was among the first to investigate the social context of economic activity. His ethnographic studies of Trobriand Island ([1922] 1961) detailed the complex rituals of indigenous exchange practices, and explored the functions of magic in instilling hope and confidence before setting out upon trade expeditions. The talent Malinowski possessed as an ethnographer, however, did not save him from drawing some erroneous conclusions.

Malinowski ([1922] 1961) rejected the notion that Trobriand Islanders were motivated by self-interest. In fact, he held economic theory in disdain and characterized the "primitive economic man" concept in mocking tones. In his account of the Trobriand Islanders' yam harvest, Malinowski argues that rather than self-interest, the prestige behind the title *tokwabagula* or "good gardener" was the primary motivation.

> The most important point about this is, however, that all, or almost all of the fruits of his work, and certainly any surplus he can achieve by extra effort, goes not to the man himself, but to his relatives-in-law . . . [I]t may be said that about three quarters of a man's crop go partly as tribute to the chief, partly as his due to his sister's (or mother's) husband and family.
>
> But although he thus derives practically no personal benefit in the utilitarian sense from his harvest, the gardener receives much praise and renown from its size and quality, and that in a direct and circumstantial manner. For all the crops, after being harvested, are displayed for some time afterwards in the gardens, piled up in neat, conical heaps under small shelters made of yam vine. Each man's harvest is thus exhibited for criticism in his own plot, and parties of natives walk about from garden to garden, admiring, comparing, and praising the best results.
>
> (Malinowski [1922] 1961, reprinted in
> LeClair and Schneider 1968: 20)

The contradictions within these paragraphs appear evident to any student of modern economic theory. Malinowski missed the point that economic ends do not necessarily have to involve monetary or material ends, and that all wants, whether monetary, material, or social, are part of the fundamental economic problem if scarce

28

means must be employed to satisfy them. The gardeners Malinowski described use scarce means (land, labor, time, seed, equipment, etc.) to achieve the ends of prestige and social obligation. Rather than denying the self-interested rationality of the Trobriand Islanders, Malinowski's own account serves to demonstrate the keen efficiency they display in the pursuit of the ends they found most important.[2] Yet, as apparent as these mistakes seem today, others followed Malinowski's disdain for economic theory. "By following Malinowski, anthropologists were systematically and uncritically cutting themselves from the one body of theory which sought to illuminate economic phenomena" (LeClair and Schneider 1968: 5).

Within the period of a single year, however, three anthropologists independently offered devastating critiques of Malinowski. D.M. Goodfellow (1939), Melville Herskovits ([1940] 1952), and later Raymond Firth (1951) made use of rational choice theories in their studies of economic phenomena in South Africa, West Africa, and Polynesia, respectively. To varying degrees, all three followed a Robbinsian approach to the nature of the economic problem. The universal nature of economics, according to Robbins (1932), does not lie in a universal pursuit of material wealth. The universal nature of the economic problem lies in the fact that human wants are virtually boundless, while the means to satisfy these wants are relatively scarce.

Firth, Goodfellow, and Herskovits recognized that economic differences are generated by different cultural influences. Gifts in religious ceremonies and dietary restrictions will influence demand for specific goods, for example. Similarly, production may be shaped by beliefs and traditions which do not necessarily serve to maximize output or profit. Herskovits ([1940] 1952) cites, for example, Dolmatoff's account of the Kogi Indians in the Sierra Nevada. According to Dolmatoff, the Indians abstain from cultivating productive terrace land for supernatural reasons. Lastly, the ends which individuals find worthwhile will be determined in part by the cultural context. All three argued, however, that this does not change the fundamental economic problem. Though they agreed that cross-cultural implications of the universal phenomenon known as "economizing" exist, they argued that economic theory is valid in all settings. Firth described the Muslim "preference" for risk sharing and profit in providing capital over the charging of interest, but he argued that the Muslim is no less rational than the Western

29

entrepreneur. Here, what is demonstrated is not a lack of self-interest, but rather "a positive desire for conformity to moral and religious ideals" (Firth 1951: 152–3). Thus, they argued, neoclassical maximization models are universally valid, even though what is being maximized will differ according to the social context. Whether the end is to maximize profit, social status, or security, the process can be modeled with the calculus of optimization.

Of the three, Goodfellow was the most ardent supporter of the neoclassical paradigm. He relied heavily upon the Robinson Crusoe construct of economic theory to make his point.

> It has been shown that Robinson Crusoe has something more than a strictly methodological significance; that an individual in his position would indeed feel the pressure of needs upon resources, would in fact make choice between the applications of his various resources, would encounter varying returns and would have to choose between present and future and between work and leisure. Wicksteed . . . has shown how the greater part of the apparatus of economic theory may be evolved without going outside a single household. This being so, it would be surprising if modern economic theory failed to apply to the peoples known as primitive.
>
> (Goodfellow 1939: 6)

The value of the Crusoian or single household construct is that it demonstrates the all-pervasive reality of scarcity—an important point which, as it turns out, was missed by many within economic anthropology. Yet, another lesson which is often taken away from such constructs is the notion that economic processes operate independently of the social and cultural context. Further, this notion implies that any differences which do persist from one society to another are simply benign differences in preference.

From the start, Crusoian economics assumes that cultural or institutional differences are irrelevant. As Goodfellow argued,

> [T]he phenomena of social science are nothing if not universal. The groups, the behavior, the fundamental social relationships such as those of kinsmen, and neighbors, are qualitatively the same the world over. Wherever we look at Mankind we see motives of accumulation, of competitive display, of obligations towards kinfolk, of religious organization and political activity; these, and such, make up the body of fact with which

social science must deal. The fundamental differences between "civilized" and "savage" . . . have now been so effectively exploded that we need not here waste space upon them.

(Goodfellow 1939: 4)

It should not come as a surprise that many cultural anthropologists objected to the use of economic constructs which effectively assumed culture and the rest of their subject matter into the background. Many economists have also objected to Crusoian economics on the grounds that it cannot address the extended economic order which is generated among millions of disparate human beings. The elements of the extended order, including the price system, financial markets, and international trade, are facilitated by social institutions such as law, property, and monetary systems. As these and other social institutions do not arise out of an acultural context, an acultural model will not adequately serve in their study.

Both Firth and Herskovits were somewhat critical of Crusoian economics. Yet, without a clear alternative, neoclassical economic theory was better than no economic theory.

One of the principles of early economic theory was to regard the individual as the point from which all development of theoretical principles must begin. We have come to realize that the individual never exists alone; that a society, as it has been put, is more than an aggregate of Robinson Crusoes; and that social interaction in terms of cultural tradition dictates reconsideration of the earlier starting point. The process of economizing, we recognize, is essentially based on the broader organization of society. Yet, the individual can not be left out of the picture, for all forms of social behavior, in the final analysis, must be referred to the behavior of individual members of a given society in specific situations.

(Herskovits [1940] 1952: 6–7)

Thus, even the neoclassical economic anthropologists were somewhat aware of the paradigm's shortcomings. However, the mistakes which were made in the absence of any economic theory were reason enough to defend it.

The late 1950s gave rise to the "substantivist" school of thought as a counter-attack upon the formalist or neoclassical paradigm within anthropology. But rather than moving the debate forward by exposing the acultural nature of the neoclassical paradigm, the debate continued to revolve around the basic issue of scarcity. This retrenchment unfortunately drew attention away from the substantivists' point that economic processes in pre-industrial societies are embedded within a complex cultural context. The implications of this point for neoclassical economics were never fully considered, and thus alternatives to acultural economics were never explored.

Economic historian Karl Polanyi (1957) argued that societies are "integrated" in one of three ways: through the market mechanism, through reciprocal relationships such as kinship, or through redistribution via a central authority. Polanyi and his associates argued that neoclassical economics is only applicable if the primary form of integration is the market. Polanyi argued further that market integration is a relatively isolated and recent phenomenon. Thus, neoclassical economic theory, he argued, is only applicable to the modern Western context from which it arose. In *Trade and Market in the Early Empires*, Polanyi *et al.* (1957) were primarily arguing against the use of modern economic concepts in historical contexts, but economic anthropologists such as George Dalton (1961) and Marshall Sahlins (1960, 1972, 1976) were quick to employ similar arguments in non-Western contexts.

Polanyi suggested two meanings of "economic":

> The substantive meaning of economic derives from man's dependence for his living upon nature and his fellows. It refers to the interchange with his natural and social environment, in so far as this results in supplying him with the means of material want satisfaction.
>
> The formal meaning of economic derives from the logical character of the means-ends relationship, as apparent as in such words as "economical" or "economizing." It refers to a definite situation of choice, namely that between the different uses of means induced by an insufficiency of those means. If we call the rules governing the choice of means the logic of rational action, then we may denote this variant of logic, with an improvised term, as formal economics.
>
> (Polanyi 1957: 243)

Formal economics, then, refers to technical efficiency between means and ends—the logic of rational action. Whether or not an economy is faced with scarcity, Polanyi argued, is an empirical question. This is where he saw the flaw of formal economics—in its application to areas in which scarcity induced choice is not significant, such as in tribal societies. Polanyi stated that only in market societies will scarcity be present. Thus, only the substantive meaning of "economic" matters to empirical investigations of pre-industrial society.

In response to Polanyi, two points need to be made here. First, most societies exhibit all three forms of integration to one degree or another. Markets do not control the distribution of all resources in advanced Western society. Accelerated tax rates, charitable organizations, and family obligations speak to the redistributive and reciprocal forms of integration operating in this context. Nor are Soviet-type systems merely redistributive. Market coordination, in the form of black markets, second and shadow economies, often determines the flow of resources in such contexts (Grossman 1982; Katsenelinboigen 1977). Second, even if redistribution or reciprocity dominate in any particular context, scarcity is still a determining factor in choice. Even the heaviest of welfare states faces scarcity. The difference is the allocation mechanism, not the presence or absence of scarcity. The very fact that an allocation mechanism is necessary suggests that scarcity is present. The benevolent king must still decide who gets what and how much.

Essentially, the substantivist school emptied economic theory of its core concept: choice. Polanyi argued that substantive economics does not necessarily entail choice, nor does it imply insufficiency of means:

> [M]an's livelihood may or may not involve the necessity of choice and, if choice there be, it need not be induced by the limiting effect of a "scarcity" of the means; indeed, some of the most important physical and social conditions of livelihood such as the availability of air and water or a loving mother's devotion to her infant are not, as a rule, so limiting.
>
> (Polanyi 1957: 243–4)

Polanyi's own examples defeat his point, however. It is exactly the usual abundance of air and, in some circumstances, water that place their acquisition outside of the economic problem. Further, scarcity persists in many things other than material resources. The example of a mother's love is an excellent case in point. The sentiment that love knows no bounds is pleasant, but any mother of two knows that she is unable to offer the second infant the same amount of attention that she was able to offer the first. Even if love is boundless, a mother's time and energy certainly are not. Scarcity necessitates choice, as one course of action must be given up in pursuit of another. In short, any definition of "economic" which

33

does not have both the elements of scarcity and choice is meaningless. It is precisely at the point in which scarcity is not a factor that the situation is outside of the fundamental economic problem.

In line with Polanyi, Dalton (1961) argued that scarcity is socially, not physically, defined. Dalton challenged the formalist assertion that wants are unlimited. He argued that market organization compels the individual to seek self-gain. Outside of a market context, he asserted, individuals would not be compelled to increase their material wants, so the issue of scarcity is not relevant. Similarly, Sahlins (1968, 1972) argued that by restricting wants, hunter-gatherer societies could enjoy relative affluence, characterized by high consumption of leisure time, even in the absence of material abundance.

An important point was being made in this literature: which criteria are associated with self-interest, which activities, goods, or services provide satisfaction, and what material circumstances constitute "affluence," are all culturally defined. As Sahlins (1976) later argued, in order to understand non-Western societies, it is necessary to understand the natives' own cultural constructions as the starting point of analysis. Such constructions will indeed have real effects on the relative scarcity of some things, as scarcity of any particular resource must be defined in relation to the demand for that resource. A society which has no use or desire for chickens will not experience a scarcity of chickens, no matter how many or how few exist in close proximity. Yet, even though culture helps to define the relative scarcity of resources in the particular case, no society is immune from the basic circumstance of scarcity in the general sense. Even for an ascetic people whose material wants have been fully satiated, limited time and energy must always be allocated to competing ends. Time spent preparing meals is time that cannot be spent in prayer, for example. Or in response to Sahlins (1968, 1976), even people of affluence must decide how to spend their perhaps abundant, but still limited, leisure time. What Dalton and Sahlins could have argued is that commodity fetishism is not a universal phenomenon. But this does not mean that only some societies are subject to the constraints of scarcity.

In short, the substantivists made many of the same mistakes Malinowski made years earlier, and the formalists were quick to recognize them (Burling 1962; Cook 1966). Such corrections were necessary, but the retrenchment of the debate into the basic issue of scarcity continued to divert attention away from the very real shortcomings of neoclassical economics. Sahlins' (1963) work on the role of kinship in economic relations, for instance, demonstrated the failure of maximization models to characterize adequately economic decisions which were embedded within the social context. The substantivists argued that in pre-industrial societies, all economic decisions were made within a complex web of social institutions and customary rules. For this reason, applying maximization techniques in pre-industrialized contexts emptied the analysis of any substantive content. While neoclassical economics was on solid ground in its defense of the fundamental economic problem, the limitations of the theory to characterize complex decision making outside of the acultural model presented a more challenging critique—a critique that was never fully addressed.

Perhaps one of the reasons this part of the substantivist challenge was not addressed directly in the debate was that the substantivists did not take their challenge far enough. The substantivists emphasized the cultural specificity of neoclassical economics as its major shortcoming. But the Western origin of neoclassical economics is not the source of its limitations. The reason why many economic anthropologists find neoclassical constructs at odds with their work is that it represents an acultural model of the economic process. The substantivists did not recognize the radical potential of their own critique. Not only are pre-industrial economies embedded within a complex cultural context, so too are advanced capitalist economies. Neoclassicism is just as ill-suited to address the cultural context of Western markets as it is ill-suited to address the cultural context of West African markets.

The formalist–substantivist debate was never fully resolved. As Plattner (1989: 14) suggests, economic anthropologists "did not stop doing empirical research but stopped arguing about how to go about doing it." Neoclassical economics did not provide a satisfying theory for social scientists interested in economics and culture, yet the substantivist position did not offer a better alternative. Thus, rather than pushing the debate further, most simply left the discussion.

By the 1970s, the vacuum left in the wake of neoclassical theory was quickly filled with Marxist and neo-Marxist theories attempting to explain economic phenomena in the developing world. The so-called "new economic anthropology" redirected the discussion away from the formalist–substantivist debate towards economic development issues. Marxism, in part through the influence of the "new French school" of economic anthropology was reintroduced into the discipline (Althusser 1969; Dupre and Rey 1973; Godelier 1972; Meillassoux 1972, 1976; Terray 1972, 1974). Marxist economic anthropology sought to shift the focus from transactions (either ceremonial or market transactions) to production and the class relations which emerge out of the particular mode of production.

Marxist economic anthropologists rejected the formalist reliance upon neoclassical theory, but they were equally critical of the substantivists for arguing that industrialized and pre-industrial societies were fundamentally different. The Marxist critique of capitalism was taken for granted. The point of the new economic anthropology was to explain how the developing world fit into a generalized Marxist paradigm. As developing countries became defined in terms of world capitalist domination, Marxian concepts of class, class dominance, and exploitation in the mode of production were applied across the globe. Marxist theory also had a significant influence in economic anthropology through the "dependency school" of the 1970s. Underdevelopment, it was argued, was not the outcome of internal deficiencies, but a direct consequence of Western growth and affluence, and/or neocolonialism (Cockcroft *et al.* 1972; Frank 1969; Kahn 1978). In either case, economic anthropology essentially had become applied Marxism in the context of underdeveloped countries. As Godelier argues,

> [I]t is the concept of the mode of production which constitutes the primary concept of economic anthropology. The task of the latter is to determine the types of mode of production which exist in the societies it studies and which transform themselves through articulation with, and under the domination of, the capitalist world economy.
>
> (Godelier 1972: 195)

In describing the new economic anthropology of the 1970s, among which he counts himself a contributor, Seddon says it best.

> For the "new economic anthropology" is neither "economic" in the usual limited sense, nor is it "anthropology." It is rather a branch of historical materialism predominantly but not exclusively concerned with the dynamic and structure of pre-capitalist social formations and the conditions of their transformation.
>
> (Seddon 1978: 62–3)

The crucial issue here is that as economic anthropology became increasingly dominated by the influence of Marxism, the questions regarding the interplay of culture and economic processes, or more importantly, the embeddedness of economic processes within culture, which were never adequately addressed within the formalist–substantivist debate, were completely subverted. No sacred cows were spared in this pursuit. For instance, Marxist anthropologists sought to de-throne the central role of kinship held within anthropology. Of far greater importance to the Marxist is the control of the means of production.

> Classical Marxism has a definite conception of the necessary structure of society. A society is conceived as a social forma-tion, an articulated structure of three interdependent levels, dominated by the structure of a particular mode of production consisting of an economic, a political–legal, and a cultural level. The levels are thought to be related in such a way that the first (i.e. economic) always plays a primary role, that of determination in the last instance.
>
> (Cutler *et al.* 1977: 174)

The mode of production is central to Marxist social theory, as it is the engine which drives all other social phenomena. "The key ques-tions are: what is produced, by what social groups? How are the groups organized and by whom? What is the purpose of production (e.g., use or exchange)?" (Frankenberg 1967, quoted in Clammer 1978: 7). The concept of "class relations" took the place of any cultural theory. The attempt to overthrow kinship as a key compo-nent within economic anthropological analysis was only one celebrated example. Within the Marxist paradigm, the mode of production drives and takes precedence over social relations, custom, kinship, religion, ideology—all of which were central to cultural analysis. What ground cultural theory had lost in the formalist–substantivist debate in the 1960s was reinforced by the resurgence of Marxian economic anthropology in the 1970s.

BEYOND ACULTURAL ECONOMICS: NEW INSTITUTIONAL ECONOMICS

To the broader field of anthropology, the lack of attention paid to culture among formalist and Marxist economic anthropologists was not a tremendous loss, given that cultural anthropology was still a thriving sub-discipline within the field. More significantly, the opportunity to introduce cultural analysis into economics was not pursued. Certainly, many would argue that this was no great tragedy—that the acultural nature of neoclassical economics is an asset. After all, exogenous policy shifts such as price controls, import quotas, and restricted government licensing generate systematically similar results, no matter what the cultural context. Indeed, cultural analysis is not necessary for all questions an economist might ask, and in this respect, the neoclassical paradigm often serves us well.

Yet advances such as those made by the "new institutionalist" school of economics have revealed some important limitations of neoclassical economic theory. Following on the insights presented by Ronald Coase (1937, 1960), new institutional economics argues that neoclassical conclusions will rarely hold in the real world, as positive transaction costs are almost always present (Wallis and North 1986). Wherever transaction costs exist, institutions become relevant as individuals seek out ways to minimize the costs associated with exchange. Establishing enforceable contracts, for instance, reduces moral hazard problems associated with long-distance and inter-temporal exchange. New institutional economics has effectively argued that the social institutions neoclassicism assumes into the background of analysis, such as contract and dispute resolution procedures (North 1987, 1990), property rights (Alchian and Demsetz 1973), and the role of the state (Bates 1981), are the key to understanding economic history and development. The division of labor and the expansion of trade depend upon institutions which reduce transaction costs associated with production and market exchange. As an economic historian, North (1994) identifies another important limitation of neoclassical theory in that it has no time dimension—no way of understanding how institutions and economic performance change. This emphasis has allowed new institutional economics to influence development economics (Harris *et al.* 1995; Nabli and Nugent 1989; North 1989, 1995) and, to a lesser extent, anthropology (Ensminger 1991, 1992).

In order to understand economic development in any particular context, the economist must investigate entrepreneurship and the social institutions that mediate the development process. The smooth functioning of the market relies on enforceable contracts, a method of resolving disputes, financial safety nets, and a conducive environment for entrepreneurship; advantages which all arise from the cultural context. Institutional analysis at its best is that which provides rich historical and cultural detail of this process. Yet, it is precisely in this regard that neoclassical economics exhibits its limitations, because it has no way of addressing complex, institutionally defined, culturally informed choice within the market.

North recognizes the pivotal role culture has in supplying informal enforcement mechanisms (North 1990) and in generating the path-dependent nature of institutional change (North 1994). For institutions to work, they must be supported by cultural norms that reduce the costs associated with formal enforcement mechanisms. Contractual obligation, private property rights, and the justice system cannot function in a society without a commonly held notion of what a contract actually is, what can and cannot legitimately be bought and sold, and what constitutes fairness. The market process depends on the underlying culture, as it provides the source of legitimation for the social institutions crucial to a successful economy. Further, the renegotiation of institutional rules will take place within the given cultural context, so the past will always exert its influence upon the present and future institutional context.

Nowhere is North clearer about the significance of culture than in his discussion of culturally defined "mental models." In his work with Arthur Denzau, North argues that

> [i]deas matter; and the way ideas are communicated among people is crucial to theories that will enable us to deal with strong uncertainty problems at the individual level. For most of the interesting issues in political and economic markets, uncertainty, not risk, characterizes choice-making. Under conditions of uncertainty, individuals' interpretation of their environment will reflect their learning. Individuals with common cultural backgrounds and experiences will share reasonably convergent mental models, ideologies, and institutions; and individuals with different learning experiences (both cultural and environmental) will have different theories (models, ideologies) to interpret their environment . . . [I]n order to understand decision making under such conditions of uncertainty we must understand the relationship of the mental models that individuals construct to make sense out of the world around them, the ideologies that evolve from such constructions, and the institutions that develop in a society to order interpersonal relationships.
>
> (Denzau and North 1994: 3–4)

While the role culture plays in shaping institutions and entrepreneurial perspective is recognized, it is far from the central focus of the new institutional economics. In this sense, the present project can be seen as complementary to the work of North and others interested in the role institutions play in markets. The present project turns our focus not only to the fact that markets are embedded within a particular institutional context, but to the *cultural* embeddedness of markets as well.

In another sense, however, this project represents an alternative approach to that taken by the new institutionalists, in that North and others have continued to adhere to a "relaxed" version of the neoclassical paradigm, rather than abandon it for one that might directly address the crucial questions they raise. Even within the "relaxed" version of the neoclassical paradigm, institutions are still characterized as separable from the cultural context from which they evolve. Alchian and Demsetz (1973), for instance, merely see culture as a less than desirable substitute for property rights. If, for example, a community fails to establish private property rights, they would then have to rely on cultural indoctrination to alleviate the tendency to shirk and free-ride off others' efforts. Thus, Alchian and Demsetz argue that a system of values and behavioral norms will compensate (though imperfectly) where property rights fail to emerge.

By characterizing the possible solutions as *either* coordination through private property rights *or* cultural indoctrination, Alchian and Demsetz imply that culturally informed systems such as values or informal rules of behavior are not at work in the formation of private property rights. The point is not that values are at work in one situation and not the other, but rather, that different value systems are at work in each. A strongly held ethic of "earn respect and honor through sharing" may work to ration resources in a setting of communal rights. But an equally strong ethic such as "respect the fruits of your neighbors' labor as their own" is just as necessary for the private property setting. These ethics are part of the cultural framework which gives rise to and supports effective rules of property. Without this framework, rules of property—private or otherwise—have no source of legitimation and are therefore not sustainable. Stein (1995), for example, argues that socialist policies in parts of Eastern Europe and Africa have eroded the cultural sources of legitimation for private property, explaining the often disappointing results of privatization efforts. To be complete, investigations seeking to understand the success or failure of social institutions to generate economic growth must make reference to the particular cultural context in which the institution emerged (or was imposed). Private property rights can only be expected to generate economic development if the community at large accepts such arrangements as legitimate.

Similarly, contractual arrangements which involve credit, partnership, or supply agreements will expand markets, but only if a reliable system of conflict resolution is in place. Entrepreneurs are not likely to offer resources and supplies on credit if they have no recourse in the case of default. Thus, economic progress cannot emerge in a world of rational maximizers without guarantees of property and justice. Yet, accepted attitudes towards the sanctity of private property, shared notions about who to trust, what constitutes justice, or appropriate behavior in trading relationships do not surface out of thin air. They evolve out of a specific cultural context. Tribal, and religious traditions, for example, may provide the justification for what is fair, or how land is divided and passed from one generation to the next. Kinship structure may determine the individual's financial obligation to the community and vice versa. In short, markets are an extension of culture because it is culture that shapes the rules necessary for a market to function.

By trying to add culture into what is essentially an acultural model, the new institutional economics often suffers from the same shortcomings as standard neoclassical economics. North and others explicitly reject the narrow view of mechanistic rationality inherent within neoclassical constructs, charging that

> such version[s] of the rational actor model have simply led us astray. The actors frequently must act on incomplete information and process the information that they do receive through mental constructs that can result in persistently inefficient paths.
>
> (North 1990: 8)

Yet, as we see here, North sets up the neoclassical world of zero transaction costs as the only context in which "correct" or perfectly efficient decisions can be made, because it is only within this context that we do not have to deal with the distorting effects of the cultural lens. Rather than seeing culture as the context in which contentious interpretations of the world are worked out, culture is seen mainly as distorting an otherwise clear and objective reality.

Though the time dimension that new institutional economics

41

adds is a critical improvement to standard theory, this still retains a mechanistic and narrowly rationalistic approach to institutional change. For example, in her study of institutional change among the Orma of Kenya, Ensminger characterizes institutional choice as follows:

> In all cases, institutions impose costs (social, political, or economic) on certain forms of behavior, and therefore those who wish to engage in such proscribed behavior have an incentive to change the institutional structure. Furthermore, individuals try to structure institutions toward their own ends . . . by committing resources to bring about change to the institutional environment.
>
> (Ensminger 1992: 19)

To be sure, it is important to recognize that in certain contexts, particularly political contexts, those who are in a position to concentrate benefits upon themselves by changing formal institutional rules, while dispersing the costs to an uninformed and/or unorganized public, may very well seek to do so (Olson 1965, 1982). But to view all institutional change as if it is the outcome of cost-benefit calculus is misleading, in that it suggests that institutions emerge out of a cultural vacuum. Ensminger (1992: 167) later addresses the role of ideology in institutional change, but again, the role takes on an instrumental quality. She argues that the Orma recognized that by converting to Islam they seized an opportunity to reduce transaction costs and reap the economic benefits. It may indeed be the case that some such "calculus" was going on inside the heads of the converted. As Berger and Luckmann (1966) note, the construction of social reality is rarely a disinterested enterprise. Yet in this accounting of institutional change, culture *qua* ideology is treated as another argument in the objective function, as if any society could make a similar choice. In this objectified view of institutional choice, no account is taken of the cultural symmetries between indigenous and Islamic belief structures that allowed for the acceptance of both the "letter" of Islamic practice and the "spirit" of its teachings. In other words, why did Islam, with all the economic benefits it conveyed, "fit" the indigenous cultural context? While ethnographies such as Ensminger's represent critical contributions to the literature on institutions and development, they are still limited by the neoclassical framework.

BEYOND ACULTURAL ECONOMICS: THE AUSTRIAN SCHOOL OF ECONOMICS

The best way to move beyond acultural characterizations of choice is to abandon the neoclassical model altogether. It is here that we turn to the Austrian school of economics. The Austrian economics literature reaches back to contributions made by Carl Menger in the marginalist revolution of the 1870s. Along with William Stanley Jevons and Leon Walras, Menger changed the course of economic inquiry. The marginalist revolution marks a pivotal point in the history of economic thought, as it replaced the objectivistic labor theory of value with the subjective marginal theory of value. The implications of this transition are far reaching. For instance, Marx's descriptions of exploitation under capitalism and the eventual transformation into socialism are crucially dependent upon the debunked labor theory of value. Such implications are explored in detail elsewhere (Kolakowski 1978). For our purposes here, the significance of the subjectivist turn rests with the recognition that the value or meaning of objects presented in the physical world must be interpreted by the human subject. Human beings impute value to goods and services in accordance with their perception of how such goods and services will satisfy their wants. Further, the value attached to any particular unit of the good or service will depend upon the context in which the human decision maker finds herself. If the item in question is in relative abundance, human beings will in general attach a lower level of value to the last unit than if the item is relatively scarce. The valuation of raw materials and other inputs works in much the same way, except that in this case, the value human beings attach to such "goods of a higher order" depend upon the value consumers attach to the final goods and services the inputs help to produce.

Jevons, Walras, and Menger came to essentially these same conclusions, yet as other scholars followed, different elements of the marginalist revolution were emphasized. Those following Jevons and Walras further mathematized economic theory in models which emphasized equilibrium solutions, while those who followed in the Mengerian tradition—what came to be known as the Austrian school of economics—continued to emphasize and expand upon the subjective or interpretive aspects of the marginalist revolution. Following in Menger's footsteps, Ludwig von Mises ([1922] 1932, [1933] 1981, [1949] 1966) sought to expose what he saw as the weakness of economic theory which narrowly defined choice as the outcome of maximization of a particular goal within a given set of means and ends (Robbins 1932). Mises argued that such an approach rendered choice a mere mechanical computation and missed the interpretive dimension of human decision making. A broader conception of *human action*, as opposed to the narrow Robbinsian notion of economizing, would not only allow us to recognize the computational aspect of choice within a given framework of means and ends, but would also allow us to recognize the novelty and creativity at work when the individual proactively altered that framework. For Mises, this sort of reinterpretation of the available data was the essence of entrepreneurship. Entrepreneurial perception—that which allows for the creation of a new means/ends framework—lies outside of the mechanical depiction of choice as optimal resource allocation.

Building upon the Misesian conception of human action, Israel Kirzner (1973, 1979) advanced the Austrian theory of entrepreneurship as an alternative to standard neoclassical portrayals of the market. Kirzner's critique of neoclassical theory centers on the model's inability to account for entrepreneurship—a critical challenge considering that the entrepreneur is the driving force behind the learning process of the market, and ultimately behind economic development itself. Standard economics emphasizes not the process by which market coordination takes place, but rather the end state equilibrium in which all resources are said to be efficiently allocated. If equilibrium solutions are the central focus of economic inquiry, one must pay considerable attention to identifying and describing the limited conditions under which such results might emerge. In particular, one must assume that all economic actors possess the relevant information for making perfectly efficient decisions. Only then will equilibrium be guaranteed within the theoretical construct. Yet it is precisely at this point that we fail to understand the market as a process. With all the information readily available to economic actors, individuals immediately jump to the new point of perfect allocation. F.A. Hayek ([1946] 1948) recognized the irony that within this so-called "competitive solution," there is in fact no behavior we would actually call competitive—no advertising, no product innovation or differentiation. Further, Kirzner recognized that in such an economy, no entrepreneurship need exist, as the equilibrium solution is always obvious. Once the equilibrium solution is achieved, competition—in the sense of seeking to provide customers with more attractive options—ceases to be a meaningful concept, as no more adjustment is needed or even possible.[3]

Yet here on the ground, human beings live in a world of fundamental ignorance. It is only within this context of ignorance, in which human action is shrouded by uncertainty, that entrepreneurship exists. In the absence of full information, individuals cannot immediately adjust their plans so as to perfectly dovetail with the plans of other market participants. Producers in search of the highest possible returns in one market may not know of consumers in another market willing to pay more. Such ignorance leads to a lack of coordination on the one hand, and profit opportunities on the other. Some people will be alert to the opportunities that exist, buying in the first market, selling in the second, and facilitating an overall trend towards increased coordination. For Kirzner, the quintessential characteristic of entrepreneurship is this alertness.

Kirzner argues that entrepreneurial alertness is not a resource to be deployed in the course of maximizing profits or some other goal. When one is alert to an opportunity, they have discovered something previously unrecognized. To characterize entrepreneurial alertness as Robbinsian optimization within given means and ends is to suggest that the profit opportunity was already within the means/ends framework, and in no need of being discovered. The alertness which allows some to discover arbitrage opportunities before others is extra-economic, as it lies outside of the optimization problem. The significance of this is that if we are to understand the market process, we must move beyond the standard account of economic decision making which depicts choice as isolated, mechanistic calculations. By seeking out profit opportunities missed by others, Kirzner argues, the entrepreneur moves the market from a position of relative disco-ordination to one in which plans and expectations are more coordinated. Standard neoclassical economics cannot account for entrepreneurship because it assumes away uncertainty within the market. If all market participants have perfect information, no profit opportunities are left to be exploited, and thus no entrepreneurship and no competitive process need exist. The point is not simply that the assumption of perfect information is unrealistic. Rather, the assumption of perfect information assumes away the very thing that sets the market clearing forces into motion.

Also essential to Kirzner's representation of entrepreneurship is the discovery aspect of the market process. Following Mises ([1933]

1981, [1949] 1966), Hayek (1948, 1967, 1978), and other Austrian theorists, Kirzner recognizes not only the allocative role markets play, but also the role they play in enabling market participants to discover the proper course of action.

> [O]nce we become sensitive to the decision-makers' alertness to new possibly worthwhile ends and newly available means, it may be possible to explain the pattern of change in an individual's decisions as the outcome of a learning process generated by the unfolding experience of the decisions themselves. An analysis confined to allocative explanations must fail entirely to perceive such continuity in any sequence of decisions, since each decision is comprehended purely in terms of its own relevant ends-means framework. With purely allocative explanations, no earlier decision can be used to explain later decisions on the basis of learning ... We must recognize what I have called the entrepreneurial element in order to perceive that the changing patterns of ends-means held relevant to successive decision are the possible understandable outcome of a process of experience in which the decision-maker's alertness to relevant new information has generated a continuously changing sequence of decisions.
>
> (Kirzner 1973: 36–7)

Human action can only be understood within the context of an individual's overall plan or set of plans, not as isolated moments of optimization. In the course of working out those plans—through action and imagination—the individual learns and adjusts his or her plans, constantly reinterpreting the data. It is here that Kirzner makes his principal contribution: the linking of the Misesian concept of human action, one which reaches far beyond a narrow allocational role of economic choice, to the discovery process inherently tied to entrepreneurship (Lavoie 1991).

Though Kirzner's contributions represent some of the best work on entrepreneurship, it is still in need of modification if we are to take culture into account. Kirzner largely ignores the role of culture in entrepreneurship. Lavoie (1991) argues that because Kirzner still holds to the equilibrium construct set out by neoclassical theory, he has failed to see the cultural implications of his own argument. Though Kirzner shifts the emphasis away from equilibrium solutions, he maintains that the role of the entrepreneur is an equilibrating one. If exogenous shifts were to cease, entrepreneurial

46

activity would result in an equilibrium solution. Kirzner is quick to point out that such an end state will never occur, as change is inevitable, but the tendency of the market process and entrepreneurial discovery is towards a pre-existing equilibrium. While on the one hand Kirzner characterizes entrepreneurship as a creative process and the source of genuine novelty, on the other hand Kirzner holds to an objectivistic view of entrepreneurial opportunities.

"Alertness" as the quintessential aspect of entrepreneurship has drawn criticism. Rather than an equilibrating force, entrepreneurship might very well be the simultaneously creative and destructive force inherent in Schumpeter's view of entrepreneurship. For Schumpeter, economic development is more about disrupting the status quo than bringing the economy closer to an equilibrium position.

> Development in our sense is a distinct phenomenon, entirely foreign to what may be observed in the circular flow or in the tendency towards equilibrium. It is spontaneous and discontinuous change in the channels of the flow, disturbance of the equilibrium, which forever alters and displaces the equilibrium state previously existing.
>
> (Schumpeter [1934] 1983: 64)

Further, High (1982) argues that entrepreneurship also involves judgment and a capacity to envision new possibilities. McCloskey (1994; McCloskey and Klamer 1994) argues that persuasion, and not simply alertness, is crucial to entrepreneurship. For an entrepreneurial venture ever to get off the ground, the entrepreneur must persuade investors that his or her ideas are profitable ones, and consumers that the new product or service is a desirable one. Lavoie adds that interpretation is also an essential aspect of entrepreneurship, arguing that mere alertness to arbitrage opportunities, of buying low and selling high, are

> misleading in that the interpretation is trivial and has already taken place. Kirzner likens the arbitrageur's discovery of profit to finding a twenty-dollar bill on the beach. [Kirzner's] example reinforces the impression of profit that one gets from mainstream economics, that it is an objective "find" that does not require interpretation. Most acts of entrepreneurship are not like an isolated individual finding things on beaches; they require efforts of the creative imagination, skillful judgments

of future costs and revenue possibilities, and an ability to read the significance of complex social institutions.

(Lavoie 1991: 44)

How the entrepreneur teases out the meaning of all the bits of information available to him or her is a complex interpretive process largely shaped by culture. Economic inquiry within the Austrian school centers on human action, whether it be entrepreneurship, investment, or the acquisition of credit. An acultural depiction of these and other actions assumes away their very substance. An entrepreneur's decision to offer a new product or service is not an objectively defined course of action. The entrepreneur is not simply following an algorithm. Rather, he or she must interpret the meaning of the information available. As Lavoie suggests, entrepreneurial decisions are less calculus and more akin to a close "reading" of profit opportunities from a complex social context.

Entrepreneurial activity and the discovery process which follows from it, are of course carried out by real human beings operating within a specific context, not the cultureless and institutionless *homoeconomicus* of neoclassicism. Nor are entrepreneurial decisions a mechanical uncovering of something already in existence as Kirzner's alertness seems to suggest, but rather, a creative process— a series of judgments—which results when the individual entrepreneur brings his or her own interpretive framework to bear upon the situation as it is presented.

An established Ghanaian cloth trader named Beatrice who wished to expand her business provides an apt illustration. By supplying newcomers in the market with cloth, Beatrice could take advantage of the discounted wholesale price she was able to secure after years of high-volume trading. As new entrants are usually young and cash poor, she would have to provide the cloth on credit. Beatrice then had to make a judgment as to whether this truly represented a profit opportunity or not. She lamented, "The new market women will sometimes run away—back to their village. If they go, there goes my profit." When asked how she determined to whom she would extend credit, Beatrice replied, "You can tell by the way they look, if she is neat, if she has people. If she has friends in the market, I will talk to them to see."

In order to acquire credit, an entrepreneur must establish his or her credit-worthiness according to the rules operating in that community. The key indicator for this trader was the network of local connections, both of family and friends, the newcomer could demonstrate. In turn, the trader has to judge whether she can trust the word of those who vouch for the newcomer—whether they feel responsible for the welfare of the young entrepreneur or their own reputations. In other cultures, the judgments governing the assessment of credit-worthiness may be quite different. Kinship status may be the dominant factor elsewhere; a documented credit history in still another.

Good entrepreneurial decisions are not simply a matter of noticing a price discrepancy, as we might conclude from Kirzner's depiction of the entrepreneur as arbitrageur. As Richard Ebeling explains,

> A seller finds himself with unsold inventory of a product in excess of desired levels at a particular price. But what exactly is the market telling him at that price? That he needs to relocate his store? That he has failed to advertise the existence or availability of the product sufficiently? That the price is "right" but the quality or characteristics of the product is "wrong"? What the price has conveyed is information that *something* is wrong, that the seller's plans and expectations are inconsistent with those of others. It has not unambiguously told him in which direction the error lies. The price's information, in other words, needs *interpretation as to its meaning* concerning the preferences and plans of others.
>
> (Ebeling 1986: 45)

Prices are not marching orders which entrepreneurs blindly and mechanically follow. Opportunities for profit are forged through an interpretive process which is dependent upon the cultural framework. Good entrepreneurial decisions require that judgments be made about trustworthiness, risk, potential demand, reliability of supply lines, and countless other factors. Each of these elements will at least in part be tied to the specific cultural context. Culture provides the framework within which entrepreneurs not only notice, but also creatively piece together profit opportunities from the world around them.

What is called for is an economic paradigm which accounts for this interpretive process. Kirzner's concept of alertness is helpful here, but is in need of modification. Rather than seeing alertness as a monitoring device that is either "switched on" or "switched off," entrepreneurship is more like *directed* alertness. Even the most astute entrepreneur is never fully alert—capable of noticing all profit opportunities. Rather, an individual entrepreneur will be alert to certain kinds of opportunities. An urban money lender in Accra (called a *"susu*-man") will be alert to a certain sort of profit opportunity, as his focus is directed towards particular aspects of the market process, while the focus of a fish retailer will be directed elsewhere. The difference in what two entrepreneurs see—the differences in how they creatively piece together profit opportunities—may be generated by their different positions within the market, their unique life histories, their gender or obligations to family. In summary,

> Profit opportunities are not so much like road signs to which we assign an automatic meaning as they are like difficult texts in need of a sustained effort of interpretation. Entrepreneurship is not only a matter of opening one's eyes, of switching on one's attentiveness; it requires directing one's gaze. When an entrepreneur sees things others have overlooked, it is not just that he opened his eyes while they have theirs closed. He is reading selected aspects of a complex situation others have not read. And this raises the question of what gives a predirectedness to the entrepreneur's vision, of why he is apt to read some things and not others. I submit the answer to this question is culture.
>
> (Lavoie 1991: 46)

This is the point to which Austrian economics brings us with respect to the question of culture and the market process. Austrian contributions to entrepreneurship and the economic methodology of radical subjectivism have carved out a space within which we might now introduce cultural analysis as a part of understanding market processes.

BUILDING UPON TWO INTERPRETIVE TRADITIONS

In building a "cultural economics," we bring together two interpretive traditions—one economic, the other anthropological. The most vocal proponent of an interpretive economics was Ludwig Lachmann (1971, 1976, 1978; see also Lavoie 1986, 1991; Ebeling 1986). Lachmann extended the notion of subjectivism to all perception and action within the market process. Both Austrian and neoclassical economics are subjective in the sense that values are determined by the wants and desires of market participants. Yet, Austrian economics, as influenced by Lachmann, is *radically* subjective in that strategies for profit, perception of information, and the construction of individual plans are also subjectively determined. Prices and other market signals are only meaningful inside a particular context in which human beings are interpreting their significance.

The main voice in the call for an interpretive anthropology belongs to Clifford Geertz. The role of the social scientist, Geertz (1973) argues, is to sort out the "structures of significance" among those who hold them—to render that which is, at first unintelligible to the outsider, intelligible. Borrowing from Gilbert Ryle, Geertz provides an example of two boys, both rapidly moving their eyelid. For one, the movement is an involuntary twitch, the other a conscious wink. The two movements look the same, yet

> the difference, however unphotographable, between a twitch and a wink is vast; as anyone unfortunate enough to have had the first taken for the second knows. The winker is communicating, and indeed communicating in a quite precise and special way: 1) deliberately, 2) to someone in particular, 3) to impart a particular message, 4) according to a socially established code, and 5) without cognizance of the rest of the company. As Ryle points out, the winker has done two things, contracted his eyelids and winked, while the twitcher has done only one, contracted his eyelids. Contracting your eyelids on purpose when there exists a public code in which so doing counts as a conspiratorial signal *is* winking. That's all there is to it: a speck of behavior, a fleck of culture, and—*voila!*—a gesture.
>
> (Geertz 1973: 6)

More recent work in anthropology has developed a culturalist method of economic analysis which also applies an interpretive approach. By studying the primary metaphors at work within a particular culture, the social scientist comes to understand the subjects' perspectives (Gudeman 1986; Bird-David 1990, 1992). In her study of modern hunter-gatherer societies, Bird-David argues that

> [t]he primary metaphor of "sharing" is thus a concept with which *we* can make sense of hunter-gatherers' economic arrangements and moreover, a metaphorical concept by which *they* make sense of their environment, one that guides their action within it.
>
> (Bird-David 1992: 31)

Much of the apparently wasteful behavior exhibited by modern hunter-gatherer societies makes sense within their own interpretive context. This alone says nothing as to whether a particular primary metaphor leads to economic stability or volatility, capital accumulation, or subsistence production. Yet it may provide a means of understanding the subjects' cultural perspective which renders the economic environment meaningful for them, and thereby guides action.[4] This is not to suggest that pre-industrial societies operate in the "false" world of metaphors, while industrialized society experiences the "real" world directly. Similar to what Denzau and North (1994) describe as "mental models," metaphor is just as essential to the modern entrepreneur in order to makes sense of his or her world. Money, for instance, depends upon the power of myth. The monetary system only works because people believe that account balances and currency represent value. The world is never experienced directly. It is always interpreted through the cultural lens.[5]

As Geertz argues, the value of an interpretive anthropological investigation is determined by whether it can solve a piece of the mystery; "whether it sorts winks from twitches."

> The claim to attention of an ethnographic account does not rest on its author's ability to capture primitive facts in faraway places and carry them home like a mask or a carving, but on the degree to which he is able to clarify what goes on in such places, to reduce the puzzlement—what manner of men are these?—to which unfamiliar acts emerging out of unknown backgrounds naturally give rise.
>
> (Geerts 1973: 16)

What might be lost in such an enterprise is the neatness and exactitude abstract and acultural theory so often affords. But what is gained is understanding.

CONCLUSION

The formalist–substantivist debate never definitively answered the question of whether economic theory was applicable to the non-Western developing world. On the one hand, neoclassical theory seemed inadequate given the sorts of questions being asked. The cultural foundations and the endogenous nature of economic development have little if any place within the neoclassical paradigm. Yet, to many, economic theory seemed too important to abandon altogether, even considering its shortcomings. With no apparent resolution and no clear alternative, the debate faded into the background of economic anthropology.

The Austrian school of economics has the potential to provide an alternative. Austrian methodology provides the link by which we can incorporate cultural analysis into economic investigations. The radical subjectivism posed by the Austrian school embraces the fact that markets are inhabited with creative interpreting beings, not atomistic reactive agents. Culture and interpretive perspective never emerge as relevant concepts in the neoclassical paradigm, as atomistic agents have no culture, indeed, they have no perspective. With the exception of Friedrich Hayek's work on the role culture plays in facilitating the extended order (to which we turn in the next chapter), cultural analysis has not yet played a principal role in the body of Austrian economic thought. Yet its position of radical subjectivism meant that it was only a matter of time before Austrians turned to the cultural framework that shapes the subjective perspective that defines Austrian economics.

2

ECONOMIC AND CULTURAL KNOWLEDGE

Ghanaian economic performance through an Austrian lens

> The curious task of economics is to demonstrate to men how
> little they really know about what they imagine they can design.
> (Friedrich Hayek 1988: 76)

Tracking Ghanaian economic performance in the post-colonial era is a veritable roller coaster ride. In 1959, real per capita GDP was growing at an annual rate of 10 percent. Yet, even with considerable development planning efforts immediately following independence, what resulted was a virtual collapse in the economy. By 1965, growth rates were not just declining, they were actually negative and continued to be so until 1968. After a lackluster recovery in the late 1960s, the early 1970s met with even more economic hardship. The same pattern is repeated in the late 1970s and into the 1990s in which weak recoveries were followed by severe economic downturn (Frimpong-Ansah 1991: Table A6.7). Macroeconomic adjustments in the 1990s have enhanced Ghana's economic performance, but present attempts by the state to improve local market conditions continue to falter (Aryeetey *et al.* 1994).

Ghana's post-colonial experience has been the subject of extensive study (Ahmad 1970; Chazen 1983; Frimpong-Ansah 1991; Killick 1978; Pellow and Chazen 1986; Rimmer 1992). Our purpose here is not to offer another comprehensive account of post-colonial economic history, as the facts of the period are well established and largely undisputed. What is still in question, however, is the interpretation of those facts; specifically, *why* Ghanaian economic performance has been, on net, so disappointing.

The aim here is to explore this period from a perspective not often applied to the developing world—that of Austrian economics. An Austrian approach to economic development will focus principally on

54

two themes. First, the process of economic development is inherently tied to entrepreneurship, particularly the creative, culturally engaged, and persuasive sort of entrepreneur that Schumpeter ([1934] 1983), Lavoie (1991), McCloskey (1994; McCloskey and Klamer 1994) and High (1982) describe. Second, and for the purposes of this chapter the most salient, an Austrian approach to economic development will focus on the nature of knowledge in the extended order; the "extended order" being not just the growing market economy, but the rules, institutions, morals, and cultural foundations which evolve to support the market. The work of Friedrich Hayek provides the best starting point for understanding economic development from this perspective. Further, an Austrian reading of Ghanaian economic performance in the post-colonial era will provide new insight as to the reasons why development policies so often fall short of their intended results.

THE DISPERSED NATURE OF KNOWLEDGE IN THE EXTENDED ORDER

Throughout his life's work, Friedrich Hayek's principal concern was that human society avoid what he was to eventually call the "fatal conceit"—the belief that human reason is capable of successfully replacing or redesigning the institutions of the extended order which have emerged through the process of social evolution (Hayek 1973, 1988). By "extended order" Hayek (1988: 72) literally means, "that which *far surpasses the reach of our understanding, wishes and purposes, and our sense perceptions*, and that which incorporates and generates knowledge which no individual brain, or any single organization, could possess or invent." Here he is referring to the self-ordering rules and institutions that emerge to support (among other things) the expansion of market relationships. Within the context of an extended order, individuals find themselves producing for and benefiting from millions of other human beings whom they will never know.

This extended order is as opposed to the small groupings of early social organization, structured and held together principally by the common purpose of survival. Rather than being dependent upon common ends, the extended order is structured and held together by common rules, such as those involving property, contract, honesty, privacy exchange, trade, competition, gain, and privacy (Hayek 1988: 12). The critical difference is that the extended order allows for enormous complexity and change. As the rules and institutions of the extended order evolve, survival is no longer dependent upon a unity of purpose within society. Individuals are free to experiment as they pursue their diverse ends. This experimentation will result in both individual and social learning as successful strategies are imitated and failing strategies are abandoned. Rules which allow for competitive experimentation facilitate adaptation to unknown and unforeseeable circumstances, and the discovery of new solutions.

This, then is a key to understanding economic development. Though development is most easily measured by an increase in material goods and services, the heart of the matter is a society's ability to adapt to unknown circumstances and accommodate greater and greater levels of complexity. Thus, in seeking to understand the foundations of the extended order, Hayek seeks also to understand the foundations of economic development. Given the extraordinary degree to which the extended order has evolved in modern industrialized society, it is tempting, Hayek admits, to credit human reason as the source of such remarkable order and progress. Likewise, it is tempting to assume that it is human reason that will eradicate poverty in the developing world. Yet, on the contrary, Hayek argues that the extended order depends not on the rational design of human beings, but on the unplanned evolution of culture and morality.

Effective constraints which allow for the expansion of markets, such as systems of contract and property are not chosen, rather they evolve through trial and error; their rules passed down and adapted in the process of enculturation.

> Most knowledge . . . is obtained not from immediate experience or observation, but in the continuous process of sifting a learnt tradition, which requires individual recognition and following of moral traditions that are not justifiable in terms of the canons of traditional theories of rationality. The tradition is the product of a process of selection from among irrational, or, rather, 'unjustified' beliefs which, without anyone's knowing or intending it, assisted the proliferation of those who followed them (with no necessary relationship to the reasons—as for example religious reasons—for which they were followed). The process of selection that shaped customs and morality could take account of more factual circumstances than individuals could perceive, and in consequence tradition is in some respects superior to, or "wiser" than, human reason.
>
> (Hayek 1988: 75)

Cultural evolution is "wiser" than human reason in that it allows society to take greater advantage of the accumulated knowledge of past generations and otherwise distant individuals. Social institutions are informed by new experiences, not only our own, but by the experiences of millions of others unknown to us. Cultural evolution is an ongoing process, continually adapting to unknown circumstances. No human mind could possibly take account of all the accumulated knowledge embedded within this cultural process, much less rationally direct its evolution. Our culture is "smarter" than we are, in that it can accommodate a level of complexity no human mind ever could.

Cultural systems can accommodate such complexity because the knowledge contained within them is fundamentally dispersed. Cultural "knowledge" is not possessed, as one might possess a list of explicit rules, rather it is perspectival. Two individuals may share a common culture, but this does not mean that they share the same positions within that culture. For example, in the Ghanaian context, traditional divisions of labor govern the sorts of crops men and women will grow. In general, cash crops such as cocoa will be grown by men, while women grow local food crops. A male cocoa farmer is not likely to have the same perspective as a female cassava farmer, even though they operate in the same cultural context. Different positions within a particular culture generate different perspectives, which in turn generate a multiplicity of goals and strategies. Cultural "knowledge," or more appropriately, cultural perspective is fundamentally dispersed among the people who share that culture, and is never given to a single mind.

It is this dispersed nature of cultural perspective that allows the extended order its ability to adapt to an ever-changing environment, as every individual is a potential nodal point by which new interpretations can be fed into and inform existing social norms and institutions. The gradual nature of cultural evolution frustrates the visionary who wishes, instead, to wholly redesign the extended order. Yet, the dispersed nature of knowledge in evolved social processes such as the market, common law, and moral rules radically limits the ability of humankind wholly to redesign and reconstruct the extended order. For such a reconstruction will be limited by the capacity of human reason which cannot accommodate the complexity and collected wisdom contained within the evolved order.

The most significant contributions Hayek and others within the Austrian school have made are epistemological. Understanding the nature of knowledge embedded within social processes, both cultural and economic, has been a focal point of twentieth-century Austrian literature. Ludwig von Mises ([1922] 1932, [1933] 1981, [1949] 1966) began his systematic investigations into the epistemology of the economy by arguing that the principal function markets perform is one of discovery. In his critique of central economic planning, Mises ([1922] 1932) recognized not only the allocational role of prices, which is well-recognized within standard theory. He also argued that the prices which emerge in the competitive bidding process enable individuals to discover the ends market participants value most, and the best method by which to achieve those ends. The latter issue is the most significant. For while we might imagine that without a system of market prices, a society might find some method of identifying the most highly valued ends (though only for a small subset of society), we still have no rational means of determining the most efficient method of achieving those ends. If, for example, we were to build a house without the benefit of meaningful market prices, we would have no way of discovering the best mix of inputs so as to use society's resources most efficiently. Should the house be built with lumber? Steel? Stone? Brick? Some combination of each? If so, which combination? Absent a system of market prices, we have no way of discovering the best course of action.

The work begun by Mises was continued by Hayek. In response to those who proposed the state could effectively replace both market pricing and production (Lange [1936] 1964), Hayek ([1935a, 1935b, 1940, [1945] 1948) explored the nature of knowledge embedded within a system of market prices. Hayek argued that the price system is essentially an information network by which billions of market participants unintentionally transmit relevant signals to one another. Changes in the relative scarcity of resources—whether due to changing consumer preferences or catastrophic events—require that market participants adjust their plans, perhaps by conserving on some resources, offering substitutes into the market, or even abandoning some lines of production altogether. The relevant point is that no central decree or command is needed to inspire these adjustments. Market signals (and the corresponding incentives) are spontaneously transmitted such that market participants can respond accordingly.

Further, market participants feed information into the price system, just as they read information from it. The price system is updated at all points of the market process. As individuals choose one product over another, pursue a particular career path while abandoning another, or select a specific combination of inputs from all the options available, new information enters the price system. The flow of information within the price system has no hierarchical structure. It is in a constant process of revision because every market participant informs the price system through the choices they make.

Not only does the price system work *despite* the lack of a central authority, the price system works so well precisely *because* of the fundamentally dispersed nature of knowledge embedded within it. As market participants can rely on the signals transmitted through the price system, they are freed from having to track all the particulars of market change. An entrepreneur does not need to know exactly who has an increased demand for their product to know that such an increase has taken place. This is not to suggest that entrepreneurial decisions are merely mechanistic responses to changes in price. Rather, the creative element of entrepreneurial decisions necessitates that the entrepreneur's attention be freed from the impossible task of knowing all the details of market conditions. By having access to a system of meaningful prices, the entrepreneur is free to develop an area of specialized local knowledge out of which profit opportunities can be creatively pieced together.

As individuals specialize in their market activity, the knowledge each encounters is only a piece of the whole. No two individuals have exactly the same set of information at their disposal, thus any two entrepreneurs may devise distinctly different profit strategies based on the information they have in hand. Further, a second-order difference also operates here. Even if entrepreneurs have access to the same information, divergent interpretations of those data may still emerge. The subjective nature of knowledge will often generate dramatically different strategies for profit. Just as every reader of a text sees something new and distinctly different from every other reader, every entrepreneur will "read" economic data differently. This is not to say that all interpretations are correct. The market will ultimately determine whether any particular reading of the data is a profitable one. Yet a multiplicity of interpretations may ultimately lead to profitable solutions. The rivalrous competition in the market is a rivalry among competing interpretations of the data (Ebeling 1986). Economic knowledge is generated as individual market participants offer their own interpretations out into the market through buying, selling, embarking on new business ventures, and closing failing ones. Thus, competing interpretations of the data will reinforce the already dispersed nature of knowledge within the market.

Hayek's critique of central economic planning centers, then, on the state's inability to harness and use effectively the economic knowledge required to replace the market process. Like the knowledge embedded within cultural systems, economic knowledge is never given to a single mind or organization. Economic knowledge is *fundamentally* dispersed, as it is generated by billions of individual market participants, each principally operating within the context of their local sphere of knowledge. If we were to imagine that all the information flowing into the price system had to be funneled through a central authority, or if market participants had to know all the specific details of market conditions before they could take action, economic activity would quickly cease.

In response to Hayek, many argued that improved technology would eventually overcome this problem, such that one day, all economic knowledge could be given to a single computer, if not a single mind (Lange 1967). Yet even if this doubtful scenario were to emerge, the basic problem remains. For not only is economic knowledge never given to a single mind, any attempt to centralize such knowledge will face two insurmountable obstacles. First, a central planning apparatus cannot gather the particular sort of knowledge necessary for successful economic decisions. Second, even the information that can be collected will be meaningless once stripped from the particular context of time and place.

On the first point, much of the knowledge relevant to economic decisions is tacit in nature, and not readily conveyed to a central authority. Not all the information relevant to wise economic decisions comes in the form of explicit data, but rather in the form of inarticulate rules of thumb, subtle judgments informed by years of experience, even intuitive hunches. Certainly some explicit data would be employed in any business decision, but the explicit quantifiable data are only a small subset of the knowledge needed to generate success in the market. Even with the most sophisticated data gathering techniques, the actual cognitive process by which market decisions are made can never be conveyed to the center.

On the second point, any information that could be collected by the central authority would be rendered meaningless once it was stripped away from the local context in which it made sense.

[T]he sort of knowledge with which I have been concerned is

knowledge of the kind which by its nature cannot enter into statistics and therefore cannot be conveyed to any central authority in statistical form. The statistics which such a central authority would have to use would have to be arrived at precisely by abstracting from minor differences between the things, by lumping together, as resources of one kind, items which differ as regards location, quality, and other particulars, in a way which may be very significant for the specific decisions. It follows from this that central planning based on statistical information by its nature cannot take direct account of these circumstances of time and place . . . .

(Hayek [1945] 1948: 83)

The ability of market participants to access easily the vast network of information contained in the price system, and the development of local knowledge of time and place give the market order its ability to adapt to unknown and unforeseeable circumstances. To centralize the fundamentally dispersed nature of economic knowledge is to destroy the market's ability to accommodate such adaptation.

While Austrian arguments regarding the nature of economic knowledge were made in response to arguments favoring socialist planning, the lessons are no less relevant for understanding the prospects of *development* planning. In the 1950s and 1960s, Ghana's leadership pursued such a path, with the advice and council of what were then the mainstream voices in the field of economic development. The reasons behind Ghana's economic decline during this period are the subject of much debate. An Austrian interpretation of this period will cast new light on the experiences of the past, as well as offer some insight as to the direction development policy might take in the present.

THE FAILURE OF DEVELOPMENT PLANNING

After World War II, British colonial rule in Ghana came under increasing pressure, not least from educated Africans protesting their exclusion from power. In 1947, the United Gold Coast Convention (UGCC) was established to challenge the colonialist presence gradually to withdraw their control. Yet, gradual transition to independence was not sufficient for the more radically minded of the UGCC. Chief among the radical voices calling for "self-government now" were those of Kwame Nkrumah and his

Convention People's Party (CPP), which was established in 1949. The CPP earned wide popular support, and the colonialist government correctly perceived the movement as a threat to their hold on power. In 1950 the colonial authorities arrested Nkrumah and others within the CPP, only to release them following widespread protests. In February 1951, a national constitution allowed for limited self-government and local elections, which the CPP easily won. Though the (mostly) elected Legislative Assembly enjoyed wide authority in determining matters of public policy, Nkrumah continued to lead the charge for full independence. In 1954, the Governor's authority was progressively reduced, transferring power to an entirely elected Legislative Assembly, and an Executive Council and Cabinet whose members were to be nominated by the Prime Minister. On 6 March 1957, the Gold Coast won full independence under the name "Ghana." Kwame Nkrumah and the CPP won a decisive victory in the first full and free elections.

Kwame Nkrumah and the CPP offered Ghana a uniquely African leadership, returning control to the indigenous peoples so as to usher in economic prosperity. On the eve of independence, Ghana's economic structure was fragile by the standards of the industrialized world (Seers and Ross 1952), yet relative to the rest of the developing world, Ghana was considered to have tremendous potential. Between 1950 an 1958, imports rose by 60 percent, indicating a significant improvement in the standard of living (Rimmer 1992: 66, Table 4.1). Ghana's export industries, particularly cocoa, were relatively successful on the eve of independence. As world cocoa prices rose significantly in 1954 and 1958, farmers responded by expanding their existing crops and cultivating new land. Ghana enjoyed considerable endowments of natural resources, including gold, bauxite, and manganese, and boasted one of the highest levels of per capita GNP in the developing world. Rimmer points to other indicators that suggest long-distance communication and transportation services had expanded to accommodate this growth.

> The volume of letters handled by the Post Office increased from 14 million to 37.2 million between 1949 and 1958, and the number of telephones in use rose from under 6,000 to over 19,000. Motor vehicle registrations increased from 5,318 in 1950 to 8,360 in 1958. Road mileage maintained by the Public Works Department grew from about 3,525 in 1950 to

4,277 in 1958 (but there were many other roads, and the total mileage in 1958 was put at 18,866).

(Rimmer 1992: 66)

Rimmer also points out that between 1950 and 1958, enrollments more than doubled at every level of education—a significant indicator of improved living standards, as school fees and the opportunity costs of losing productive child labor can represent a considerable drain on family resources.

Further, Ghana had considerable international political support, not only as a former colony, as Nkrumah had also garnered political support from the Soviets and the Eastern bloc countries. One of Ghana's principal obstacles was overcoming the backward conditions within agricultural food production (Frimpong-Ansah 1991). Yet Nkrumah argued that the present conditions in agriculture were the legacy of colonial rule, and that under independent African leadership, Ghana would eliminate "backward" methods of agricultural production.

Nkrumah's vision was to adapt Marxist socialism to the unique cultural and historical context of Africa. In order to step out from under the shadow of colonial rule, Ghana needed to establish economic as well as political independence. A socialist platform, Nkrumah argued, was the avenue by which both could be achieved. Through socialist economic planning, Ghana could undergo rapid industrialization and break her dependence upon primitive agricultural modes of production. At the same time, Ghana could break the grip of Western domination and international capitalism by providing for her own capital equipment needs. Thus, establishing a strategy for planned economic development across all sectors was a central piece of Nkrumah's vision towards scientific socialism.

Mainstream Western economic development theory provided the foundation for Nkrumah's strategy to achieve economic growth (Killick 1978). In particular, the prominent themes which emerged from development theory during the 1950s—a principal role for an industrialization policy, the importance of establishing linkages across economic sectors, and replacing inadequate private entrepreneurial and investment decision making with a state planning apparatus—were all central to Nkrumah's strategy to generate economic development.[1]

In order to formulate the Seven Year Development Plan, Nkrumah hosted a conference which included Arthur Lewis,

Nicholas Kaldor, and Albert Hirschman, among other prominent Western development economists. Despite some minor disagreements, the conference participants endorsed the overall development strategy.[2] Although Nkrumah's goal was to establish socialism, economic development would be the essential step in achieving this goal (Killick 1978). The fact that much of mainstream development theory supported a heavy interventionist role for the state was ultimately in consonance with Nkrumah's socialist ambitions.[3]

Killick (1978) surveys mainstream development theory of the 1950s and finds a common theme of heavy interventionist policy recommendations. Development economists challenged the efficacy of market pricing and private investment to provide adequate incentive and direction in the development process. Lewis (1959, 1965), Chenery (1959, 1960), Scitovsky (1954), Leibenstein (1957), Myrdal (1953, 1956, 1957), Hirschman (1958), and other prominent development theorists of the 1950s carved out a significant and central role for the state as investor, entrepreneur, and resource coordinator.

> [M]ainstream development economics was at many points highly congenial to Marxism. This is of considerable importance when we turn to examine economic policies in Ghana during the Nkrumah period . . . . [Marxists] embraced the [development theorists'] arguments which led to a rejection of marginalism and the open economy. The idea of the big push was also in their writings, together with their emphasis on the need for major increases in saving and investment, and a process of development which emphasized industrialization . . . . All in all, the congruence of Marxian and non-Marxian thought on the development issue was a rather remarkable and mutually reinforcing one.
>
> (Killick 1978: 24–5)

The planning strategy advocated by the advisors included far-reaching legislative controls on imports, capital transfers, licensing, and wage, price, rent, and interest rate controls. Further, the state was to mobilize resources for the industrialization drive through increased taxation, deficit financing, and an overall decrease in private consumption in favor of increased public investment. Thus, Western theorists provided Nkrumah with the theoretical justification for pursuing socialism and economic development as simultaneous and mutually reinforcing goals.

Yet, with few exceptions, the economic performance of post-colonial Ghana is considered to have been disastrous. As Killick (1978) reports, virtually every state enterprise was a financial catastrophe. The State Fishing Corporation, State Gold Mining Corporation, Ghana Airways, and the Food Marketing Corporation all consistently operated at a significant loss, even though they each enjoyed substantial monopoly power. By 1966, only four out of the sixty-four state enterprises demonstrated any margin of success. The state built tomato canneries, even though the types of tomatoes grown in Ghana were not suitable for foreign trade. A sugar factory could not operate because it was built in an area where there was no water supply. The state built a mango processing plant, even though there were no mangos to process (Killick 1978). (They eventually planted some mango trees, yet this was of little help, as the maturation process takes seven years.) State enterprises represented one economic blunder after another.

Highly mechanized state farms were equally disastrous. Even though the State Farms Corporation had command over vast capital assets and controlled inputs relative to private agriculture, the state farms performed dismally by comparison. Whereas private farms produced 0.94 tons per acre on average, state farms produced only 0.21 tons per acre. The productivity of labor on private farms also outstripped state agriculture with 3.33 tons per worker versus 0.59 tons per worker, respectively (Killick 1978: Table 8.2). Frustrating the farmers they supervised, political appointees with little or no knowledge of farming methods held the management positions within the large state cooperatives (Frimpong-Ansah 1991: 83). The state imported expensive farm machinery which was wholly inappropriate for the local hard soil conditions. Further, a small malfunction would render the equipment inoperable as no replacement parts were available. Nor did the technical know-how to make repairs exist on site (Dadson 1973). On average, only 20 percent of the 4,000 imported tractors were functioning at any one time (Killick 1978). Meanwhile, interventionist agricultural policy was destroying the one sector which had demonstrated promise for its growth potential—the private agricultural sector.

By the 1966 military coup which threw Nkrumah from power, the Ghanaian economy had virtually collapsed, despite the considered attempt to promote economic development. From the late 1950s to the mid-1960s, the Ghanaian economy fell from being one of the fastest growing in the developing world, to one of the worst cases of economic calamity (Roemer 1981). From 1959 to 1965, the per capita growth in GDP fell from 10 percent to –2.4 percent. Yet, from 1957 to 1965, government expenditure rose from 15.4 percent of GDP to 25.3 percent. During the same period, net exchange reserves fell from 25.9 percent of GDP in 1957 to –0.05 percent in 1965, as the state increasingly had to resort to deficit financing to cover its expenditures (IMF Data Fund 1988; data reproduced in Frimpong-Ansah 1991: Tables A6.1, A6.3, A6.6). Thus, as Ahmad (1970) describes, Ghana suffered the paradox of investment without growth. From 1960 to 1966, real income had declined 41 percent for minimum wage earners, and a staggering 66 percent for cocoa producers (calculated from Killick 1978: Table 4D). By 1966, Ghana was facing rapidly growing inflation and a foreign debt of $858 million. Little debate remains as to the disastrous results of post-colonial development efforts. The economic collapse is largely credited as the cause of Nkrumah's political downfall. What remains unresolved are the reasons why such economic chaos ensued.

Douglas Rimmer (1969, 1992) suggests that neither African socialism nor economic development were ever the underlying goals of the Nkrumah regime. Rather, the economic platform which was pursued was designed to maintain power and to foster large-scale wealth transfers from the private agricultural sector to the leadership and bureaucratic elite. Given that overall economic progress was never the goal of the regime, Rimmer argues that it should not be surprising that the economy finally buckled under the weight of a heavy bureaucratic structure.

David Rooney (1988), on the other hand, takes issue with Rimmer's flat dismissal of Nkrumah's ideological motivations. Rooney paints a portrait of Nkrumah as a convinced Marxist socialist, seeing the only path for Ghana as a radical split from Western capitalism.[4] Nkrumah's failure, Rooney argues, rested with his inability to set strict controls on corruption within the state enterprise system. According to Rooney, Nkrumah's efforts at industrialization would have been successful if he had been able to establish a disciplined adherence to the goals of the plan and not the personal aggrandizement of the political leadership and bureaucratic functionaries.

Tony Killick (1978) likewise recognizes Nkrumah's sincere commitment to African socialism. The economic policies which Nkrumah implemented were directly tied to this end. The massive thrust towards industrialization, the push away from small private farming in favor of large state cooperatives, these were all elements of a considered attempt to destroy the colonialist economic structure. According to Killick, economic development planning failed because of improper implementation techniques in state agriculture and industry, not because of the self-serving motivations of the planners themselves.

By drawing upon Hayek's ([1935a, 1935b, 1940, 1945] 1948) argument concerning the nature of economic knowledge, yet another interpretation emerges. An Austrian interpretation reconciles the contradictory views of the standard accounts. Further, such an interpretation provides a more sound explanation for the economic chaos which ensued in post-colonial Ghana. The position taken here is that Nkrumah believed he was following the most judicious path towards African socialism and economic prosperity. Yet, given the goal of central planning for economic development, proper implementation would have been impossible, as the planning apparatus removes the ability of an economy to make use of the knowledge required to generate coordination and economic growth. Thus, while the policies Nkrumah followed were ideologically motivated, as Killick and Rooney suggest, ultimately these objectives could not be achieved. The only criteria left to the political leaders and bureaucratic elite were those suggested by Rimmer—to skew the process to their own personal advantage, regardless of the devastating effects to the rest of the economy. The advantages were then concentrated within the political elite, as the costs were disbursed throughout the population.

Corruption as the source of failure

In reviewing Nkrumah's "Program for Work and Happiness," the outline for the Seven Year Development Plan, it is difficult to dismiss Rooney's argument that Nkrumah was a devoted Marxist attempting to introduce socialism into the African context.

> The strategy [is] for the public sector, which control[s] key areas of the economy, gradually to overtake the private sector until the private sector [is] entirely eliminated . . . . The main tasks of the Plan are: firstly, to speed up the rate of growth of our national economy. Secondly, it is to enable us to embark upon the socialist transformation of our economy through the rapid development of our state and cooperative sectors. Thirdly, it is our aim by this plan, to eradicate completely the colonial structure of our economy . . . . [T]his Seven Year

67

Development Plan which I now lay before you is the first really integrated and comprehensive economic plan ever drawn up for Ghana's development after a thorough examination of our needs and resources. It embodies a long view of the path which should lead to a self-sustaining economy, based on socialist production and distribution.

(Nkrumah 1964: 182, 189–90)

Nkrumah associated capitalist production with colonialism. According to Nkrumah, economic exploitation under commodity production was simply a variant of the political exploitation which took place under colonial rule. Thus, as long as Ghana still relied upon the international capitalist structure, the country was not truly independent.

Rooney argues that Nkrumah believed a socialist platform would provide a radical economic and political break from colonialism.

Nkrumah suggested that state operated enterprises were needed to compete with the power of the multinational companies . . . . A policy of scientific socialism would aim to free the economy from alien control, to protect the people from alien exploitation, to control the means of production and distribution.

(Rooney 1988: 183–4)

The way to achieve scientific socialism in the African context was to achieve economic growth and independence.

According to Rooney, ultimately it was the lack of administrative control of the state enterprise system and the resulting corruption of the Nkrumah regime which fostered the eventual political and economic chaos.

[T]here is little doubt that corruption was one of the most important single factors in causing the failure of [Nkrumah's] attempt to create a socialist state . . . . Nkrumah's indifference to financial discipline and accounting gave endless opportunities for unscrupulous people. This led to what can only be called a madness—a belief that there was a totally unlimited supply of money. Appalling examples from Ghana's ambassadors and high commissioners are echoed through every rank in the government and every party, down to the lowliest party agent at the village level corruptly using his power to enrich himself.

(Rooney 1988: 194)

Rooney argues that four separate government commissioned reports—the Akainyah Report on Corruption (1964), the Abrahams Report on Trading Malpractices (1964), the Jiagge Report on Corruption (1966), and the Ollennu Report on Malpractices Over Import Licenses (1967)—characterized Nkrumah's "indifference to financial discipline," particularly since the recommendations made within these reports were largely ignored. Rooney suggests that if Nkrumah and his leadership had secured tighter administrative control, the wealth would not have been diverted to the hands of private individuals, but rather, would have been directed into the socialist industrial sector. It was here that Nkrumah would have been successful in providing the foundations for socialist planning, and therefore development. While the leadership did provide the ideological foundations for socialism, in the absence of effective controls to curb corruption, the newly established socialist economy did not survive.

Yet, as an explanation for failure, corruption does not provide a convincing story. Historical evidence suggests that if the leadership had embarked upon a massive anti-corruption campaign, it is unlikely that the economy would have improved. In fact, reform efforts designed to curb corruption in the Soviet Union, such as those implemented under Andropov and Gorbachev actually resulted in further economic chaos. As Grossman (1977, 1982) suggests, it is the ability to engage in bribery, black market trade, and political favor swapping that allows agents within a bureaucratized context to acquire equipment and inputs for production in a shortage economy.

This is not to say that corruption necessarily provides optimal efficiency, but rather, that it can often act as the grease which keeps the wheels of an overly bureaucratized machine turning. To remove the corruption would be to force the economic system to a grinding halt. If the leadership in Ghana had pursued a vigorous anti-corruption campaign, historical precedent suggests that in the best case, the economic situation would not have improved, and that in the worst case, such controls would have led to further decline (Simis 1982). Thus, while Rooney presents a persuasive case that Nkrumah was committed to establishing African socialism, the lack of bureaucratic control over corruption is an inadequate explanation for Ghana's economic collapse.

Poor implementation as the source of failure

According to Killick (1978), the Ghanaian leadership was devoted to pursuing economic development, and not simply their own enrichment, as the primary goal. The fact that the plan was based upon the advice of some of the top mainstream development economists of the time indicates a true commitment to achieving economic progress. However, Killick argues, in both the agricultural and industrial sectors, poor implementation measures were the source of the economic chaos.

> [M]any of the [state cooperative] farms were established with little prior planning, their managers were political appointees knowing little of agriculture, implements were ordered from many different sources with little thought for the organizational problems of a mechanization programme, and there were many acute shortages of trained personnel and supplies . . . . [Nkrumah] wanted an agricultural revolution but neglected such elementary preconditions as the creation of an administration to conduct it . . . . He wanted a revolution; instead he got a shambles. He introduced capital and modern technology; but the technology was inappropriate and much of the investment was money down the drain.
>
> (Killick 1978: 194–5)

Killick cites a similar record for state industrial performance, particularly with reference to the general excess capacity among state firms. On average, state enterprises operated at only 20 to 29 percent of capacity. From 1960 to 1967, the average gross capital to output ratio doubled, even though the Seven Year Development Plan projected a ratio of 3:5 (Killick 1978: 96). More and more was being spent in pursuit of economic development, with little if any tangible result.

> A wide-ranging set of conditions conspired to limit the efficacy of the industrialization drive. Over-optimism about the future growth of the economy and the search for economies of scale produced an under-utilized and high-cost structure of industry. The unselective and arbitrary protection, a variety of biases favoring capital intensity and processes with few linkages to other sectors, a deteriorating quality of investment decisions, and sub-standard performance on the part of state

enterprises—when taken together provide a powerful explanation for the failure of industrialization.

(Killick 1978: 204–5)

Yet the problems Killick cites as the source of economic decline are themselves symptoms of the planning apparatus' inability to accommodate adequately the resource and coordination requirements of the agricultural and urban sectors. If Killick is correct in assessing the leadership's commitment and effort in pursuing economic development, why did Nkrumah and his followers suddenly become so indolent?

Killick does not explain why the political will was present to garner the resources necessary to introduce new technology into agricultural production, for example, but was absent when it came time to adequately assess the relative merits of the technology. Nor does he explain why the political will was present to transfer massive resources to the state industrial sector, but was insufficient to make wise investment decisions, establish vital linkages in the economy, keep costs down or productivity high. The answer lies in the fact that investment decisions which make economic sense are not a matter of political will as Killick seems to suggest.

In general, the Nkrumah leadership was relatively successful in mobilizing resources. Even as world cocoa prices were falling, on average the state managed to appropriate revenues higher than forty-nine other developing countries (Bahl 1972). What Ghana's leaders consistently failed to do, however, was to generate productive results once the resources were transferred. This general tendency indicates that the state lacks the ability properly to assess the economically efficient choice, even when the political will to do so is present. While Killick provides a convincing argument that Nkrumah believed he was following the best course toward economic development, the argument that the eventual economic collapse was simply the lack of effective implementation is unconvincing.

Development planning as rent-seeking

Given the accounts of Nkrumah's own ideological commitment to building scientific socialism within Ghana, and his considered effort to employ the best advice he could find as to how to implement a strategy for development planning, a case is to be made that the Nkrumah regime was at least in some respects driven by an ideolog-

71

ical motivation. However, when reviewing the record of corruption, Rimmer's (1969) argument that the policies pursued were merely the manifestation of rampant rent seeking also deserves serious consideration. Following the public choice tradition, Rimmer considers the real goals of the regime to be the financial and political security of the bureaucratic elite. According to Rimmer, the policies were designed to provide the maximum opportunity to exploit the private sector, while the concern for building socialism through economic growth was empty rhetoric.

> [In Ghana] it appears possible to make a very simple categorization of the redistributive motives which lie behind the growth of government expenditure. These motives are, first, the enrichment of the government itself (i.e. of the ruler, of Ministers, of party leaders, of top civil servants, and possibly of numerous subordinate ranks of public officers and party workers), and, secondly, the buying of the political support which will enable the government to maintain itself in power.
>
> (Rimmer 1969: 197)

Rimmer suggests that the Seven Year Development Plan might as well never have been written or enacted. While it was not officially dropped until the 1966 coup which ousted Nkrumah from power, no real attempt had ever been made to implement the plan in the first place. Rather, Rimmer argues that, from the start, side deals designed to enrich the political leaders were favored over the established plan.

New projects appeared which had never been envisaged in the plan but were now being pushed by contractors willing to pay commissions to the persons who accepted them. Projects were begun without feasibility studies and without competitive tendering. New enterprises were distributed among party functionaries as private fiefs, enabling them to give patronage to relatives, friends, and supporters (Rimmer 1969: 195).

As economic development was never the goal of the regime, Rimmer argues, it is not surprising that the private sector stagnated and eventually collapsed under the weight of bureaucratic interventionism. The most lucrative private sector industry—cocoa production—virtually crumbled. In his study of the United Ghana Farmers' Council (the agricultural wing of Nkrumah's Convention People's Party), Bjorn Beckman (1976) offers an account of the rent-seeking behavior which eventually undermined the productive capacity of private agriculture in general, and cocoa production in particular. The history of cocoa production in Ghana provides the best example of what Rimmer sees as the conspicuous attempt on the part of the bureaucratic elite to enrich themselves at the expense of the private sector.

Upon taking control from the British government, the independent leadership in Ghana inherited a marketing board structure, supposedly designed to stabilize agricultural income. The premise was to establish a fixed price to farmers for the purchase of cocoa and other cash-crop products, holding the reserves in a fund which would supplement farm income in times of low world market prices (Bates 1981).[5] After World War II, cocoa prices were relatively high and reserve funds grew substantially. The surplus revenues, rather than being invested in local infrastructure, were invested in British government bonds for postwar reconstruction. The farmers did eventually receive the yield on the investment, but the precedent had been set. From the outset, the cocoa farmer reserve funds were used for public finance purposes, at the discretion of state officials (Beckman 1976).

The independent government seemed to learn quickly from the example of their colonialist predecessors. Under Nkrumah, use of the reserve funds was completely at the discretion of state officials. Shortly after the CPP gained political control, the Minister of Finance, Komol Gbedmah, announced that the increase in the world price for cocoa would not be passed on to the farmers. By 1961, the Farmers' Council already controlled much of the local trade. Officially, seats on the Council were to be reserved for farmers, yet virtually all the positions were held by bureaucratic officials, who maintained increasingly lavish living conditions and created well-paying jobs for friends, political supporters, and family members.

The Farmers' Council launched a ruthless campaign against the local and foreign wholesale buyers and credit merchants by forcing through legislation which banned all cocoa trade except with the Council itself. The middlemen represented both an ideological challenge to the socialist platform, as well as a leakage of resources which could otherwise go to the state industrial sector and the pockets of the bureaucratic elite. This left only the Farmers' Council to dictate the terms at which cocoa would be purchased by the state. Supposedly the political spokesmen for the cocoa farmers, the United Ghana Farmers' Council, "volunteered" a long line of price reductions to demonstrate the farmers' patriotism and commitment to the development program.

According to Beckman (1976), the most remarkable public finance decision, however, was the compulsory savings plan. Income was to be withheld for the purpose of investing in National Development Bonds, redeemable at the end of ten years with accumulated interest. Cocoa farmers were hit with the highest confiscation rate of 10 percent. The particularly high rate faced by the farmers was, again according to the Farmers' Council, a voluntary act of patriotism. Six months after the introduction of the savings plan, farmers and urban workers were encouraged to donate their savings to the development program. The Farmers' Council, again supposedly acting on behalf of the cocoa farmers, voted not to reclaim their savings. The cocoa producers were again lauded for their patriotic zeal. By 1963, the state abandoned the compulsory savings plan in favor of a non-refundable income tax.

Further, Beckman reports that rent-seeking behavior was not isolated to the upper ranks of the political elite. Low-level functionaries benefited greatly from the monopoly position held by the Farmers' Council. With no other legal choice for alternative weighing sites, farmers were at the mercy of government clerks who systematically extorted cash and cocoa. By miscalibrating the scales, the clerks could under-weigh a farmer's load, and over the course of the day, haul in a considerable surplus to sell for their own gain. If farmers challenged the official's readings, fellow clerks would hurl insults and threaten arrest. The long and inconvenient distances to the official weighing sites provided further opportunity for extortion. Clerks deliberately created delays so as to inspire side payments to avoid overnight stays or return trips. Clerks sometimes kept poor quality beans in their pockets and claimed the load was of inferior quality, unless the farmer was able to convince the clerk otherwise with a cash tribute.

This flurry of rent seeking and corruption might support Rimmer's argument that the stated goals of socialism and economic development were mere rhetoric and that the true goals of the regime were the maintenance of political power and financial gain. Rimmer (1992: 91) cites the "administrative jungle" of fifty-three ministries, the dozen joint state/private enterprises, and two dozen public boards as examples of how decisions either did not make any sense at all, or were made on political grounds. In either case, economic reasoning was not the motivation behind any of the decisions.

Much of the investment in so-called directly productive activities was ludicrously amateurish. It might be called the result of shopping without a list. Additional causes of failure were overstaffing (state enterprises being regarded implicitly—and sometimes even explicitly—as means of providing employment); . . . the corruption that allowed obviously unsuitable deals to be made with foreign contractors; and political interference in the appointment and promotion of personnel, the giving of credit, the choice of local suppliers, and so on.

(Rimmer 1992: 91–2)

This interpretation seems to suggest, however, that *had* the Nkrumah regime been truly motivated, either by socialist aspirations, or by the desire to plan for economic development, they could have been successful. The problem, according to Rimmer, was that the political elite were only interested in maximizing their own power and financial gain, and designed a political apparatus to do exactly that.

Rimmer makes an important observation that, in general, administrative functionaries do not have the same incentives to make economically rational choices as private investors do. Yet, considering the Misesian argument regarding market discovery, Rimmer's emphasis on the political elite's lack of motivation misses a more crucial point. The "over-capitalization, wrong location choices, and failures to match product supply with market demand" to which Rimmer (1992: 91) refers as "shopping without a list" may represent more than just an incentive problem. Supposing that the Nkrumah regime were in fact motivated to advance economic development (as Rooney and Killick suggest) outside of the market context, they had no way of discovering what to put on their "shopping list." Even the most motivated planners have no way of determining the appropriate mix of resources and factory locations, and certainly no way of matching product supply with market demand, if in fact there is no functional market. The Misesian insight is that even if the Nkrumah regime were truly motivated to advance economic development (as may have been the case), they would have had no way of determining what the economically rational course of action was.

The rent-seeking interpretation of this period begs a further question: if the systematic transfer of wealth to the political elite was the calculated goal, why did they allow the pricing and taxation policies to destroy their goose that laid the golden egg, i.e. the private agricultural sector? Certainly, it would have been better if the leadership could have continued this wealth transfer in perpetuity. Rimmer's (1992) criticism of Killick's argument that the leadership was committed to long-term economic development (and implicitly Rooney's argument that the Nkrumah regime was motivated by truly socialist aspirations) is that such arguments cannot explain the results of rampant rent seeking. Yet a similar criticism could be made of Rimmer's analysis. The interpretation that the political and economic structure was designed to maximize the wealth of the political leadership does not coincide with the fact that they eventually destroyed the source of their wealth and their own hold on power. On the other hand, an Austrian interpretation can reconcile the various interpretations, while at the same time provide a more plausible explanation for the eventual failure of the regime to foster economic development.

Development planning as the source of failure

The most convincing elements of Killick's and Rooney's arguments are that Nkrumah was an ideologically motivated socialist committed to establishing economic planning and development. Yet, how might we reconcile this with the most convincing element of Rimmer's argument, that rent-seeking behavior was a principal characteristic of the regime? The answer lies in understanding Hayek's argument as to why centralized economic planning cannot succeed.

Nkrumah called for the eventual replacement of private decision making with state planning in virtually all sectors of the economy, including the agricultural, industrial, and financial sectors. On the advice of development theorists, the Ghanaian state was supposed to fill the "entrepreneurial gap" characteristic of pre-industrial economies. Given the long history of trade and entrepreneurship within sub-Saharan Africa, and Ghana in particular, it is questionable whether such a gap ever existed. Yet even if it did, the detailed accounts of industrial failure offered by Killick (1978) and others, suggest that the state is apparently incapable of filling this gap. The reasons Killick cites for industrial failure include inefficient plant size, high-cost production techniques, failure to establish links across industries, diminishing quality of investment decisions, and low productivity. Within a Hayekian interpretation, these are not causes of industrial failure, but rather symptoms or characteristics of industrial failure. The symptoms are caused by the state taking over the role of entrepreneur. As entrepreneur, the state is ill-suited to recognize profit opportunities across sectors, the most prudent production technique, or the most advantageous investment decision. The state has neither the incentive nor the knowledge required to make economically viable decisions. Such is the case within the state agricultural cooperatives as well. The state cannot make economically sound decisions because it is operating completely outside of the context in which the knowledge necessary to inform those decisions is generated.

Development planning is not only incapable of designing new economic sectors, such as state industry and state agriculture, it is also incapable of controlling the unintended consequences of its interventions within the private sector, as illustrated by the decay within private agriculture. In the development planning process, indigenous entrepreneurship is systematically undermined as the state attempts to direct the course of the market process. The knowledge contained within the indigenous market, in the form of prices, interest rates, and practical advice, is annihilated. This is particularly the case in post-colonial Ghana where the political leadership targeted both local and foreign entrepreneurs as foes to the socialist objectives of the state. In launching deliberate attacks upon middlemen buyers and credit merchants, the Farmers' Council eliminated the mechanism by which price and interest rate signals could convey meaningful information.

Further, the annihilation of the so-called "bourgeois class interests," or the private lenders in the agricultural sector meant the loss of an essential network of credit, supplies, and practical farming advice. In the "Programme for Work and Happiness," Nkrumah proposed that the private money lenders be annihilated, as they represented a form of colonial exploitation.

> I know that many of those who are carrying on this business of lending money at criminal rates of interest are non-Ghanaians. But, unhappily, not a few of our own people have joined the ranks of those who make quick and easy money out of the difficulties and misery of others. Money-lending and usury are intolerable and inconsistent with the ideals of a socialist state. We should see to it that this practice is eliminated from our society.
>
> (Nkrumah 1964: 203)

The state banking sector was to take over this role, so as to direct investment into state industry and not the hands of capitalist middlemen.

> Individuals who can command capital use their money not in productive endeavor, but by the purchase and re-sale at high prices, of such commodities as fish, salt and other items of food and consumer goods which are in demand by the people. This type of business serves no social purpose and steps will be taken to see that our banking resources are not used to provide credit for this type of business.

> (Nkrumah 1964: 202)

The various campaigns against the middlemen and private bankers dealt a devastating blow to the private agricultural sector in particular. Their annihilation meant the destruction of a network of price information and advice for growing techniques. By wiping out the role of the private banker, the state also destroyed a valuable futures market in produce which provided farmers with capital in a lump sum to embark upon the next growing season (Beckman 1976). Yet, as Killick points out, the state banking system proved to be disastrous as a replacement for private investment decisions. Whereas the private bankers had intimate knowledge of the market conditions, the state planning apparatus and banking system were divorced from the process which generated such knowledge. As such, the state banking sector was incapable of making economically sound investment decisions.

Development planning itself was responsible for the failure of state industry, the failure of state farms, and the destruction within private agriculture. Yet, it was also responsible for the rent-seeking behavior so prominent in post-colonial Ghana. Certainly Nkrumah had difficulty justifying the corruption taking place, while he simultaneously promoted the ideals of African socialism. Though the two run contrary to each other in the minds of the public, they are by no means mutually exclusive in actuality. Whereas the market is a self-regulating and self-coordinating process, development planning depends on conscious control. As centralized development planning efforts replace the private planning of market participants, a larger and larger administrative sector is called forth. The growing bureaucracy affords the *nomenklatura* greater opportunity to skew the political process to their own narrow advantage, yet no greater ability to direct the development process rationally. Even if the regime is committed to the high ideals of economic prosperity and socialism, making economically rational decisions is not an option. Political rationale *must* replace economic rationale once decisions are taken out of the context of the market.

Though it may appear that the political elite consciously designed and controlled the political apparatus to enrich themselves and maintain their power, there is in fact no way to control the unintended effects of state intervention. The predacious actions of the state toward private agriculture aptly illustrate both the opportunity of political functionaries to engage in rent-seeking behavior and the inability to control the effects of such activity. If the political elite could have consciously controlled the systematic exploitation of the private sphere, they would have constrained their activities enough to maintain their political and economic advantage. Yet in the end, both were lost, suggesting that the political elite could no more control the outcome of their rent-seeking behavior than they could successfully control the process of economic development.

The original goals of Nkrumah's platform were impossible to attain. The economic failure of state agriculture and industry was inevitable as the state tried to substitute the entrepreneur with a centralized planning agency, necessarily operating outside the context of well-defined property rights and meaningful market signals. The private agricultural sector also failed as the market mechanism was systematically circumvented and the discovery process at work in the economy was annihilated.

Given the failures big-push industrialization drives have produced in the twentieth century, the development planning literature of the 1950s has fallen out of favor. Localized development projects have replaced sector-wide planning. Policy makers are now seeking ways to direct resources to the local private sector rather than a state industrialized sector. But we have moved ahead without a clear understanding of why sector-wide development planning failed in the first place. We have moved ahead without a full appreciation for the role markets play in generating the knowledge necessary for economic development. Below, we will assess the potential for the new thinking in development policy which targets local entrepreneurs with easier access to credit and other services. But first we will briefly review the major political and economic changes which have taken place in the years since Nkrumah.

79

THE POLITICS OF ECONOMIC DECLINE

The political backlash against the corruption and economic decline experienced under Nkrumah were relatively swift and certainly severe. While making a state visit to China on 24 February 1966, Nkrumah was swept from power in a military coup, which installed Lieutenant-General J.A. Ankrah as the head of state. Support for the coup came from all reaches of society, including farmers who had lost their incomes, traditional leaders whose power had been eroded by state legislation, workers and labor leaders feeling the effects of failed industrial policy, intellectuals who protested the increasing use of arbitrary force and preventative detention, and trade organizations representing business interests which did not benefit from the system of privilege promoted under the Nkrumah regime (Pellow and Chazen 1986).

The new government, called the National Liberation Council (NLC), consisted of eight members, and was entirely made up of police and military officers. Yet it proclaimed itself to be a transitional regime with the primary purpose of eliminating corruption, which would eventually turn the country back to civilian rule. The NLC appointed a commission to draft a new constitution that would establish liberal democratic rule as had been envisioned toward the end of the colonial period.

The tenure of the NLC was not without its problems. The predominantly Ga and Ewe Council members were accused of promoting the interests of their own tribes over that of the Ashanti and other Akan peoples. Though the economy improved somewhat with a devaluation of the cedi and an increase in prices paid to cocoa farmers, Ghana still suffered the effects of Nkrumahist policies. Yet, the NLC did deliver on its promise to return the country to civilian rule. In 1968, an electoral commission was established. In May 1969, the ban the CPP had imposed on political parties was removed, and in August of the same year, elections were held and Ghana was returned to civilian control.

The Progressive Party, led by K.A. Busia, was elected to power. Busia and the Progressive Party drew most of their support from the Akan peoples, including the Ashanti who had opposed Nkrumah. Busia publicly favored policies of liberalization, and in fact reduced the budgets of both the military and civil service. While the cuts were large enough to alienate most members of the military and civil service, they were not radical enough to turn the economy

80

around. Further, Busia and his Finance Minister, J.H. Mensah—who had been a principal architect of the Seven Year Development Plan under Nkrumah (Frimpong-Ansah 1991)—considered it politically prudent to pursue policies of government-led growth, reminiscent of the Nkrumah years. The increases in capital spending were financed through inflationary borrowing practices (Rimmer 1992). Despite rapidly rising inflation, falling cocoa prices in the world market (and corresponding decreases in tax revenue), the Busian government persisted with its expansionary agenda. Further, no serious attempt was made to close inefficient state industry or reform protectionist international trade policies. Forty-three of the fifty-three state enterprises that had been created under Nkrumah were still operating in 1971, and five more had been created (Killick 1978: 313). As Rimmer notes, this prominent role was given to state intervention

> despite the aversion of the NLC and the Busia government to "socialism" and their declared partiality for private enterprise . . . . At the end of 1965 the public sector had provided 70 percent of the recorded employment total of 396,000; at the end of 1971 it provided 72 percent of a total of 402,000. And the public sector continued to take the lion's share of bank lending . . . .
>
> (Rimmer 1992: 126)

Though attempts were made toward the devaluation of exchange rates and the removal of restrictive import licensing, throughout the NLC and Busia years, no great progress toward liberalization was made. Market controls, including exchange, price, rent, and wage controls, remained in place, and the systematic expulsion of non-Ghanaian retail and wholesale merchants continued as it had under Nkrumah. Though in word Busia advocated a liberal political economy, in deed his policies were strikingly similar to those advanced by Nkrumah.

The expansionary policies under Busia led to growing budget deficits, the accumulation of short-term international debt, and a growing balance of payments deficit. An overvalued currency raised the relative price of Ghanaian cocoa and other exports in world markets. Ghanaian cocoa continued to lose world market share. Seeing the problem to be short term, the Ghanaian leadership sought bilateral resolutions with the United States and Britain to provide a line of credit to support the balance of payments deficit.

Wary that Ghana was returning to the precarious economic policies of Nkrumahism, the United States and Britain refused, insisting that assistance be secured through the IMF, which would in turn insist on measures to reverse the balance of payments problem. In the early part of 1971, it was clear that Ghana's balance of payments deficit would not be supported by external donors (Frimpong-Ansah 1991: 107). In December of 1971, Busia acknowledged that the balance of payments deficit was a pervasive problem, stemming from the expansionary policies the government had put in place. The principal corrective measure Busia initiated was a massive 42 percent devaluation in the exchange rate, rendering imports more expensive and export industries more competitive on the world market. The austere corrective measures were never allowed the opportunity to work, however, as a military coup removed the Busian government from power.

The National Redemption Council (NRC) seized power in January, 1972. Led by Colonel Ignatius Acheampong, the NRC capitalized on populist and nationalist sentiments, particularly within urban centers, as they appealed to those most adversely affected under Busian policies, including members of the military and civil service. The principal motivations behind the coup, according to Acheampong, were the inexcusable reductions in military compensation and benefits, the arbitrary reductions in public sector employment, and the cowardly concessions made to international interests and the domestic export sector, as evidenced by the exchange rate devaluation. This platform immediately won him the allegiance of former CPP supporters. Acheampong increased public service employment and military compensation, partially reversed the exchange rate devaluation, and repudiated Ghana's international debt. The government nationalized the majority shareholdings in four of the largest foreign-owned timber companies, and the largest gold mining company. Further, they reinstituted restrictive import licensing, "restoring a powerful instrument of [political] patronage" (Rimmer 1992: 135).

Like his predecessors, Acheampong was interested in economic expansion, but he pursued a rather different strategy. Acheampong developed policies to stimulate domestic food production. On the surface, such a move might have seemed surprising, in that his support rested in the urban centers, not in agriculture. Yet, with the repudiation of international debt, external sources of capital investment for industrialization were not forthcoming, thus promotion of domestic agriculture was the only option left (Frimpong-Ansah 1991). At first, the policies seemed to be working, as agricultural production increased and imports decreased. But this was to be expected as foreign producers would no longer send their goods on credit and domestic consumers had no choice but to rely on local agriculture.

Market signals were increasingly circumvented. The discrepancy between controlled prices of agricultural output and real market values increased as inflationary pressures rose. Both consumers and farmers increasingly sought out black markets, circumventing official distribution controls. Eventually, interventionist policies would all but destroy what was left of the productive capacity of the private sector. The fragile economy could not withstand the poor growing conditions of 1972 to 1974. By 1975, the increase in oil prices had exacerbated the balance of payments deficit. Fiscal deficits also grew as they absorbed the difference between world market prices for petroleum and local controlled prices. Further, the negative growth effects of the rent-seeking economy were apparent in all sectors, and economic decline was more pronounced than it had ever been. In 1975, per capita growth of GDP was an unprecedented *negative* 15 percent (IMF Data Fund).

The NRC faced increasing opposition, against both the crumbling economy and its abhorrent record of corruption. Acheampong's response was to replace the National Redemption Council with the Supreme Military Council (SMC), giving exclusive control to the military, and advancing himself to the rank of General. This move effectively eliminated all ties Acheampong had to political parties and the civil service. By 1976, organized opposition had emerged, particularly among the intelligentsia and professional classes (Rimmer 1992: 136). The antagonism had reached fever pitch by 1978, as opposition movements were banned and its members imprisoned. Sensing opposition even within its own ranks, the military leadership deemed Acheampong to be a liability. Acheampong was forced out by the SMC, to be replaced by Lieutenant-General F.W.K. Akuffo. Though his regime was somewhat less oppressive, the change in leadership did not appease the opposition. In November of 1978, civil servants went on strike, bringing almost all public services to a resounding halt.

It was clear to everyone, including Akuffo, that transition was inevitable. By the beginning of 1979, Akuffo had made some moves toward returning democratic elections to Ghana. But before any elections could be held, junior officers within the army staged a successful coup on 4 June 1979. Flight-Lieutenant Jerry Rawlings led the Armed Forces Revolutionary Council (AFRC) to power, once again appealing to populist and nationalist sentiments. Rawlings' charisma also won him instant support. Rawlings presented the AFRC as a necessary corrective to the rampant corruption in the upper ranks of the military regime. The rhetoric of the AFRC struck a popular chord with the average citizen who had been locked out of the system of privilege, yet was spending more and more for basic requirements. Once order was restored, Rawlings promised, national elections would be reintroduced.

Establishing order for the AFRC included the execution of Acheampong, Akuffo, and other members of the Supreme Military Council. Fifty senior officers within the military, government officials, and businessmen were tried and imprisoned on corruption charges. Charges of corruption were not limited to the elite ranks of government and business, however. Market traders selling above the state controlled price were also targeted for their "profiteering" (Robertson 1983). (As will be discussed in Chapter 4, the effects of this and other campaigns against urban market traders are still being felt.) Promising to remain neutral to the outcome, the AFRC then held elections on 18 June 1979. Five parties ran in what are largely considered to have been fair elections. The People's National Party (PNP), the heir apparent of Nkrumah's Convention People's Party, won the majority of the seats. The victory was largely credited to the party's leader Dr. Hilla Limann, who presented an image of high moral character.

The period of civilian rule was to be short-lived, however. Political tensions were pervasive, particularly with regard to economic policy. The devaluation which was needed for economic reasons posed political problems. Attempts by previous regimes at devaluation had resulted in coups d'état. Further the watchful eye of the military posed a continual threat. Limann attempted to use political maneuvers to reduce this threat. For example, he had Rawlings and the other AFRC appointees in the police and military "retired" from service. Rumors that Limann might repeal the portion of the Constitution which gave the AFRC immunity for actions taken in 1979 served as the final split between the government and the military (Rimmer 1992: 142). On 31 December 1981, Rawlings and his Provisional National Defense Council (PNDC) staged another coup, throwing Limann from power.

Still drawing upon his populist support, Rawlings stepped up his anti-capitalist rhetoric. The declared enemies of Rawlings' revolution were the entrepreneurs, the larger farmers, the liberal intelligentsia, and professional classes (Frimpong-Ansah 1991: 112). Drawing on a mixture of dependency theory, anti-Westernism, and Nkrumah's neocolonialism, Rawlings favored at least a partial withdrawal from the global economic system (Haynes 1989). International capitalist interests conspired to keep Ghana in a dependent position, Rawlings argued. Never did he blame domestic interventionist policies for the continued economic decline.

By 1983, the rate of inflation was 122.8 percent, as credit expansion was used to accommodate growing budget deficits. Per capita growth in GDP had been negative for five years running, and the currency was grossly over-valued. Cocoa production also continued to fall. While cocoa accounted for about half of the cultivated land and provided employment for about a quarter of the work force, cocoa production was half of what it was at the end of the Nkrumah years. Distortionary interventionist policies in agriculture and over-valued exchange rates reduced Ghana's share in the world cocoa market to a fraction of what it had once been in the 1960s. Only in 1983, when he was in considerable danger of losing political control, did Rawlings grudgingly accept the conditions of an IMF Economic Recovery Program (ERP).

The principal aims of the ERP were to introduce trade reforms, to stabilize macroeconomic factors such as inflation, budget deficits, and exchange rates, and to reduce market distortions within the domestic economy. All of this was to be supported by an inflow of structural adjustment aid. Though not immediately, the adjustments led to an improvement in economic conditions. By 1984, growth rates finally turned positive for the first time since 1978, and eventually reached 5 percent by 1985. Many price and distribution controls were eliminated. Inflation was lowered from more than 75 percent in the early 1980s to 25.2 percent in 1993. Exports increased in cocoa, gold, timber, and electricity. From 1983 to 1988, the value of total exports doubled (IMF Data Fund). The more recent phase of the ERP has been directed toward institutional change, such as the downsizing of the bloated civil service sector and privatization of state industries.

The improvements have been significant, but the aggregate statistics do not tell the whole story. The public sector may be shrinking, but as of 1992, government was still the largest employer and government continues to represent a significant burden on private development (EIU 1995). The private sector continues to suffer the burdens of government plunder. In fact, from 1981 to 1984, rent seeking had increased, despite the initiatives set forth by the ERP (Ampofo-Tuffuor *et al.* 1991). With the transition to democratic elections in 1992, in which Rawlings and his National Democratic Congress (NDC) emerged victorious, the pressure to reward supporters with government positions and lucrative government contracts has only increased. Privatization efforts have been anything but successful, with only a handful of state enterprises actually having been privatized. While agriculture and exports have improved in relative terms, the actual levels remain weak. Even if the 5 percent growth rate continues, it will take thirty-five years to double the current per capita income and reach a disappointing $900 by the first third of the twenty-first century (Armstrong 1996: 2).

Further, Ghana is still heavily dependent on foreign aid. By 1991, total external debt had already exceeded $4 billion. Between 1987 and 1993, donor assistance averaged over $800 million per year, representing 10 percent of GDP per year (Armstrong 1996: Table 3.1). As the aid must be funneled through the public sector, an aid dependent economy will continue to be one characterized by government projects rather than private sector entrepreneurship (Bauer 1981). Reports from both the IMF and the World Bank suggest that sustainable development in Ghana will require a greater reliance on private investment rather than continued support of government initiatives (Aryeetey *et al.* 1994; Armstrong 1996). Indeed, there is even some recognition on the part of international aid agencies that they may be part of the problem. In its own review of assistance to Ghana, the World Bank suggests that

> [t]he Bank should give greater consideration to minimizing the potential adverse effects of "too high" levels of external aid, including upon the behaviors of government officials. Excessive aid may allow governments to postpone adoption of needed but politically difficult reforms, thus reducing savings and private investment and delaying the expected supply response. But it may also lead to excessive numbers of projects relative to the country's absorptive capacity, dependency behaviors (such as "let the donors do it"), distortions in incentives created by multiple scales of donor-financed supplements

and allowances, and the dominance of donor-driven objectives
and donor-specified performance indicators.

(Armstrong 1996: 9)

Given these and other dangers of government development initiatives,
the IMF and World Bank are now searching for ways to promote
savings, investment, and growth in the indigenous private sector.
Insufficient access to credit has been identified as the number one
problem local entrepreneurs face. While macroeconomic and institutional adjustments continue, the IMF, World Bank, and the Ghanaian
government are also focusing their attention on the private sector in
hopes of promoting economic development from the ground up,
rather than the top down. It is to these efforts that we now turn.

STATE PROMOTION OF INDIGENOUS
ENTREPRENEURSHIP

In the history of economic development as a field of inquiry, never
has there been greater attention paid to the prospects and limitations of indigenous market economies than in the 1990s. Several
reasons can account for the change in thinking that has taken place
since the development literature of the 1950s and 1960s. First and
foremost has been the dismal failure of centralized, government-led
development planning strategies, not only in Ghana, but in many
parts of sub-Saharan Africa, Asia, and Latin America. Though the
role of government (whether domestic or through donor agencies) in
development efforts is still taken as a given by most scholars and
policy makers, the notion that government ownership is the key to
industrialization or agricultural productivity is, by and large, no
longer considered to be a feasible strategy.

A second reason why indigenous private markets are capturing
the attention of development analysts is that for better or worse,
local informal markets represent the principal source of labor
absorption in the face of structural adjustment programs (Parker *et
al.* 1995). As was noted earlier, the International Labor
Organization estimates that 61 percent of the urban labor force in
sub-Saharan Africa are employed in the informal sector (ILO 1990:
43). The report continues,

> The remaining part is either employed by the modern sector
> (21%) or is unemployed (18%). Knowing that (i) a quarter of
> the regional labor force is urbanized and is growing at 6

percent per annum, and that (ii) two-thirds of all wage employment are located in urban areas and is growing at 2 percent a year, it follows that a staggering 93 percent of all additional jobs in urban Africa will need to be generated in the informal sector during the 1990s.

(ILO 1990: 43)

ERP reforms designed to reduce the bloated public sector mean that increasing numbers are turning to the informal sector for employment. Whether this transition will result in overall growth (as labor is released into the productive sector) or simply in greater constraints on existing microenterprises (as they face increasing competition) depends in part on the demand for goods and services supplied by microenterprises. Issues such as these warrant serious attention as Ghana continues the necessary though difficult reform process.

A third reason for the increased attention paid to indigenous markets is that the potential of small-scale entrepreneurship is slowly receiving its long overdue recognition. Relative to large-scale production, microenterprises utilize inputs such as unskilled labor more intensively and are more responsive to changing market conditions, given their low level of capital intensity. Further, they channel savings into capital investment, and they provide a training ground for future entrepreneurs (Balkenhol 1990). This is not to suggest that large private firms do not have their own advantages— economies of scale being the most obvious—but it does suggest that contrary to earlier development theory, there is no "entrepreneurial gap" that only the state or large firms can fill.

Policy advisors within international aid agencies are arguing for strategies which will enable the market to lead Ghana toward economic development, rather than expanding government projects. Yet such a course is not without its challenges. A consensus seems to be emerging within the development literature that a principal challenge facing private entrepreneurs in almost all developing countries is the limited access to capital and credit markets. In Ghana, this is cited as the single most serious problem among small enterprises (Steel and Webster 1991: 17). Steel and Takagi (1983) conclude that the higher productivity rates enjoyed by private large-scale firms, relative to smaller firms, is not an inherent advantage. Rather, the observed association between size and productivity is explained by the pervasive difference in access to capital. According to Kurwijila and Due (1991), restricted access to capital becomes more acute, the smaller the firm; and female entrepreneurs tend to have even more trouble than their male counterparts in securing credit (Berger 1989; Morewagae *et al.* 1995; Simms 1981). In addition, as most small-scale entrepreneurs have little in the way of collateral, formal education, or training in business practices, the formal banking sector has not stepped in to fulfill their credit needs (Morewagae *et al.* 1995).

However, across the globe, programs developed to meet the credit needs of small farmers and entrepreneurs—including the Badan Kredit Kecamatan in Indonesia, the Fundacion Carvajal in Colombia, the Accion Communitaria in Peru, FEDECREDITO in El Salvador, and the Self-Employed Women's Association (SEWA) and Working Women's Forum in India—offer reason for optimism (Berger 1989). The most celebrated example—the Grameen Bank in Bangladesh—is the rural success story to which many point as the model to be emulated for urban entrepreneurs. Indeed, the record of success is compelling. The Grameen Bank makes loans on a group lending basis, relying on mutual persuasion and support, rather than on collateral, to ensure repayment. Supported by private foundations, the Grameen Bank began as an experimental project in 1976. By 1992, it had established 974 branches, covering 28,879 villages, serving 1,271,461 members, of whom 1,186,826 were women. Since the year it began, the Grameen Bank has maintained a remarkable 98 percent loan recovery rate. The Grameen Bank is still dependent on donor aid which has fueled the horizontal growth of the organization. But the significant difference in interest the bank pays in the world market, and the 20 percent rate at which it lends in Bangladesh offer the potential for eventual self-sufficiency (Wahid 1994: 2). Yet, even if it were to remain dependent on foundation support, the program would be much less expensive and far more successful than comparable state programs.

The positive impact the program has had upon the participants and the local economy is evident. Employment and productivity is higher among Grameen Bank members than non-members, principally because of the emphasis placed on job training and farming techniques. The per capita growth in income of Grameen Bank members, particularly women, are the highest in Bangladesh, even when compared to participants in state-supported development programs. Grameen Bank members also tend to have better quality housing and a better diet, not only in absolute amounts, but in diversity and nutritional content as well (Wahid 1994).

International aid agencies such as the World Bank and the IMF are taking notice both of the credit constraints facing microenterprises and the records of success some programs have demonstrated in alleviating these constraints. By establishing agencies with the specific mandate to lend to small-scale entrepreneurs, or by providing incentive funds to existing banks for microenterprise lending, international aid agencies and domestic governments have attempted to mimic the success of the Grameen Bank and similar institutions. Unfortunately, such efforts exhibit a disappointing record.

In his study of West African countries which had established a fund to guarantee loans to small-scale entrepreneurs, Balkenhol (1990) found that the default rate ranged from 40 to 60 percent, significantly higher than that for regular commercial lending in the same region (and much higher than the 2 percent default rate characteristic of the Grameen Bank). Balkenhol attributes the poor performance to bureaucratic rigidities, including overly strict conditions for settlement in the face of default, and excessive delays in risk assessment. He observes that the successful programs are those which use social pressure and group solidarity to enforce the conditions of the loan. Such programs tend to be less bureaucratic and have higher loan repayment rates. Berger (1989) also finds that programs which are most directly linked to the borrowers, through social service outreach, business training, literacy programs, and the like, are more successful in securing repayment than those programs that adopt conventional banking practices. Both Balkenhol (1990) and Berger (1989) point out that only the programs run by non-governmental organizations (NGOs) or private voluntary organizations (PVOs) were able successfully to employ such methods, though no analysis was offered as to the possible reasons behind the correlation.[6]

In their critique of rural credit programs, Adams and Von Pischke (1992) warn against the dangers of instituting similar credit schemes for microenterprise. They cite a disastrous record of performance in the rural programs, reporting that loans were made on the basis of a vague perception of need rather than on what the farmer could reasonably be expected to pay back. The programs were unsustainable, both because of high monitoring costs and high default rates. Further, interest rate distortions such programs introduced gave commercial banks even less incentive to lend to farmers, and discouraged savings. A World Bank report on credit programs in Ghana seems to support this assessment.

The 124 unit rural banks have the clearest mandate for lending at the small scale level. They were set up ostensibly to mobilize deposits from rural areas and channel these into productive activities in those areas. Unfortunately, their performance has been generally disappointing, mainly as a result of poor port-folio management and ineffective savings mobilization, resulting in perpetual capital inadequacy problems and the failure to meet obligations to customers in some cases.

(Aryeetey *et al.* 1994: 29)

Yet, Adams and Von Pischke (1992) qualify their critique by suggesting that some programs have, in fact, been successful. The successful projects tend to be the NGO or PVO initiatives, though, again, they offer no analysis as to why these organizations have a better record of success.

Morewagae *et al.* (1995) find a similar pattern in their study of credit programs in Botswana. Even establishing government agen-cies with the specific mandate to lend to small-scale entrepreneurs does not ensure success. For models of success, Morewagae *et al.* turn to the Grameen Bank and the Mennonite Economic Development Association (MEDA), a non-governmental organiza-tion established in 1953. MEDA has established successful microenterprises credit programs in Haiti, Jamaica, Bolivia, and Nicaragua. Again, the private organizations seem to "get it right," whereas state and parastatal projects sponsored by the World Bank, seem to be plagued with difficulties.

The recommendations offered by these and other scholars is that state and World Bank programs should mimic the practices of the successful programs. Indeed, this was the objective of the Fund for Small- and Medium-Sized Enterprise Development (FUSMED), introduced by the World Bank in Ghana. The project offered a $25 million line of credit through the Bank of Ghana, which would be available to banks making loans to small-scale entrepreneurs. The project also offered technical assistance to improve the banks' moni-toring skills and ability to assess credit worthiness (Aryeetey *et al.* 1994: 31). Yet even with the assistance of this program, banks used the same criteria to assess credit worthiness for small-scale entrepreneurs, as they used for large-scale firms. The principal factor in securing a loan remained access to collateral; a condition that virtually excludes the majority of urban entrepreneurs.

The costs associated with collecting information on microenterprise loan applications created a disincentive for banks to engage in the FUSMED project.

> Banks estimated that screening to gather information about the applicant and project, review the feasibility study, do the credit analysis and make the decision took an average of sixteen man-days for a large-scale application and twenty-four man-days for a small-scale application. They attributed the longer time for SMEs [small and medium enterprises] to the time it took to assemble all the required information. Similar results obtained for loan monitoring and contract enforcement suggest that the transaction costs for SME lending were higher than those for large enterprises per loan (let alone per cedi lent).
>
> (Aryeetey et al. 1994: 32–3)

Further, Aryeetey et al. argue, the program did not reduce the perceived risks of lending to microenterprises, as bank staff were insufficiently trained to assess the strength of individual loan applications. To add insult to injury, banks which participated in the FUSMED program tended to incur greater administrative costs than those that did not.

Other projects established by the World Bank to cushion the effects of adjustment under the ERP, such as the Program of Actions to Mitigate the Social Cost of Adjustment (PAMSCAD), exhibited similar problems. The PAMSCAD administration had difficulty identifying the households that were most adversely affected by structural adjustment reforms. In 1990, a multi-donor evaluation of the $85.7 million project found that it had accomplished little in the way of mitigating the social costs of adjustment (Armstrong 1996: 107). In addition, PAMSCAD credit assistance programs had little success in differentiating those microenterprises which had growth and profit potential from those that did not (Aryeetey et al. 1994: 37).

In general, the problems experienced with World Bank and government efforts to promote microenterprise development fall into three categories. First, programs designed to use the existing financial structure do not seem to offer the appropriate incentives to entice banks and loan officers to expand credit to microenterprises. Even those programs specifically set up to meet the needs of credit-poor entrepreneurs lack the appropriate incentives to fulfill their mandate. Second, government and World Bank credit programs face ubiquitous information costs, and in most cases appear incapable of accessing the information needed to make sound judgments regarding project appraisal and credit worthiness. Third, World Bank and government programs continue to rely on formal (Western) methods of loan enforcement, such as collateral requirements and a documented credit history, which significantly reduce their effectiveness in reaching small-scale entrepreneurs.

Reports and appraisals of projects like FUSMED, PAMSCAD, and similar programs seek to address the problems which lead to such disappointing records of performance (Armstrong 1996; Aryeetey *et al.* 1994; Parker *et al.* 1995; United Nations 1995). Yet, inadequate incentives, the lack of useful information, and the inability to use anything but formal loan security requirements are phenomena inherently tied to the structure of such programs. As the problems are systematically linked to the projects themselves, they are not likely to be overcome through piecemeal reform measures.

For instance, in their appraisal of FUSMED and other World Bank credit projects, Aryeetey *et al.* (1994) suggest that loan officers be given greater discretion in assessing the merits of loan applications and to tie their income to the success or failure of their overall loan portfolio; in other words, give loan officers a greater incentive to meet the needs of worthy entrepreneurs. However, unless the loan officers find a way to overcome the relatively high information costs associated with microenterprise lending, they will be just as reluctant to issue credit to microenterprise borrowers as the banking institution itself. Alternatively, a United Nations (1995) report on microenterprise finance suggests that credit guarantee programs may provide banks the necessary incentive to lend to microenterprises, if they are reimbursed in the case of default. But such programs have introduced moral hazard problems, in that loan officers are even less motivated to provide the necessary oversight or acquire the information needed to determine which borrowers represent the best risk. Further, in response to the inherent moral hazard problems, monitoring agencies require more evidence that loan recipients are indeed good risks. Thus, even with loan guarantee programs in place, collateral and documented credit histories are required, and this is exactly what small-scale entrepreneurs cannot provide (United Nations 1995).

Aryeetey *et al.* (1994) also recommend that the costs of acquiring information on credit worthiness and project viability be lowered through better training of project staff. While this may improve the situation, it is not for want of training that loan officers in the formal financial sector cannot access the information necessary to making sound lending decisions. The difficulty rests in the fact that relative to informal sources of credit, formal loan officers do not have access to the local knowledge embedded within the indigenous market context. In Ghana, informal savings and lending agents known as *susu*-men, for example, acquire in-depth local knowledge of the entrepreneurs they serve. Entrepreneurs can build capital by saving a set amount with a *susu*-man[7] each day. At the end of the month, the lump sum is returned to the entrepreneur, minus the standard fee of one day's savings. *Susu*-men will also lend to their more trusted clients. Every day, *susu*-men travel through the market, meeting their clients at their market stalls or usual selling spaces to collect the day's deposit. *Susu*-men acquire in-depth knowledge of their clients' record of business success or failure, not only from their deposit activity, but from gossip and speculation they might have chance to overhear. They also acquire intimate knowledge of local market conditions, knowing which products are selling well and which are not. It is upon this basis of local knowledge that *susu*-men assess the credit worthiness of potential borrowers—knowledge that loan officers in the formal financial sector simply do not have.

Better access to local knowledge may be a reason why private voluntary and non-governmental projects achieve a better record of success than state and World Bank projects. For instance, NGOs (particularly those which are locally based) seem to avoid the need for formal lending practices, instead lending on the bases of character and group enforcement. On the other hand, state and World Bank programs seem to resort to formal criteria of collateral and documented credit histories, even when their mandate is to do otherwise. The difference may be due to the varying degree to which staff members are engaged in the local context—how closely they are tied to the lives of the entrepreneurs they serve. The following description of field workers in the Grameen Bank may provide some insight as to how non-monetary motivations often act as an incentive to be fully engaged in and build local knowledge of the community they serve.

> Critics often claim that the success of the Grameen Bank, to a large extent, depends upon the availability, dedication and loyalty of field level workers. Their training program is so

rigorous and effective that they become fully motivated before going to the rural areas to serve the cause of their institution and that of the rural poor. They regularly put in extra hours beyond their official duties and refrain from charging bribes from their clients as many of their counterparts do in government sponsored development programs.

(Wahid 1994: 12)

Local knowledge within NGO projects is built as staff members work with loan applicants and recipients in training programs, literacy programs, business mentoring, and loan oversight. Access to local knowledge, such as the reputation of the borrower for honesty and industriousness, renders the need for a documented credit history or collateral less important than if such knowledge were not accessible. Thus, the recommendation that government and World Bank programs should use character as a criterion for assessing credit worthiness (see, for example Konig and Koch 1990) misses the point that in most cases, loan officers will not have access to the information needed to make such assessments.

Of course there may be staff within the formal financial sector who are committed to improving the lives of microenterprise entrepreneurs, and who are in fact fully engaged in the local market context. They may have close friends and relatives who trade in the market. They may know in detail the character of some entrepreneurs who apply for loans. But given the institutional context in which loan officers operate, they will be less able to employ the local knowledge they have cultivated. In order to avoid moral hazard problems, the bank is likely to insist that loan officers are not to be allowed to make decisions regarding friends and relatives, the very people about whom they have in-depth knowledge. It is even more likely that the power to make such decisions will not rest with them in the first place. As Aryeetey *et al.* note,

The internal organization of most banks is such that SMEs [small and medium enterprises] applying for loans deal with branch staff who have little to say in the decision, whereas major decisions are taken at the head offices by officials who know little about the entrepreneurs. Branch office personnel only monitor loan account performance and report at regular intervals to the head office . . . . There is a high probability that many potentially good projects are turned down because distant credit officers lack enough documented information to form views on projects and, especially, on the entrepreneurs.

(Aryeetey *et al.* 1994: 34)

Thus, such programs will continue to favor those loan applicants who can meet the formal requirements of documented credit histories and collateral, because formal institutions cannot effectively access and use the local knowledge needed to make decisions based on less formal criteria.

As informal lenders and non-governmental credit projects can make lending decisions based on a broad set of informal criteria, they tend to enjoy much greater flexibility. By contrast, the bureaucratic rigidities prevalent in government and parastatal programs are exacerbated by restrictive banking regulations put in place with the ERP. According to Timberg and Aiyar, the absence of regulation is a principal reason why informal bankers in India can be so responsive to changing conditions within the market.

[T]hree salient characteristics of the intermediaries [informal bankers] in this market seem to lead to lower transaction costs: (1) the intermediaries' intimate knowledge of their clients, which reduces their information costs compared to those of commercial banks; (2) the absence of government control on lending and borrowing rates governing the intermediaries, which enables them to adjust more fully to market forces than regulated intermediaries; and (3) the absence of charges on the informal intermediaries in the form of idle or low-interest reserves, which are imposed on regulated intermediaries.

(Timberg and Aiyar 1984: 44)

In the formal banking sector, on the other hand, higher liquidity requirements, the centralization of decision making, and increased monitoring and documentation requirements have only made it more difficult for formal banking institutions to serve the needs of microenterprises (Aryeetey *et al.* 1994).

The knowledge built up by informal lenders and local NGO staff may also include knowledge of how cultural norms might be employed to secure loans, such as group lending practices in Bangladesh. As noted earlier, this particular practice may not work in all cultural contexts, and other solutions will only come by way of accessing the local knowledge embedded with the specific cultural context, thus giving private informal and local NGO programs a distinct advantage. It may also be the case that non-governmental projects have a better chance of using such cultural norms to their advantage because the projects themselves become part of the local community. Loan recipients are more likely to feel a moral obligation to live up to their part of the agreement if they perceive the agreement as a promise to a member of the local community. We might suspect that government agencies or faceless parastatal organizations elicit fewer feelings of moral obligation. Of course there are no guarantees that private organizations will be more effective in acquiring and using local knowledge of the market and cultural contexts. Private organizations can be just as formal and alienated from the local context as any government bureaucracy. But it appears that some private organizations have taken advantage of the opportunity their status affords them to become engaged in and attuned to the local context.

Recognizing the superior access of private money lenders and NGOs to the knowledge needed to assess the credit worthiness of entrepreneurs, Aryeetey et al. suggest that information costs in World Bank programs can be reduced by enlisting the help of informal savings and credit agents, and NGOs.

> Using information possessed by informal lenders may be inexpensive and very useful. Closer interaction between formal financial institutions and informal agents in deposit mobilization and lending has great prospects in facilitating transaction cost reduction while expanding the lending base and reducing the risk borne by banks. [Further], the use of NGOs in screening and preparing SME loan applications can generate information and monitoring at low cost to the lender.
>
> (Aryeetey et al. 1994: 41)

Not only does this suggestion beg the question of whether private money lenders have any interest in supplying such valuable information, it also begs the following question: if private money lenders and NGOs have access to the local knowledge needed to make low-cost decisions regarding microenterprise lending, and are in fact providing such services more effectively, what purpose do World Bank and government programs serve? In fact, Steel and Aryeetey (1994) argue that *susu*-men have already started the process of building bridges between the formal and informal lending sectors by depositing *susu* collections in the formal banking system. This is not to suggest that there is no role for the World Bank or government policy in promoting the private sector, but it does suggest that such efforts are best directed toward removing the obstacles which inhibit the development of indigenous markets, rather than toward direct market interventions which appear to be incapable of achieving the desired outcome.

The various performance reports which have been cited here do make many important recommendations which need to be considered. Besides limited access to credit, entrepreneurs face other significant constraints. Limited market demand for their output, distortionary tax policies and subsidies which favor large-scale industry, and government controls and interventions continue to limit microenterprise development. Further, political uncertainty continues to inhibit private investment from both domestic and international sources.

Steel and Takagi (1983), and Fischer-Quinke (1990) argue that by reducing taxes, duties, and fees imposed on microenterprises by national and local governments, the benefits will be two-fold. Facing lower costs, the firms themselves will be more competitive relative to larger firms. In addition, as the small-scale entrepreneurs represent a significant segment of consumer demand for microenterprises, the income they keep by reducing taxes and fees will help to stimulate local demand. Steel and Takagi also argue that eliminating state subsidies, special tax status, and other distortionary policies that favor large industries will stimulate demand for microenterprises, which often compete with large-scale industry.

The uncertainty inherent within Ghanaian politics has reduced the incentive to invest in the private sector. Even with the transition to free elections in 1992, the Rawlings regime has been unable to convince private investors that arbitrary measures which might destroy the value of their investments will not be used. Such uncertainty has far-reaching effects. The inability of the state to credibly commit to non-interventionist principles affects the decisions made by pension fund managers in Chicago, just as it affects the decisions made by local entrepreneurs who delay the purchase of new capital for fear that the market area may be moved or destroyed on the basis of political whim (Aryeetey 1994; Parker et al. 1995). Any move the state can make towards a credible commitment to non-interventionist principles will improve the market environment. Thus, complete privatization of remaining state industries and the removal of distortionary subsidies and taxes would signal to the public that the regime was in fact committed to market-led economic development.

CONCLUSION

Many of the policy decisions made in Ghana (and much of the developing world) since the 1950s have come about because politicians and scholars have not recognized the limits of human reason. The capacity of reason does not give humankind the ability to redesign wholly or to redirect consciously the market and social order. As Hayek observed, "The curious task of economics is to demonstrate to men how little they really know about what they imagine they can design" (Hayek 1988: 76). The observation needs only to be amended in that "it is the curious task of *Austrian* economics to demonstrate to men how little they really know about what they imagine they can design." The fundamentally dispersed nature of the knowledge embedded within market and cultural processes is an insight missed by most schools of economic thought. This oversight has led to many unfortunate policy initiatives, particularly in the developing world.

Lest we forget, it was on the advice of learned development economists that Nkrumah would undertake his program of development planning and government-led industrialization. Blaming the disastrous effects of development planning on corruption and inept administration, policy makers convinced themselves that *they* could do it right, only to prolong and deepen the decline into the 1980s. Efforts to liberalize market relations, to the extent that they have been achieved, have significantly improved the possibilities for the indigenous economy to lead the way towards economic development. But the policies and programs instituted to promote private sector development demonstrate that we have moved forward without learning the lessons of where we have been.

Those who participate in the market process with a vested interest in making wise economic decisions have access to the local knowledge which can allow for flexibility in judgment and the effective discretion needed to make such decisions. Though the state and parastatal organizations have the power to intervene in this process, such power does not afford them access to the local knowledge required to make sound economic judgments. As will be argued in the next chapter, the potential for a rising entrepreneurial class rests with the market women of Ghana. The principal way in which governments and international aid agencies can promote this emerging class of entrepreneurs is to eliminate state policies which inhibit the development of the indigenous private sector.

3

THE CULTURAL FOUNDATIONS OF INDIGENOUS ENTREPRENEURSHIP

As discussed in the previous chapter, the failure of government-led development efforts have turned the attention of economists and other development specialists towards the indigenous market economy. The most important role government can serve with regard to promoting the private sector is to foster an institutional environment such that entrepreneurs can rationally respond to meaningful market signals, rather than be paralyzed by distortionary public policy. It appears that the remaining tasks of market-led economic development, however, rest with the entrepreneurs themselves. The principal question this chapter asks and seeks to answer, at least in part, is whether the indigenous private sector possesses the potential to succeed in leading the way toward economic development. The focus here is to identify the cultural resources which establish both the institutional requirements and entrepreneurial orientation necessary for economic development.

In the West African context, the viability of the indigenous private sector depends upon the conditions under which women engage in market activity. Considerable advances have been made in this interdisciplinary field of inquiry. Research on women in development began in earnest in the 1970s (Boserup 1970; Guyer 1978; Hafkin and Bay 1976; Lewis 1976, 1977; Mullings 1976; Peil 1979; Robertson 1974, 1976; Sanjeck and Sanjeck 1976; Sudarkasa 1973). The United Nations declared 1975 as the "International Women's Year," which led into the UN Decade for Women, further fueling the interest in women and development. Women had at last received just recognition for their part in production and marketing. Detailed accounts of market women in urban Ghana, such as Deborah Pellow's (1977) *Women in Accra: Options for Autonomy*, Claire Robertson's (1984a) *Sharing the Same Bowl*, or

100

Gracia Clark's (1994) *Onions are My Husband*, illustrate the savvy ability of women to negotiate strategies for survival and profit in an often unforgiving environment. Yet, in other accounts the picture often painted of market activity is one in which women are marginalized and exploited, either by an international system of dependence upon Western capitalism, a domestic system of male domination, or both (Arregui and Baez 1991; Ibrahim 1991; Pala 1981). The following portrayal of women's economic and cultural subordination is representative.

> [T]he position of women in Africa is to be considered at every level of analysis as an outcome of structural and conceptual mechanisms by which African societies have continued to respond to and resist the global processes of economic exploitation and cultural domination. I am suggesting that the problems facing African women today, irrespective of their national and social class affiliations, are inextricably bound up in the wider struggle by African people to free themselves from poverty and ideological domination in both intra- and international spheres.
>
> (Pala 1981: 209)

Women are portrayed as caught between two oppressive forces. On the one hand, traditional ideas concerning the subordination of women keep them from pulling out of an economically disadvantaged position. On the other hand, modern capitalist relations aggravate their situation by exploiting this marginalized role of women. Traditional society offers the security of customary obligations, yet propagates the ideology of subordination, leaving women at the mercy of a male dominated society. Modern society offers more independence yet has no need for culturally based social systems, leaving women at the mercy of the market. Other scholars suggest that recent improvements in macroeconomic indicators under structural adjustment have only been achieved at the expense of further marginalizing female market traders. As Elson (1991) argues, structural adjustment programs designed to reduce the role of government and social services merely transfer the burden of nurturing the sick, and other forms of unpaid labor to women.

Traditional social norms can also constrain female entrepreneurship. As noted earlier, women have far less access to formal sources of credit than men (Berger 1989; Morewagae *et al.* 1995; Simms 1981). Traditionally, both matrilineal and patrilineal inheritance structures favor men over women (Mikell 1989). As their relation-ship with their kin group is interrupted by marriage, women's access to the family's resources is less than that of men (Brydon 1985). Further, there is usually no element of choice between chil-dren and career. The West African woman is expected to bear the burdens of both (Dinan 1983).

Given the constraints facing Ghanaian market traders, particu-larly female entrepreneurs, it may seem doubtful that they possess much potential for leading the way towards economic growth. Yet indigenous cultural norms and institutions within the Ghanaian context may provide the foundation for an emerging entrepreneurial class. In the urban West African context, social constructions of gender include entrepreneurial dimensions, not only in terms of what men and women trade, but why men and women engage in market activity. A woman's role within the marketplace emerges more from her customary obligation to her children than her subor-dinate status to men. Further, the female dominance of local markets is not the outcome of international influences, but is rather an integral part of the indigenous social order (Brydon 1985). The female dominance of indigenous market trading also affords market women the advantages many ethnic trading networks enjoy, such as the overseas Chinese in Southeast Asia, the Jews of medieval Europe, and the Lebanese in West Africa (Landa 1991). Combined with indigenous rules and institutions conducive to trade, it will be argued that female entrepreneurs do possess the potential to advance market-led development.

Historically, urban markets have played a central role in indige-nous West African life. In their studies of the origins of African urbanization, McIntosh and McIntosh (1984, 1993) argue that indigenous development of towns occurred as early as the first century AD, as evidenced by the key archeological site of Jenne-jeno in ancient Mali. The significance of this research is that archeolo-gists had earlier believed that trade and urbanization occurred much later, in the late ninth century AD, with the expansion of Arab trade routes from the north (Rayfield 1974). As McIntosh and McIntosh point out, market trading is an indigenous phenomenon within West Africa society.

Based on excavation data and later historical sources . . . we are able to suggest with some confidence that indigenous trade was a vital element in Jenne-jeno's development. We see the well-established settlement hierarchy in the Jenne-jeno region as a manifestation of the integration of communities into a formal, intra-regional economic network. Within this network, there probably existed a lively trade in local staples, including rice and fish, which could be exchanged for desired commodities from other regions, such as copper from the Sahara.

(McIntosh and McIntosh 1993: 638)

By the late fifteenth century, when the Europeans first arrived along the coast of what is now modern Ghana, long-distance trading into the interior in salt and fish was already well established. By the beginning of the seventeenth century, local, regional, and inter-state trade were commonplace. Certainly the growing concentration of Europeans diversified what was traded in the market, but the conventions of trade had long been established (Daaku 1971).

The argument made here is that indigenous culture within southern Ghana provides the resources essential to economic progress. The development of local and long-distance trade networks relied on the evolution of cultural traditions and institutions which facilitated the extension of trade. As in other African societies, the principal tribes of modern Ghana, including the Akan, Ga, and Ewe, all developed a property rights structure and a legal order that fostered commerce at every level. Thus, as the current political leadership seeks to improve the institutional environment in which entrepreneurs operate, the wisest course may be to turn to and support indigenous institutional forms. Further, it will be argued that indigenous kinship and religious structures provide the basis for capital accumulation and a uniquely West African capitalist ethic. To the extent that such cultural norms still operate, they further support the emergence of an indigenous entrepreneurial class. Traditional kinship and religious structures among the Akan will be the primary focus of the discussion, but an attempt will be made to point out similarities and differences among Akan, Ga, and Ewe traditions when they are relevant. Though further study may reveal that the arguments presented here are more widely applicable, the conclusions for the time being will be limited to the southern urban areas of Ghana.

The necessarily specific nature of the analysis and conclusions made here call a broader theoretical point into question. As cultural factors are incorporated into economic analysis, have we come closer to, or are we further away from, a generalizable model for economic development? Those who argue that culture is of little or no significance in development often point to political and economic institutions as the principal determinants of economic performance (Clarkson 1975; Clegg and Redding 1990; Waters 1987). An inherent optimism accompanies this perspective, since it suggests that all societies can enjoy economic success if the state follows a particular set of rules, such as enforcing contracts and property rights. If, on the other hand, culture is responsible for economic progress, the rules which work in one society might not work in another. In other words, a generalizable theory of development is less likely the more culture plays a role. This question will be considered in the closing remarks of this chapter.

INDIGENOUS WEST AFRICAN INSTITUTIONS

As North (1987, 1990, 1995) and others working within the new institutional economics paradigm argue, establishing the institutions of property and conflict resolution is key to lowering the cost of long-distance and inter-temporal trade. As many institutionalist scholars will point out, no society which has failed to establish a sound system of private property rights and a stable legal tradition has ever achieved industrialized status (Fong 1988). Yet such observations often gloss over the culturally specific nature in which institutions evolve. Though we may say in general that a reliable system of contract is essential to development, for example, the particular rules of contract that evolve will depend upon and reflect the specific cultural context from which they emerge (Bates 1995). Often, it is to the West that scholars and policy makers turn when searching for models of institutional success. Yet if the source of legitimation is missing in the local cultural context, the institution which leads to economic and social order in one setting may lead to chaos in another.

Lessons from the Native American experience are illustrative. In their comparative study of Native American economic development, Cornell and Kalt (1995) found that the social and economic success of the Apache, relative to the Sioux, is due largely to the fact that the indigenous governance structure among the Apache closely matched the constitution that was imposed by the Indian Reservations Act (IRA) of the 1930s. In contrast, indigenous governance among the Sioux is far more decentralized than that imposed by the IRA, and the lack of symmetry has been a major contributing factor in the economic stagnation and social decay within Sioux communities. While the goal of the IRA was never to foster economic development, a lesson is still to be learned here. In seeking an institutional context by which to promote economic development, indigenous forms of governance, conflict resolution, private property rights, and contract have the best chance of bringing about the desired results.

Indigenous institutions within the West African context were highly accommodating to the development of long-distance and inter-temporal trade. Traditional Akan tribal and religious structures worked together to provide a stable form of property rights and conflict resolution, long before the colonial era. Traditional judicial proceedings operated on the principles set forth by a commonly shared or "universal" concept of truth, not the arbitrary rulings of a despot (Ayittey 1991). The system was kept in check through an appeals process and ultimately impeachment or "destoolment" of a chief who did not follow these principles (Busia 1968). Likewise, land and personal wealth were secured through a right of private property. Although the degree of individual agency varied and still varies among different forms of traditional property, the operating norm was and still remains one of private property. To the extent that such institutions still operate in modern Ghanaian society, they may represent an important resource in the effort to re-establish a sound institutional setting.

Indigenous forms of dispute resolution

Common to many West African religions is the emphasis placed upon harmony among the living members of the community. According to the Akan, the cosmos operates in an orderly fashion, and it is essential for all of its parts to be in harmony. Human society is an integral part of this balance. Ideally, the legal system re-establishes spiritual as well as social order when conflicts arise. Using a combination of tribal and lineage authority, both the Akan and the Ga developed a decentralized system of arbitration for private offenses. Private offenses were disputes between two parties, including theft, contract, financial and property disputes.

Kinship ties provided the first level of conflict resolution. Minor offenses were brought before any respected person or committee of elders within the lineage, upon whom the two parties agreed. In exchange for their judgment, the disputants provided the elders with a small financial tribute or rum as a hearing fee (Manoukian 1950). Among the Tallensi, such arbitration constituted the entire judicial process. Elders within the clan relied upon "the fear of ancestors or the Earth's spirit, as well as the force of public opinion, for getting their decisions carried out" (Arhin 1985: 8). Among the Akan, more serious private offenses were brought before the lineage head. Yet arbitration and restitution were the principal issues to be resolved, not retribution and punishment (Busia 1968). When disputes between lineages emerged, the lineage heads would first attempt to settle the matter on their own, or call in another non-partisan lineage head. In either case, the maintenance of good relations among the lineages was the paramount concern. For common disputes, the decentralized arbitration system allowed for quick and trustworthy resolution without overburdening the central authority figure.

In the case of public offenses among the Akan, the chief and his council of elders presided. Among the Ga, such cases were taken to the *wulomo*, the priestly head of the extended family or settlement. Public offenses involved not only a dispute between two parties, but were considered crimes against the ancestry, and thus placed the entire living community at risk for retribution from the spiritual realm. Such offenses took the form of taboo, including murder, suicide, incest, intercourse with a menstruating woman, sexual intercourse "in the bush," treason, and witchcraft. If arbitration efforts failed in the case of private offenses, the matter was "transformed" into a public offense. In Ga tradition, someone wishing to bring such a case before the court would levy a conditional curse upon the judge in the event that he refused to hear the case. According to Manoukian (1950), such overtures were taken quite seriously, demanding the immediate attention of the judge. In Akan tradition, the accuser would take the "chief's oath" that the accused had indeed perpetrated the crime. If the accused took the oath in his defense, this placed the case on the level of a public offense as one party or the other must be lying to the chief's ancestry. Here, then, the chief and his council of elders decided the final verdict (Busia 1968).

Legal decisions were based on general principles, not the arbitrary whim of an overzealous authority figure (Ayittey 1991; Schapera 1957; Yelpaala 1983). An Akan chief had to maintain the support of his counselors in rendering political and judicial rulings. Decisions were never unilateral, but always involved the elders who represented their particular lineage. A chief who did not consult the elders or abused his power in some other way could have his sacred status revoked.[1] Judicial decisions could not contradict the higher norms believed to be derived from the spiritual realm. This appeal to principle cultivated an atmosphere of stability under which members of the community could contract and resolve disputes with confidence. At the same time, these principles did not constitute a rigid code of behavior, but rather afforded a reasonable flexibility within which the chief and the council of elders could take individual circumstance into account (Ayittey 1991).

An important question to ask is whether indigenous forms of conflict resolution can still be relied upon in contemporary society, given the profound cultural changes which have transpired since the colonial period. Indeed, colonial and post-colonial governments significantly diminished the role of the chief, and other tribal leaders. As Arhin notes,

> After 1900, the British Government assumed the power to do all that traditional rulers had been doing: the power to make war, the power to make rules for the maintenance of law and order, and the power to take measures to promote the economic and social welfare of the people. The assumption of these powers put an end to the traditional states as independent, political communities.
>
> (Arhin 1985: 89)

By 1904, the British government had effectively subverted the sovereignty of the local leadership. Traditional rulers could still be elected according to indigenous custom, but the British government had final veto power if those elected were deemed unacceptable. According to Arhin (1985: 91), "this was to ensure that the government would have the kind of traditional rulers who would willingly act as its agents in carrying out its decisions."

The position of the chief and other traditional leaders fared no better after independence. Under Nkrumah, chiefs were given only the authority to decide issues of tribal custom. Traditional leaders could not organize to discuss matters of general welfare without the government's permission. Further, the independent government reserved and exercised the right to revoke their status. While Nkrumah was in power, salaries and allowances were offered to those traditional leaders who supported government policies, such as increased taxes and lower agricultural prices to farmers. The general public often read such tributes as political payoffs, further diminishing the respect and prestige afforded traditional positions of leadership (Arhin 1985).

As devastating as colonialist and independent government policies were to indigenous political structure, some important elements of traditional control remain. Specifically, many of the traditional principles of conflict resolution are still operational. While traditional leaders have almost no official authority, the decentralized methods of arbitration and conflict resolution are more tenacious. Elders are still consulted regarding major personal decisions, and respected members of the community are still asked to arbitrate disputes.

Particularly in the marketplace, such methods of conflict resolution are regularly employed. Those in close proximity to quarreling traders have a direct interest in helping to settle the matter, as their business is likely to suffer if customers avoid the area of discontent. Disputes among traders are usually resolved by bringing the issue to a respected neighboring trader or to the head of the traders' commodity group. If the dispute involves traders from two different commodity groups, the commodity leaders will attempt to come to some resolution. Failing this, or in the case of more serious disputes, the matter is brought to the "market queen" or market head. But before matters are brought to the market queen, attempts are made to settle the dispute at the most local level first.

The position of market queen still functions in much the same way as in traditional Africa. Traditionally, the market queen is chosen by consensus. Through sustained face-to-face interaction in the market, the most trustworthy and experienced traders are easily identifiable. This is still the case in smaller markets such as Madina, which lies outside of Accra. Similarly, commodity leaders in the larger markets of Central Accra are often chosen through consensus. But the market queen, and the leader of more dominant commodities such as cloth are elected, as more than one woman may have earned the respect necessary to serve in this capacity. The results are essentially the same, however. As long as a leader maintains the respect of the traders, a market queen is likely to serve many terms.

Vida, the elected market head of Makola Number One describes her role this way:

> The [commodity] associations try to keep peace between the women. The market woman in charge will settle many quarrels. If two traders are fighting and the associations cannot

resolve it, each party comes to me. I talk to them first alone.
Then I bring them together. I try to get them to work it out. I
tell them it is not good for business to have fighting all the
time. After they talk for a while, they are more willing to
settle their dispute . . . . If the dispute is over money, we try to
agree on an amount that pleases everyone. Then we all take a
mineral [soft drink] and the matter is settled.

When asked if she requires compensation for providing arbitration
services, she replies, "No. They do not pay me directly. Often the
traders will bring me a gift. But I do not ask them to pay." The
principal benefit the role of market leader conveys seems to be the
respect and prestige afforded the position. In fact, the time it takes
to settle disputes can represent a considerable cost in terms of lost
trading time. Respecting this fact, traders and commodity leaders
make an earnest attempt to resolve disputes internally. Again, the
decentralized system of conflict resolution means that disputes are
usually settled without overburdening a central authority figure.

In Accra and Kumasi, the market leaders have no official legal
status. Their decisions are binding simply because the community
of traders regards them as such, not because the state has any
interest in enforcing them. In a detailed account of a dispute
between two Kumasi orange traders, Clark (1994: 261) illustrates
the process by which the orange commodity leader settled a
disagreement over a shipment of oranges.

Both parties received a full hearing, repeating their stories
several times . . . . The *ohemma* [head of the orange market]
asked questions and called for witnesses, but said relatively
little . . . the *ohemma* [then] took a more active role and began
to repeat the facts of the case herself to elders arriving late from
distant sections of the market. Surprisingly, her first resumes
were the shortest and also seemed strangely incomplete, until I
realized they included only the facts not in dispute. Further
repetitions soon followed, and each became longer and
smoother, as she removed more and more facts from contention.
The disputants began conversely to shorten their own accounts
and to respond directly to several proposals for settlement
presented by different elders. When the serious proposals had
narrowed to two, the *ohemma* announced her decision. She
would divide the disputed shipment between them.

Upon hearing her decision, the two disputants protested—a highly unusual response. The *ohemma* determined that this unusual response called for unusual measures. She took the shipment of oranges for herself, to the cheers of the market women who had listened to the entire lengthy process. The authority the *ohemma* needed to punish the unrelenting disputants came from the community of traders, not an official enforcement mechanism.

The lack of official status is not without its consequences. Municipal policy makers are not required to consult with market leaders before closing or moving a market area, for example; a situation unheard of in traditional Africa. The decentralized system of arbitration and the respect traditional leaders earn in the community of traders still function, however. It is much easier for a government to remove the official status of a central figure than it is to destroy the decentralized system which is entrenched in the daily lives of people. As policy makers seek to establish an institutional environment conducive to the development of the indigenous private sector, the solution may often be simply to support the existing institutions, like that of dispute resolution, already at work within the marketplace.

The evolution of property and inheritance structures

As tribal and religious structures have shaped methods of conflict resolution, they have also shaped property arrangements in traditional West African society. Traditional Akan property structure carved out three types of land, each establishing a different domain of control (Sarbah 1968). Stool land was allocated by the chief to a lineage. This land was believed to belong to the ancestry, the living being the caretakers of the property. The initial allocation established *usus fructus* rights for the lineage. This form of property right was particularly helpful in establishing rights over uncultivated land when it was plentiful and tribes were expanding. Private property rights were operative here with the one exception that stool land could not be sold. The chief could not confiscate the land once allocated, nor could he dictate how the land was used. The profits made from the land were the sole property of the lineage. With the advent of cocoa and other cash-crop farming, stool land was frequently "pledged" or leased to cultivators, thereby facilitating widespread cocoa farming without officially selling the stool land (Hill 1986). Though it was eventually replaced as the principal form of property, stool land served an important function in establishing a norm of private property to large expanses of land while it was relatively abundant.

As the new institutionalists suggest, when relative prices change, institutions evolve to accommodate the new environment. As uncultivated land became more scarce, a second level of property—lineage property—came into greater use, and eventually came to replace stool land as the dominant form of property. Here, the asset could be sold, but only with the consent of the relevant members of the lineage. Thus, lineage property is less fungible than individual property, yet it is not the antithesis to private property. The West has its own version of communal property, the only difference being the size of the community involved. One only needs to look at divorce settlements in the United States to recognize that communal property arrangements operate in the West as well. Whereas Western community property arrangements are based on the nuclear family, Akan lineage property is based upon the extended family.

Today, lineage land still serves important functions within the social system. In particular, the extended kinship structure is reinforced by maintaining some assets within the lineage. According to Hill (1986: 99), such an arrangements builds a sort of social security system, in that "the right of any member of a matrilineage to cultivate portions of lineage land is itself an aspect of inheritance." In turn, the maintenance of the extended kinship structure supports economic development, as it is often the source of capital for entrepreneurs starting out or expanding their business. The structure of lineage ties, however, limits the scope of obligations, lest it crumble under its own weight. Robertson (1984a), makes the point that while the sentiment of mutual aid is strong, the actual amounts are small. She sees this as a sign of weakness of the extended family system in providing a social safety net. However, this could also be seen as a strength of the network as it does not place too great a burden on the donors and does not foster dependence by the recipient.

Akan custom allowed for the acquisition of individual property as well. Here, a sort of Lockeian principle was at work. A private property right was established once a person's labour was mixed with an unclaimed resource. For example, a river could not be owned by a human being according to Akan custom, yet the fish caught from the river, or a dock built on the river was privately owned. Such property could then be sold to others. If unsold at the time of the owner's death, individual property was traditionally absorbed into the lineage, but while living, the owner could make a gift of the property to anyone he or she chose. In the pre-colonial era, individually owned land was relatively rare. Individual ownership was commonplace, however, when it came to other means of production, such as boats and weapons (Ayittey 1991).

As land became increasingly scarce, lineage property replaced stool land in its relative importance. Particularly as urban areas expanded, and land values increased, large expanses of land gave way to smaller fragmented plots (Hill 1986). Recently, individual ownership of land has become more prominent. As they seek alternatives to the subordinate position they hold in traditional inheritance schemes, women in particular are seeing that the acquisition of individual property affords them greater security. Traditionally, and as is often still the case, a widow will not receive the assets owned by her husband upon his death, as the two are not part of the same matrilineage. Today, more people are adopting the Western practice of leaving a written will in order to bypass traditional tribal rules governing inheritance. Such arrangements are not always honored in practice, however, and the default favors the lineage arrangement of property. If left intestate, or if the will is successfully disputed, property is absorbed into the lineage and distributed accordingly. Thus individual ownership over assets (particularly a residence) provides women an important source of security and autonomy in old age.

Traditionally, the Akan follow a matrilineal system of inheritance. The logic operating is that lineage "blood" is passed on by the mother, not the father. In the matrilineal system, a man's brothers are his first heirs, according to age (Keesing 1975). The brother may waive his right in favor of a sister's son or a maternal male cousin. (The brother's children are not successors, because they are part of a different matrilineage.) Property owned by Akan women also follows a matrilineal pattern, but here the heirs are first the owner's surviving aunts, then her sisters, then her sons and daughters, and then her nephews and nieces. The Ga follow a dual patrilineal and matrilineal system of inheritance. Property owned by men is distributed according to the patrilineage. Among the Ga, a man's heirs are first his full brothers, then his sons. Ga women follow a matrilineal pattern similar to Akan women (Kilson 1974).

Though men are privileged over women in both the matrilineal and patrilineal inheritance structures, women are adapting in ways that will concentrate accumulated capital within the hands of the entrepreneurs they train—their daughters, grand-daughters, and nieces. As women acquire more individual property, they are employing the use of written wills more frequently to override traditional inheritance structures. The Western innovation has been an important ingredient in this transition, but it should be noted that movement away from the ideal matrilineal structure had already taken place in the pre-colonial era. Clark (1994: 96–7) points out that prior to the colonial era, courtiers of the *Asantehene* (the Ashanti king) were allowed to train their own sons in the duties of the office they would one day inherit, without interference from matrilineal kin. The use of written wills to bypass traditional inheritance structure provides greater assurance that the daughter or niece who helped in building a business is compensated for her service, rather than distributed to a son or nephew who may have had little to do with the trader's prosperity and/or who stands to inherit from his maternal uncle. This offers a greater opportunity for women to benefit from their status as entrepreneurs. Not only will daughters inherit their mother's and grandmother's practical advice and training, they will also have greater access to accumulated capital.

THE ORIGINS OF A WEST AFRICAN CAPITALIST ETHIC

In Max Weber's classic essay *The Protestant Ethic and the Spirit of Capitalism* ([1922] 1958), he argued that the acquisitive practices which promoted capital accumulation and Western economic growth were fundamentally linked to the religious tenets and belief system set out by Calvinist Protestantism. The argument made here is that traditional religious belief structures in the Ghanaian context also provide a work ethic similar to, yet stemming from a vastly different doctrinal source, the Protestant ethic described by Weber. This work ethic is then reinforced by religious and kinship structures which encourage savings and the accumulation of capital.

A seemingly endless debate surrounds Weber's thesis; Frank Knight (1928), R.H. Tawney ([1926] 1972), H.M. Robertson (1933), Kurt Samuelson (1961), Christopher Hill (1961, 1966, 1969), Hugh Trevor-Roper (1963) are just a few of the more prominent contributors. The thesis has been criticized for being historically inaccurate in that Weber chose inappropriate religious texts to conduct his investigations. It has been criticized for its ethnocentrism, in that capitalistic behavior can be seen long prior to Calvinism. Further, whatever symbiosis might exist between Calvinism and capitalism seems to break down in cases like Scotland, Hungary, and Holland (Marshall 1982). The thesis has been attacked on the grounds that it has mischaracterized monastic economic production (Silber 1993). It has also been attacked on Marxian grounds, the very notion that religious ideology could shape the economic and material conditions of human society being dismissed out of hand (George and George 1958). Our purpose here is not to pass judgment on the specific conclusions Weber draws; rather, the point is to make use of Weber's approach. As Poggi (1983) argues, the real value of the Weberian thesis is that it is an attempt to understand what it is that gives meaning to people's lives; how ideas, religious or otherwise, shape the perspectives of a people and direct action. It is in this sense that we make use of Weber's essay.

The religious foundations of an indigenous work ethic

The Akan conception of man's relationship with God is that at the start of life, a person is given a unique destiny or *nkrabea* which must be realized. The means of fulfilling the *nkrabea* is by way of opening the *sunsum*, or ego, to the *okara*, or soul. In other words, spiritual progress is achieved by allowing higher truth to guide one's decisions and actions. The *nkrabea* does not constitute a deterministic structure. Each person has a choice as to whether he or she moves closer to actualizing the *nkrabea* or not. Everyday life offers countless opportunities to make an opening of the *sunsum* to the *okara*—an opening of the ego to the soul. In every decision, there is the possibility that the divine can enter into the earthly realm. Every effort at opening the *sunsum* to the *okara* brings a person one step closer to realizing the *nkrabea*, or unique personal destiny. This process may take many lifetimes. If at the end of life the *nkrabea* is not fulfilled, a person is returned to earth to carry on his mission. The progress made in each life is cumulative throughout the incarnations (Danquah 1968). Further, self-sacrifice made in the present life brings more rewards in future incarnations. As a life of good works feeds into social progress, that person will be the beneficiary of a healthier society when he or she returns to it. This more enlightened society will in turn have a positive impact on that individual's search for personal progress.

114

Traditional Ga religious belief is similar in these respects. Instead of a *sunsum*, the Ga *susuma* is the spiritual source of personality and individual character. The Ga'*kra* is similar in nature to the Akan *okara*, or soul (Parrinder1970). The Ga *gbesi* is somewhat similar to the Akan *nkrabea*, in that it corresponds to an individual's fate, luck, or life program (Manoukian 1950). Reincarnation is also important to Ga spirituality, but it is the grandfather's '*kra* that returns when the grandson is born. Girls inherit their paternal great aunt's '*kra*. Yet, the '*kra* is not a fixed quantity. The grandfather and great aunt do not have to die for their '*kra* to be passed on, and their '*kra* can be passed on to many grandchildren. It is simply said that they all share the same '*kra* (Field 1937). Thus both with the Akan and the Ga, as one bestows gifts and opportunities upon one's kin, particularly younger generations, rewards will come back, either in future incarnations or to the shared '*kra*.

The *nkrabea*, or fulfillment of one's personal destiny, constitutes the elements of a work ethic, providing a similar function as that which Weber described in relation to Protestant culture. Each person has his or her own destiny to reach the highest good, that is, the actualization of the *nkrabea*. Man is the central player in this process. God provides the challenge, yet the realization is through human action. Goodness is not a capacity, but rather is an activity. The opening up of the *sunsum*, or ego, to the *okara*, or soul, does not occur through a meditative lifestyle, sequestered off from the everyday workings of the world. The Akan belief structure is not one of mysticism but one of practicality. The opportunities for truth to be found are offered in the practical world of mundane dealings. Thus, entrepreneurial activity provides an important avenue for fulfilling the spiritual goal.

There are some significant differences, however, between the Western-based Protestant ethic and that of the Akan. Weber suggests that the Protestant ethic had a marked impact on the culture of capitalism because it offered an alternative to the Catholic cycle of sin, confession, and redemption.

To the Catholic the absolution of his Church was a compensation for his own imperfection. The priest was a magician who performed the miracle of transubstantiation, and who held the key to eternal life in his hand. One could turn to him in grief and penitence. He dispensed atonement, hope of grace, certainty of forgiveness, and thereby granted release from that tremendous tension to which the Calvinist was doomed by an inexorable fate, admitting of no mitigation . . . . The God of Calvinism demanded of his believers not single good works, but a life of good works combined into a unified system. There was no place for the very human Catholic cycle of sin, repentance, atonement, release, followed by renewed sin.

(Weber [1922] 1958: 117)

Within Catholicism, a life of sinful deeds could be forgiven at a deathbed confession so long as it was sincere. The Calvinist belief structure, on the other hand, necessitates an entire life of good works, not because it brings salvation, but because it is a sign of being one predestined to be saved.

Thus, however useless good works might be as a means of attaining salvation, for even the elect remain beings of the flesh, and everything they do falls infinitely short of divine standards, nevertheless, they are indispensable as a sign of election. They are the technical means, not of purchasing salvation, but of getting rid of the fear of damnation.

(Weber [1922] 1958: 115)

The "good works" of which Weber speaks are the vigilant and consistent fulfillment of the calling God has chosen for every believer. To do less than conscientiously pursue the opportunities that calling provides is to dishonor God's plan. This is no less true for the business person, than the minister. On this point, Weber quotes Calvin.

If God show you a way in which you may lawfully get more than in another way (without wrong to your soul or to any other), if you refuse this, and choose the less gainful way, you cross one of the ends of your calling, and you refuse to be God's steward, and to accept His gifts and use them for Him when He requireth it: you may labour to be rich for God, though not for the flesh and sin.

(quoted in Weber [1922] 1958: 162)

Thus, the vigilance required of Calvinism established what Weber called the Protestant work ethic.

To the Akan, a deathbed confession of one's spiritual failings would mean as little as it would within the Calvinist tradition. To the Akan, the point is not that the person had stored up too much evil, but rather that he or she had not yet accumulated enough good. The Calvinist notion of predestination, however, would be as equally abhorrent to the Akan. The Akan perceive a far more direct connection between earthly dealings and the spiritual realm. Not only are many of the rewards for moral behavior received here on Earth, but most significantly, the earthly world is the only manner in which the spiritual quest, the actualization of the *nkrabea*, can be realized.

To aid in this endeavor to reach the highest good, the Akan belief structure provides the concept of *opanyin*. There exists in every community the possibility of finding one who exemplifies the highest moral standard. Ultimately, the community raises such a person to the level of deity, to the *nana*, having personified the ideal good. Thus, the divine principles are at work at every moment in a living person. The status of *opanyin* is achieved only by way of living life as an ordinary citizen with honor (Danquah 1968). Thus, a hard-working farmer or a successful trader is far more likely to earn the label "*opanyin*" than one who has led a lazy existence or one sequestered away from daily productive activity. A figure with the status of *opanyin* offers a powerful role model for youth. Unlike the Christian ideal of acting "Christ-like," the traditional Akan benefit from having their ideal living among them, offering guidance, and providing a living example of the highest principles.

Both the Akan and Ga religions are practical belief structures. Each exhibits a direct connection between the earthly world and that of the ancestral spirits. The rewards of an honest life are not only granted in heaven, they are also bestowed during earthly life. Financial prosperity is seen as reward for upright spiritual behavior. Further, financial ruin can be interpreted as a punishment administered by the ancestors for some ill deed. As Field noted in 1937,

> I do not think any *wulomo* [Ga priest] is half so much afraid of his gods as a man is of his ancestors or an official of his dead predecessors. No system of "functional relationships" ever held together a body of custom half so firmly as this one idea—the idea of the ever present watchful dead and their power to smite or bless the living.
>
> (Field 1937: 197)

Prosperity, then, is not seen as the root or temptation of evil, but rather, as a sign of being in consonance with religious principles.

Capital accumulation and the stewardship of wealth

According to Weber, the essential counterpart to the Protestant work ethic was the value of asceticism, as it provided the basis for capital accumulation and community-wide economic prosperity.

> [T]he religious valuation of restless, conscientious, systematic work in a worldly calling as the highest means to asceticism, and at the same time the surest and most evident proof of rebirth and genuine faith, must have been the most powerful conceivable lever for the expansion of that attitude toward life which we have here called the spirit of capitalism. When the limitation of consumption is combined with this release of acquisitive activity, the inevitable practical result is obvious: accumulation of capital through ascetic compulsion to save.
>
> (Weber [1922] 1958: 172)

Though the Akan do not share this ethic of asceticism, what they do practice is an ethic of support among kin. Wealth and even expenditures on luxury items are acceptable within the Akan belief structure, yet only if family obligations are fully met. For example, traditionally, the taking of a second or third wife is seen as acceptable only if all families are adequately provided for. Luxuries are effective status symbols only so long as a member of the kin group is not experiencing severe hardship.

Indigenous religious structure is the principal foundation upon which this ethic is built. If there exists a common core to indigenous West African religions, it is the shared tradition of ancestral worship. The traditional gods of the Akan, Ga, Ewe, and other West African tribes are all quite different. Yet, to one degree or another, ancestral spirits play an active role in regulating the behavior of the living community in most, if not all, West African religious traditions. In the sense in which Gudeman (1986) and Bird-David (1992) suggest, it may be that the watchful eye of ancestral spirits constitutes a primary metaphor in that it regulates and directs the action of the living, though much more research, particularly linguistic research, would have to be conducted to draw any conclusions.

Ancestral spirits traditionally believed to inhabit the land can wield reward and punishment in response to proper and improper use of the land and the fruits derived from it. If, for example, a member of the lineage demonstrates stinginess with the proceeds from a bountiful crop, the ancestors are traditionally believed to

118

have the power to strike the deviant with misfortune. Given this threat, norms regarding the proper stewardship of wealth emerged and continue to operate as a dominant theme within West African culture. Market traders commonly reflect that business success obligates them to share their good fortune with relatives starting out in business or in financial crisis. Awareness that ancestral spirits may be monitoring the entrepreneurs' response to their obligations serves to reinforce this ethic.

The sense that the dead seek to correct the behavior of the living is still common, as illustrated by the comments of Louise, a jewelry trader in Accra.

> My aunt's husband treated her very badly. He beat her and used her money to drink beer and gamble. His [deceased] father came to him every night as he slept. He told him to stop doing all these things or he would never let him have a night's rest. He was scared so he stopped beating on her, but soon he left. I think he went crazy because he could not sleep.

Christian churches actively preach against such beliefs, preaching instead that Jesus Christ is the sole path to spiritual salvation. Many Christians know that they are not "supposed" to believe in the power of ancestral spirits, yet entrenched beliefs are not easily eradicated. Esther, a scarf trader in Accra, adamantly denies the power of ancestral spirits, yet there was one exception of which she personally knew.

> My sister was possessed by a spirit once. She was acting like a crazy person. She was talking and laughing to herself. My family took her to a fetish priest. This did not help her at all. We took her to [Christian] church and prayed for Jesus Christ our Lord and Savior to cleanse her soul. After that, she was much better.

Such accounts support Ayittey's (1991) thesis that Christianity has not replaced traditional religions. Rather, Christianity has created another layer on top of the indigenous belief system. By Esther's account of her sister's possession, ancestral spirits were weaker than the power of Jesus Christ, but they did nonetheless exert influence upon the living.

Clark's (1994: 262) account of Kumasi traders' attitudes toward the use of oaths (which call upon the power of ancestral spirits) further corroborates the persistence of indigenous beliefs in the modern context. By ingesting earth or pouring water onto the ground, the party swearing the oath calls upon ancestral spirits to cause the death of the guilty party.

> In one case, a woman trading vegetables from a stool and basket missed some money she had left tucked under her ground cloth .... [A]pparently, [she] had some reason to suspect her neighbor. Since she lacked proof, her willingness to swear served to dramatize the incident and give an indirect warning. Other neighbors laughed at her flamboyant gestures but also made sure to grab her arms and release the dangerous pinch of earth each time before it came near her mouth. Their comments made it clear that they thought the oath would work, even if inappropriate. As one said, "If we swore an oath every time something was stolen, there would be dead bodies lying all over the market."

The acceptance of many Western religious beliefs fit well within the indigenous context. The traditional beliefs that ancestral spirits would punish those who did not share their good fortune with those in need was fertile soil in which to plant the concept of Christian charity, for example. Market traders who identify themselves as Christian often speak of help provided to kin and other traders in religious terms. When asked how her plans would change if she were to achieve the level of financial success for which she hoped, Florence, a small-scale cloth trader, responded,

> I would still come to the market and sell cloth. I would use the money to help my friends who had not been as blessed. If, by the grace of God, I become rich I would want to give my sister and my brother some money. Besides, if I did not come to market, I would have too much time to spend the money. It would be finished very soon.

When asked why she would not simply keep the money for herself, Florence said, "I am a Christian, and when I was baptized I learned that Jesus does not like us to be greedy."

Ruth, a successful cloth trader, recognizes her responsibility to be a proper steward of her wealth in terms of a religious obligation. When asked about her sponsorship of her brother's carpentry business, she replied, "I am settled in my trade. God has been good to me and so I am happy to help my brother. He may help me someday if I am in need." Those who enjoy good fortune are morally bound to contribute a greater proportion to the "family pot," which provides emergency funds in times of financial distress and start-up capital for commercial ventures.

Thus, the origins of capital accumulation arise not from an ethic of asceticism, but from an obligation for the proper stewardship of wealth. Through the mechanism of the family pot, a similar end to that of asceticism is met. Of course migration to the urban environment and the influence of Western religions have had a tremendous influence upon indigenous belief structures. In the urban context, one is much more likely to encounter people who are well-versed in the teachings of Jesus Christ than people who can articulate the principles of indigenous religion. Nevertheless, many of the concepts which arose from indigenous religious practice still operate to regulate the behavior of individuals, particularly when it comes to trade and the stewardship of wealth.

The concept of *opanyin*, or one who exemplifies the highest moral standard, is still operative as evidenced by the respect and authority market traders confer upon market queens and other respected elders. First, as the respect one receives is more likely to increase with age in this context, older women are still regarded as productive even when they retire from the market. Retired market traders regularly perform child care and other domestic services for their grand-daughters, providing them with greater opportunities to expand their activities in the market. Second, the ethic of mutual obligation among kin still persists, and remains an essential source of capital for young entrepreneurs. Migrant women who are separated from the familial source of financial support transfer their sense of mutual obligation to close friends in the market, again providing an important source of capital accumulation. Thus, while many of the concepts of indigenous religion and kinship have been transformed by the modern urban context, many of the core principles are still operative.

FEMALE ENTREPRENEURSHIP

The overwhelming female character of indigenous markets in West Africa derives directly from cultural expectations regarding gender. The identity of the West African woman in large part revolves around her role as entrepreneur.[2] Understanding indigenous entrepreneurship and its prospects for further development requires an appreciation of both the constraints and opportunities Ghanaian women face in work and at home.

Gender relations and market autonomy

Most Western concepts regulating gender relations are inapplicable within the West African context (Vellenga 1983). Whereas Western concepts of marriage and household ideally bind the nuclear family into a single economic unit, West African concepts of marriage and household establish distinct economic spheres for husband and wife. The separation of the family purse means that the financial achievements made by men do not necessarily translate into a better economic position for their wives (Robertson 1984b). The reverse case, in which women achieve greater economic success than their spouses may also occur. As Hill (1986) points out, wives are often in a position to lend money to their husbands. Further, marriages often end in divorce or the husband may take a second wife. In such cases, the husband may cease providing any support for his first wife and her children. Even if he does continue to make provisions for the children of his first wife, the same size pie is now likely to be shared among more women and their children.

In the traditional context, the expectations of what husbands and wives would each contribute were well defined. Women provided staple vegetables from their garden or farm, and husbands provided the sauce ingredients, usually meat, fish, and salt. In the urban context, the husband's contribution is now a financial allowance called "chop money." Husbands are also expected to contribute to large expenses such as school fees for his children, but this still leaves the bulk of the day-to-day expenses in the wife's hands. Further, many informants in Accra reported that the chop money they received from their husband was not regular enough or substantial enough to meet the needs of the family, even for the one meal. For all these reasons, women must actively engage in the market to secure an independent income. While the burdens are high, these arrangements afford women a relatively high degree of autonomy and financial independence; both important assets in market trading, as women are relatively free to travel, to invest their resources as they see fit, and to acquire sole ownership over capital resources.

In the West African context, marriage will not constitute the principal relationship in a woman's life cycle as it (ideally) does in the West—the exception being educated or elite women who may adopt Western concepts of family (Oppong 1974). For most of their lives, men and women, both literally and figuratively, live in separate worlds. Multi-locality in marriage, as practiced in traditional

Ga, Ashanti, and other Akan societies, is still an accepted norm (Robertson 1984a; Clark 1994). Traditionally, men and women would cohabit for the early years of the marriage or until the first child was born, after which women returned to live with their matrilineal kin. This was true even among the patrilineal Ga, though the Ga husband would return to his patrilineal kin's compound. In the present context, the formal compound system is eroding, as the competition for urban housing increases, but this has only meant an increase in the separation of the sexes. Men successful enough to establish a lineage residence often move further outside the urban area, thereby increasing the distance between husband and wife (Robertson 1984a).

Under multi-local arrangements, wives still cook for their husbands and engage in sexual relations. But these occasions are arranged ahead of time, in part to avoid the potentially volatile circumstance of another wife (or girlfriend) arriving on the same evening. Romantic love is seen as a pleasant indulgence while young, but is not considered appropriate for the more mature woman. Clark's (1994: 103) informants described older adults who gave higher priority to marital and sexual matters than trading and other practical concerns as "immature, self-indulgent, and frivolous, and they often used sexual insults in such descriptions."

It is not unusual for an older woman simply to "retire" from marriage, relinquishing her obligations to cook and engage in sexual relations. In fact, Hagan (1983) finds that divorce rates gradually increase as both men and women age. In Clark's (1994: 340) study, only 59 percent of the women who reported being married actually lived with their spouse. In a similar study, Abu (1983) found that only 45 percent of married women lived with their husbands.

Women did recognize some benefits of cohabitation in that men were more likely to contribute to the support of their children if they lived in the same residence, but there are also benefits associated with living alone or with female kin. As Abu (1983) notes, the common perception is that men and women manage to avoid conflict by living separately, thereby building the strength of a lasting relationship. Finances and expectations regarding domestic duties are principal areas of conflict among spouses who live together. Husbands are more likely to extract financial resources and unpaid domestic services from their wives if they reside together. These gender-based conflicts are no recent phenomenon. According to Etienne (1983), pre-colonial Baule women who migrated to the cities of the Ivory Coast demonstrated a reluctance to marry, and correspondingly enjoyed an increased ability to achieve economic autonomy. Multi-local marriage arrangements afford many women the opportunity to accumulate capital which is safely beyond the reach of their husbands, enabling their advancement in trade.

Further, multi-locality releases women from many of the daily domestic services they would have to perform if they lived with their spouses, again giving them more time to engage in trade. While wives can use older children, female kin, and domestic help to perform child care, cleaning, and laundry tasks, the close association between cooking and marital sexual relations makes it inappropriate for a wife to depend upon anyone else to cook for her husband (Clark 1994). As cooking the traditional evening meal is a lengthy and involved process, being expected to cook for a husband every evening represents a significant drain on a market trader's time. Multi-locality in marriage tends to reduce the proportion of evenings on which women are expected to fulfill this aspect of the marital relationship.

Sororital alliances among market women

Relative to bonds of marriage, lineage ties are perceived as far more enduring. Particularly when it comes to financial matters, the mother–daughter or aunt–niece relationship is frequently the most dominant in the course of a woman's life. Mothers provide their daughters training and start-up capital at the end of a long apprenticeship. A mother keeps the proceeds from child labor, but saves for her daughter's entrance into business. In return, daughters and grand-daughters provide marketing services for her business while she is young, and financial security when she can no longer work. Business partnerships are often based upon this relationship.

Friends and respected traders in the market can also serve in this system of inter-generational training. Mothers will sometimes send their daughters to live with markedly successful traders to apprentice under them. In this way, daughters can be exposed to new and perhaps more profitable industries.[3] Mavis, who sells tomatoes and other vegetables from a tabletop just outside the main market area in Accra, plans to send her daughter to live with her friend who makes and sells prepared foods.

My sister [friend] went to a school to learn baking. She has two sons, but she does not want them to sell for her. When

Hadjia [Mavis' daughter] is old enough, she can sell for her . . . . Baking is better than selling tomatoes. The profits are too small. But baking is much better.

As the child matures into adulthood, the mentor will continue to serve as a source of advice and, often, financial partnership.

While a husband may provide start-up capital for his wife upon marrying her, he is not likely to fill the role of confidant. When asked what part her husband has in her business, a mid-level dried goods trader named Felicia, responds this way.

He stops by the stall from time to time, but he knows I don't like it. He says that I deceive him when I say I have no money. I may have a few thousand cedis but I need it to pay for the goods.

Again, though much more research would have to be completed to draw any conclusions, it may be that "rivalry" constitutes a primary metaphor for how urban market women interpret their strategies, opportunities, and constraints in relation to men (Gudeman 1986; Bird-David 1992). The term "rivalry" is chosen as a first approximation, because it connotes both competition, in terms of access to scarce resources, and the excitement associated with a competitive game. On the first point, a wife is generally hesitant to divulge information about her financial dealings to her husband, for fear that he may see just cause in increasing her obligations to the family. Clark's (1994: 340) informants report a preference for multi-locality in marriage, reasoning that husbands are less likely to inquire about financial details. The profiles of market women presented by Robertson (1984a) and in this volume (Chapter 5) often demonstrate a marked and consistent distrust between women and men, particularly among women who identify men as a potential threat to their financial independence. Yet the term rivalry also carries with it the connotation of a game, an engagement which can be the source of pleasure and drama. As Clark (1994: 38–9) points out, women consider divorce or adultery to be justifiable responses to sexual neglect. Though gender relations can be the source of sustained conflict, southern Ghanaian women are anything but indifferent to sexual pleasure and male companionship.

A metaphor such as rivalry would also carry over to the tight bonds of trust and confidence within female networks of friends, or "sororital alliances" and kin. Such networks enable market traders to respond strategically to the particular constraints they face.

125

Through collective action, women provide each other with access to capital and labor, reduce the burden of caring for small children, and, via pyramid schemes of financing, provide access to higher-status positions in trade. The importance of collective action among women reaches deep into West African history. Certainly, within the home, a woman's opinion was always subordinate to that of her husband's. Yet, in retribution for some shameful act committed by a man, for instance rape or the beating of an elderly or pregnant woman, the Igbo women of Cameroon would come together to call upon the spirits of female ancestors to avenge the deed in a ritual called "*anlu*." The ritual involved tainting the perpetrator's water supply and cooking utensils with excrement. The man was effectively ostracized until restitution and a gesture of "atonement" was made to the victim (Wipper 1984).

Wipper also points to the power of female cooperation as seen in everyday activities, such as rural cooperative arrangements for female agricultural plots. By pooling resources, women are able to hire teams of migrant workers. Women have also developed intricate child care networks. As mentioned earlier, older women retired from the market will often look after grandchildren or great grandchildren. Women with no children will take others into their home in exchange for marketing services the older children might provide. Some women offer child care services in exchange for a percentage of the mother's daily profit, or a group of market women will take turns caring for each other's children (Sudarkasa 1981). Through one or a combination of these arrangements women work together to provide efficient child care without substantially interrupting marketing activity.

Business connections among women also provide opportunities to acquire start-up capital. Creative methods of financing have evolved to overcome the high costs associated with entrance to some industries. Particularly in the textiles industry, importers require a substantial initial outlay of collateral before they will front a trader enough cloth to sell. Further, the stall fees are potentially inhibiting to capital-poor entrants. Often, successful textiles traders will put up the initial collateral or "passbook money" and rent the stall for a young woman, in return for the bulk of the proceeds (Robertson 1984a). Initially, the young woman is not much better off than if she were hawking on the street, yet over time she has the opportunity to build up a regular clientele and goodwill with distributors who will be more willing to issue greater and greater amounts of

126

cloth. Eventually she can establish an independent role for herself in the industry. Ruth, the successful cloth seller mentioned earlier recounts her early experience.

> At first I sold women's underclothes. Then I sewed fabric into bed linens and sold them. I also sewed school uniforms and scarves. When two friends and I had each saved ₵100,000 we bought a large quantity of cloth and split it up. We did this many times because the [wholesale] prices are lower when you buy in large quantities, but it was too much to sell by myself. I sponsored my niece and her two friends. This was much better because I could stay in the shop while the girls sold on the road.

Sororital alliances serve market women on two levels here. First, the bulk purchase agreement Ruth describes is similar to Shanmugan's (1991) description of the purchase of consumer durables in Malaysia. Ten to twelve women will arrange to buy a refrigerator or some other large consumer item every month, until each member has received one. Each member contributes only her share every month, thereby spreading her payments over the entire year. Further, the volume purchase gives the group bargaining power in securing the best price for the appliance. Similarly, by working in concert, successful market women are able to secure a better price for their supplies.

In turn, this arrangement benefits capital-poor market traders by providing entrance into the cloth industry. When asked if her niece and friends were still selling for her, Ruth replied, "No. My niece will often buy cloth from me to sell. But all three have their own stalls and they can buy direct from the wholesale trader." By providing the initial credit, high-volume cloth traders enable the advancement of new entrants into the market, as well as their own businesses. Further, such arrangements benefit older traders who have the capital but not necessarily the strength or energy to engage in day-to-day trading. In this way, many successful traders have built their business enough to invest in real estate and eventually a comfortable retirement.

These arrangements do not exclusively involve women. After accumulating enough capital, many women buy fishing boats and hire male crews to work them. In the case of production on a traditional Ga female compound, the women of the compound will smoke or salt cure the fish, and in turn, the young women of the compound will sell the finished product (Robertson 1984a). It may seem puzzling that in this traditional society men would be open to an arrangement in which they were working for a woman. Traditionally, the intelligence of women was not in question. Women were often quite influential in tribal decisions. For example, among the Akan, the *ohemma* (head woman) essentially chose the occupant of the "male stool"—the tribal leader. In some cases, the *ohemma* herself occupied the stool (Arhin 1983). The subordinate status of women was traditionally linked to the uncleanness associated with the menstrual cycle and the talents some women were believed to have in witchcraft. The market woman's ability to make good business decisions, however, was never in question.

As another means of acquiring capital, the rotating credit association is a variation of the family pot tradition, by which savings, credit, and mutual assistance are established on a kinship basis. Female access to the family pot is limited, particularly in the case of those who have migrated from the rural setting to the city. Separated from their family ties, urban migrants find trade and social networks fill the supportive gap left in the absence of close kin (Little 1973). Even the traditionally urban Ga have reached beyond bonds of kinship to secure bonds of friendship. As Kilson notes,

[Friendship] is a concept which is quite alien to older members of Ga society but which is important in the recreational life of young and middle-aged men and women. Bonds of friendship, rather than kinship, constitute the basis of voluntary associations, such as mutual aid societies . . .

(Kilson 1974: 33)

Thus, while kinship is a source of financial support and start-up capital, networks of friendship represent yet another.

Rotating credit associations, which will be discussed in greater detail in Chapter 4, evolved out of the structure traditional trade associations provided. For centuries, voluntary trade associations have regulated market traders by enforcing standards of cleanliness and honesty. The associations also provide a valued social function, thus raising the costs of noncompliance. Further, trade associations provide a network of advice and mutual support among market traders. Ostracism from the association results in the loss of credit as well as the loss of commercial and social contact. The traditional authority held by the market queen, which helped to maintain order and smooth functioning of the marketplace, established a basis of trust and stability necessary to attract members. Unlike formal savings institutions, a member does not need to be literate or own property to qualify for financial assistance. She proves her credit worthiness by building trust relationships through face-to-face interaction within a community of traders.

In his study of urban voluntary associations, Little (1965) describes the credit association called Nanemei Akpee (meaning "club of friends") in Accra. Each week members raise a loan for one person in order of seniority with the association. Each member who has not yet received a loan puts in what she thinks she can afford for the week. This amount is recorded in a general ledger, and the list of names and contributions is also given to the current recipient. The recipient is obliged to give each person on this list the same amount they contributed when her turn comes. Such obligations are upheld by the threat of ostracism and the loss of borrowing privileges if the rules are not followed.

Early entrants to the society have the advantage of receiving an interest-free loan without first saving in the form of contributions to other members. During inflationary periods, the earliest entrants are at an advantage as the real amount they receive is more than what they pay back. However, later entrants gain the advantage of a growing membership by collecting more contributions. Alternatives to waiting are available if a woman needs a loan before it is her turn to collect. In an emergency, a person can be bumped ahead in line. Some associations have also established health, pregnancy, and death benefits for its members, thus providing a financial safety net in the urban setting where migrants may be cut off from rural kin. A second alternative method is available by borrowing from the "club box." Each week, the recipient makes a donation to the club, from which small loans can be made to other members. A third alternative is to sell one's right to their turn. Such agreements are signed by the two parties and witnessed by the head woman of the association. This is similar to what Shanmugan (1991) describes as "discounting rotating credit associations" in Malaysia. The order in which group members receive the pot is determined by a sort of auction. If a group member wishes to receive the pot early, the member will offer to relinquish a certain percentage back into the till which would be shared equally among the remaining group members. The member willing to discount the most will be the next recipient. (Also see Hiebert (1993) for a similar practice in Vietnam.) In Nanemei Akpee and other Ghanaian credit associations, the order is determined by seniority in the club, and any side payment will go directly to the woman selling her turn.

At one time, Nanemei Akpee was claiming membership in the thousands. The prevalence of such large rotating credit associations are not as vast as they once were. The harsh anti-market policies implemented under Nkrumah and later Rawlings, and the overall economic decline from the 1960s to the 1980s, dealt serious blows to such institutions. Today, small credit, savings and mutual assistance associations are the norm. Yet these modest organizations still have the potential to foster economic development, as they provide an essential source of credit closed off by official channels.

In her work on ethnically homogeneous middlemen groups, such as the Jews in medieval Europe, Indians in South Africa, and overseas Chinese communities, Landa (1991) argues that certain characteristics enable some groups to achieve distinct entrepreneurial success. An ethic of mutual obligation and trust, shared cultural values, shared and accepted notions of authority and methods of conflict resolution, and a sense of solidarity in opposition to the larger outside world all tend to reduce the costs of enforcing contracts, and provide a source of training and capital for the young members of the ethnic group. In the urban West African context, female entrepreneurs share many of these characteristics. The sense of mutual obligation which has emerged out of indigenous kinship structure is strongest between same sex members of the lineage, the people most likely to train girls and young women in the rules, techniques, and strategies of market trading. Urban market women share and perpetuate commonly accepted values which enable relatively smooth conflict resolution and the enforcement of mutual agreements. Although women represent a far larger percentage of the population than the ethnic groups Landa describes, women perceive their position as one in opposition to male society, resulting in a sort of solidarity characteristic of smaller ethnic groupings. This by no means suggests that conflicts among women do not arise, but it does mean that networks of advice, business partnership, and mutual support among women do represent gender-specific solutions to the constraints they face. Thus, female entrepreneurs in the Ghanaian and larger West African context represent a potentially powerful entrepreneurial force.

CONCLUSION

The general lesson to be drawn here is that cultural analysis can help us to identify indigenous sources of wealth and development potential within an emerging economy. The institutions necessary for economic progress emerge out of a specific cultural context. Rules governing law and property reflect commonly shared perceptions of legitimate authority, justice, and the relationship of the individual to society. Rules generated outside this particularized context (for instance, those passed down by well-meaning development specialists) are not likely to meet with success. Only if the values inherent in the social institutions are generally accepted, will the system of rules convey any benefit to society. Out of cultural structures such as religion, kinship, and tribal affiliation may also emerge a common orientation towards work, commerce, and saving conducive to capital accumulation and wealth. Culture guides and directs the attention of entrepreneurs by placing them in a specific position within the social order and providing them with an interpretive framework to piece together profit opportunities creatively.

As has been argued, the capitalist ethic and the entrepreneurial mindset at work within the southern Ghanaian context is not the result of Western imperialism, but is rather an outgrowth of indigenous culture. Thus, economic development is not necessarily tied to becoming more Westernized, with a diminished reliance upon indigenous culture. Rather, the reverse might be the more promising solution, by taking advantage of the cultural resources inherent within an emerging economy.

Larger considerations might also be addressed in this context. As we incorporate cultural analysis into development theory and policy, it raises questions regarding the generalizability of a development model. Can the lessons learned by investigating southern Ghanaian culture be transferred to East African, Asian, or Latin American cases? It is indeed likely that some of the lessons learned will have relevance for urban areas quite distant from the Makola markets in Central Accra. For instance, many African, Asian, and Latin American cultures have generated rotating credit organizations of some sort (Hiebert 1993; Timberg and Aiyar 1984; Shanmugan 1991). The rules of engagement, however, will necessarily differ from one context to the next, and each warrants its own investigation. As for a generalizable model, the prospects seem quite limited. It is likely that much of what has been argued here in the case of southern Ghana will ring true for

131

many other African societies. Yet, the further one is removed, either by distance, time, or historical experience, from the cultural context out of which the observations were generated, the less general applicability those observations will have.

This is not to say that no general lessons exist, however. Institutional arrangements which foster international trade, the clear establishment and enforcement of property rights, a stable legal and political environment—all these elements are necessary conditions if economic progress is to be achieved (Clarkson 1975; Waters 1987). Yet institutions essential to development may take different forms, perform different functions, and be legitimized in different ways, according to the specific cultural context in which they have developed. Further, an institutional arrangement vital to economic success in one culture might not have any impact in another. The favored source of start-up capital and financial support in one culture might be the nuclear family, yet in another it might be the extended family. In still other cultures, the best source of financial capital might be a church or a cooperative organization. The position advanced here is not that *only* culture matters in economic performance, nor is it that *only* institutions matter. The position taken here is that both cultural analysis and institutional analysis are essential to building relevant development theory and sound development policy.

4

INDIGENOUS CREDIT, MUTUAL ASSISTANCE SOCIETIES, AND ECONOMIC DEVELOPMENT

Prospects and impediments[1]

The sight of Barclays Bank, Standard Chartered Bank, Ghana Commercial Bank, and other Western-type banking institutions in the larger cities of Ghana is impressive. It appears as though the international financial community is deeply entrenched in the Ghanaian economic process. To be certain, these institutions play an extremely important role in financing large-scale industry and high-volume import and export exchange. But the majority of entrepreneurs in the informal sector never enter the doors of such institutions. The inability of formal institutions to serve this segment of the market is not a matter of market failure, rather it is a matter of a poor cultural fit. Formal institutions such as these have grown out of and reflect a particular cultural context, one in which the entrepreneurs they serve are more often than not educated, literate, and male. Entrepreneurs in this context demonstrate their credit worthiness with a documented credit history and access to collateral. Thus, Western investors, the local business elite, and government contractors who match the Western profile of an acceptable borrower are served well by the formal banking community.

However, formal banking institutions do not fit the indigenous cultural context in which the typical entrepreneur is a small-scale female trader with limited education, and is often incapable of writing in the language of the banking community. As discussed in Chapter 2, formal banking institutions do not have access to the local knowledge embedded within the kinship and "sororital" alliances required to assess the credit worthiness of microenterprise entrepreneurs. To acquire such knowledge is largely considered to be prohibitively expensive relative to the low-cost loans they can extend to formal and international industries.

The rejection, however, is not one-sided. Microenterprise

133

entrepreneurs are just as reluctant to accept the practices of formal banking institutions as the formal banking institutions are reluctant to serve the needs of small-scale entrepreneurs. The majority of market women cannot afford the initial deposit required even to establish a savings account within the formal sector (Lycette 1985). In 1991, both Standard Chartered and Ghana Commercial Bank required an initial deposit of ₵10,000 ($23.53)[2] to open a saving account. They would not consider a loan for less than ₵100,000 ($235). For a first-time loan, they require cash collateral of half the amount of the loan, plus property or a guarantor. In addition, the borrower must insure the business and goods such that the loan will be paid off in the event of extensive accidental damage or theft. In 1992, Barclays Bank required a minimum initial deposit of ₵50,000 ($118) to open a savings account and would not consider lending less than ₵1,000,000 ($2,353). Again, the first-time borrower is required to provide cash collateral of half the amount of the loan, plus property or a guarantor. Barclays Bank requires the borrower to purchase life insurance in order to secure the loan. In 1992, a policy for a healthy thirty-year old would cost approximately ₵150,000 ($353). Barclays Bank also requires potential borrowers to carry out the bulk of their transactions in the form of checks. Small entrepreneurs deal only in cash both when purchasing supplies and when accepting payments.

Those who have attempted or contemplate establishing a savings account often remark that they fear they will be made to feel ignorant if they have difficulty understanding banking procedures or filling out complicated written forms. Further, many market women speak only their local language and not English, the official language of both the country and apparently the formal financial sector. The financial, cultural, bureaucratic, and linguistic barriers formal institutions present—just to open a savings account, much less take out a loan—mean that most market women do not consider acceptance into the formal financial sector as an appealing option, even as a long-term goal. Even if microenterprise entrepreneurs are able to establish a savings account, any loan amount for which they would be eligible would not be worth the bank's time to process and administer.

As was discussed in the previous chapter, indigenous financial arrangements provide an alternative to the formal banking system. The potential of these alternative arrangements is not widely considered to be promising, however, given that the amount of credit most often extended is no more than a few dollars (Robertson

1984a). Yet there is a case to be made that such indigenous arrangements ought not to be dismissed out of hand. First, the bulk of investment activity is financed through indigenous arrangements and not the formal banking institutions. Thus, even if the indigenous sector faces strict constraints, it is nevertheless serving a valued function in the market that is not met elsewhere. Credit, savings, and mutual assistance networks are essentially information networks. The associations make a wide range of information about credit risk, time preference, and investment potential more intelligible; just as the price system makes the vast array of disparate knowledge concerning scarcity of resources more comprehensible. Such organizations are essential elements in the expansion of trade, and are therefore essential to the development process. For not only do the numbers of trade relationships grow, but the ability of the market system as a whole to accommodate increasingly distant and complex trade relationships also expands.

Second, it is not necessarily the case that larger loans are needed. The relative success of development programs such as the Grameen Bank and similar projects indicates that small loans of just a few dollars can make a substantial difference (Wahid 1994). Third, if the indigenous arrangements are stunted this is often the result of state regulation and restrictions on trade. Thus, an investigation into the operations of indigenous financial solutions will help us identify which regulatory practices cause the most disruption to their ability to function.

The size, scope, and function of indigenous credit and mutual assistance societies will first be detailed, indicating the essential features for their proper functioning. Then, the major obstacles attenuating the progress such societies might deliver will be discussed. Lastly, institutional and policy considerations will be addressed.

INDIGENOUS CREDIT AND MUTUAL ASSISTANCE SOCIETIES

Women's associations vary in size, scope, and function. As was discussed in the previous chapter, such societies are traditionally based in kinship and tribal structures. It might be said that migration both into the city by those from the rural areas, and out of the city to the suburban areas has caused irreparable damage to the kinship and tribal systems, such that they can no longer perform the advisory and credit functions to the degree that they once did. To the extent that these structures provide less support for those in the urban environment, other culturally based support systems are evolving to fill the void.

Christian churches, particularly in Accra, provide another layer of community involvement. Almost all the Christian church organizations provide some form of mutual aid on a regular basis. Many also play an advisory role for traders looking to expand their business, either through advisory committees made up of church members or through a referral process by which the ministers introduce younger market traders to more established businessmen and women.[3] Some even provide an opportunity to acquire credit through church programs specifically designed to start people in business. Thus, as the ability of kinship and tribal structures to provide these services is faltering in the urban areas, the religious institutions are stepping in with similar services of their own. Just as Western religious institutions have influenced traditional beliefs, Western religious organizations have had to adapt and expand their role in the new context. Specifically, they have had to take on at least some of the functions previously performed by traditional structures.

The second important support system that is filling the void left by the decline of tribal and kinship structures in the urban areas is the formation of female societies which cut across tribal and kinship lines. These can range from small clusters of three to five women who trade near one another on the street to the elaborate trade organizations of several hundred women in the established markets. In Accra, inclusion in the clusters or organizations is not determined by tribal affiliation or kinship ties, though such relationships are still important when they exist.[4] Repeatedly successful face-to-face interaction engenders the trust necessary for the formation of close bonds. Physical proximity allows traders in a specific area to observe one another's behavior, as well as to establish a reputation for themselves.

The fact that such networks of women cut across tribal lines is significant, in that it points to the possibility that gender identification is becoming more dominant than tribal affiliation in relationships which are forged in the urban market context. In other words, gender itself constitutes a cultural category in this context, and is increasingly defining market and personal relationships.

Even in the Western context it has been argued that gender constitutes cultural specificity (Tannen 1982, 1990a, 1990b). Tannen argues that same-sex play groups during childhood lead boys and girls to develop distinct cultures from one another, accounting for many of the systematic differences in adult male and female relationships. As children establish same-sex peer groups, boys and girls develop separate language patterns and use language in systematically different ways. Whereas male peer groups use language to establish status, or hierarchical relationships, female peer groups use language to establish connection, or more lateral relationships. As these different language patterns develop, so do distinct cultures. As Western children enter into adulthood, the male–female relationship tends to replace the same-sex peer group as the primary relationship. Yet each retains the behavioral and linguistic patterns learned as children. Thus, communication between men and women, Tannen concludes, is essentially cross-cultural communication.

If gender differences constitute distinct cultural categories in the Western context, such distinctions are even more pronounced in the West African context. The conjugal unit, while not incidental, generally does not diminish the importance same-sex peer relationships play in the lives of West African women. Marriage does not weaken the ties women have to their female kin or even to their friends, particularly among market traders. The high degree of multi-locality for young married women and the "retirement" from marriage by many older women maintains the dominance of same-sex relationships on into adulthood and old age. The strict division of labor across gender also perpetuates the importance of same-sex peer groups into adulthood as women work side by side with one another. The traditional role female cooperation plays in production, child rearing, and the enforcement of social norms (Wipper 1984; Sudarkasa 1981) also perpetuates the influence of a gender-specific culture into adulthood. Thus, the degree to which gender constitutes a cultural category is far more pronounced in the West African context than in the Western context.

Most market women, particularly hawkers and mid-level stall traders exhibit a strong sense of camaraderie with the women who trade in their immediate area. The traders form themselves into close-knit groupings, or clusters, sometimes as small as three to five women. These connections serve a vital economic function of mutual support. Even direct competitors will sell for one another in the case of sickness. Most traders are socially as well as financially linked with other traders.

Game theory analysis has been employed to explain the mutual support and cooperative behavior such group members exhibit

(Axelrod 1981; Klein and Leffler 1981; Kronman 1985). Kronman (1985: 21) describes this method of reciprocal behavior as "union," whereby individuals seek to "reduce divergence [of interests] by promoting a spirit of identification or fellow-feeling between the parties . . . ." As opposed to other arrangements designed to combat opportunism, "union" does not assume opposition of interests. Rather "[union] seeks to eliminate the condition of separateness that makes the opposition of interests possible in the first place" (Kronman 1985: 22). Thus, casual chat, gossip, and discussions which involve traders in one another's lives, serve more than just a social function. The rituals of female friendship are also an important prerequisite for securing mutually supportive financial relationships.

Axelrod (1981) describes how a high probability of repeated interaction generates cooperation under conditions in which there exist 1) no sanctions for breaking the rules of cooperation, 2) no methods of gauging the behavior of other players outside of the game, and 3) no opportunities to change the other players' utility function. While Axelrod's analysis is internally consistent, it is not as applicable to the specific case of West African market women as Kronman's "union."

First, West African market women do indeed have sanctions for breaking the rules of a rotating credit society. Indigenous arbitration methods and the threat of ostracism are time-honored methods of minimizing such opportunistic behavior when it does occur. Second, the ability of traders to gauge one another's behavior in their day-to-day trading activities is a vitally important source of information. Simply bumping into another trader day after day is not enough to ensure a successful cooperative link. Building trust requires more than repeated interaction. Trust involves careful assessment of another's character, not simply calculating the probability of seeing the same person again. An exchange with Gladis, a bead seller, illustrates the scrutiny involved in building trust.

CHAMLEE-WRIGHT   Do you save in group *susu*?[5]

GLADIS   No. I save with a *susu*-man.

CHAMLEE-WRIGHT   How much does he charge you?

GLADIS   I save ¢200 a day. At the end of the month he gives the whole thing back except for ¢200.

CHAMLEE-WRIGHT   Why do you pay someone to help you save when you could save with your friends in group *susu?*

GLADIS   [In a hushed tone] When I had other friends in the market I used to save in group *susu.* I do not trust the women here now. Every night they go to the discos and drink. They ask me if I have money for group *susu,* but I always say "no."

A trader may faithfully return to the market day after day, but if she is frequently rude to her customers, is a spendthrift, or drinks heavily on a regular basis, other traders are not likely to see her as a good risk. The repeated interaction enables this assessment, but by no means constitutes trust in and of itself. Third, Axelrod's condition that the players cannot interact outside of the game, or in other words, cannot influence the feelings one has for the other, is clearly not applicable in this case. The bonds of friendship are paramount in establishing the financial support networks.

Women at the upper end of the scale who have been financed by their husbands, however, often do not show as much interest in joining together with other women. Mary, a prosperous batik trader refused to take part in any of the trade or credit associations. In fact, she reported that she did not gossip or go out of her way to be sociable with the neighboring traders.

I used to belong to these groups, but the women were always meddling in my affairs. I do not need the advice of illiterate women about how to run my business. I learned bookkeeping at school. These women just want to look at my books so they can gossip about me.

Mary suggested that trade and commodity associations were more for the illiterate traders, not for someone as well educated as she. In some respects, she is correct. Mary's business was financed by her husband who holds a prominent civil service position. The fact that her husband was able to buy a large house gave her the opportunity to produce the batik herself, as the process requires a large protected space.[6] Mary's attitude regarding trade and commodity associations is indicative of a general pattern. Of the stall traders interviewed, 83 percent belonged to trading associations, whereas only 42 percent of the more prosperous lock-up shop operators belonged. This indicates that the female camaraderie which does exist plays more than just a social role, but serves a financial function of which relatively wealthy women need less.

The hawkers

The smallest forms of indigenous credit and mutual assistance occur among clusters of women who sell in the same area. Trust and reputation are the essential elements in all of the informal arrangements, as this reinforces a system of reciprocal behavior. For this reason hawkers, or women who sell on the streets or sidewalks, tend to form the smallest groups of three to five women. Traders must be in close enough proximity to one another to be able to interact on a social basis. Out of these social relationships evolve financial arrangements.

Such clusters will gather to engage in group *susu*, or a rotating credit organization. Members of a group *susu* association make either daily or weekly contributions to a common pot. The pot is then distributed to members in turn, usually on a monthly basis. Group *susu* can be ongoing or set up for specific purposes. Hawkers who have no fixed trading position tend to save anywhere from ₵200 to ₵500 ($0.47 to $1.18) per week. Thus, in a four-member group, each will receive ₵800 to ₵2,000 ($1.88 to $4.71) once a month. One member is chosen to hold the money over the month. This woman must not have a reputation of being a spendthrift. Yet other considerations, such as her living arrangements are also important. If she lives with a husband who is known to gamble or drink heavily, the women will know that the fund is in danger under her care, so another choice is made.

If the trust relationships can be formed, group *susu* has an advantage over saving with a *susu*-man, as he charges a commission of one day's savings per month. Further, depending on the rules the group wishes to follow, the women who receive the pot first have a source of interest-free credit. The women last in line to receive the pot have a way to keep themselves and their family members from spending their profits too swiftly. In the smaller groups, the order is generally determined by consensus, allowing the woman with the most urgent need for the resources to receive the money first. In larger, ongoing groups, the order is determined by order of entrance into the organization. In many Asian communities, the order one receives the pot in a rotating credit organization is determined by lot (Shanmugan 1991). This was not the preferred method among market women in Accra, who instead wanted to be able to take individual circumstances into account.

While the *susu* arrangement offers a financial resource, credit can also come in the form of goods. Women who have lost their capital will often rely on friends to advance them produce or other goods for which they will pay at the end of the day or week. Abiba, a street vendor who lost her capital through fines levied by the city council helps her friend sell rice in return for a small sum at the end of the day. This amounts to a transfer, as there is no financial benefit to the rice seller for "hiring" her friend, yet the ethic of mutual support is reinforced so that the rice seller could rely upon similar support if such a situation were to befall her. Besides financial support, this arrangement also affords the opportunity for Abiba to maintain her position in the peer group. When she is able to secure her own goods for sale, she will be able to ease back into the market culture more easily than if she were to drop out of market activity completely.[7]

Generally, street vendors have little opportunity to belong to an ongoing mutual assistance society, as they do not have the financial capital necessary to make regular contributions, but they will take up collections to aid friends who have given birth, are getting married, or who must provide funeral arrangements for a family member. Some women will still have this sort of support within their home village. But access to such support would most likely require returning to the village, as much of the assistance is given in kind rather than in cash. Women are reluctant to take advantage of this source of support if it means they must give up the independence and financial prospects the urban setting offers.

The illegality of trade on the street gives this sector of the market a distinctive character. As the city council guards make their way down the street, the hawkers pass an audible signal to alert each other to the guards' presence. As if choreographed by Busby Berkeley himself, the traders hoist large trays of fruit, vegetables, fish, utensils, etc. atop their heads. Women who sell goods too heavy to place on head trays need to secure a position close to the entrance of the established market. Once the signal is heard, she can quickly move her goods inside and lose the city guards in the maze of the market— a maze far more familiar to female traders than the male guards.

No one can officially own a selling spot on the sidewalk, yet a system of *de facto* property rights has nonetheless emerged. Many women "inherit" these positions in the market from their mother, an aunt, a sister, or a friend. This *de facto* property rights system enables larger and more permanent *susu* organizations, as women can count on their peers returning to the same spot in the market. When a position is well established, any woman who attempted to encroach upon this space would be harassed out of the spot by the surrounding women with a barrage of insults, as the following exchange demonstrates. Grace sells beans in the same spot every day. She is situated directly outside the officially designated market. The amount of beans she brings to market is far too great to carry around. When asked about her selling place on the sidewalk, several of her friends join the conversation.

CHAMLEE-WRIGHT	What happens if you are too sick to come to the market, or are traveling to get more supplies?
GRACE	My friends will sometimes sell for me. If there is enough, I share the profits with them.
CHAMLEE-WRIGHT	What would happen if another trader decided to use your spot? What if they refused to move when you returned to the market?
HAWKER1	Ooh, another trader tried to steal her [another hawker's] spot when she was away.
HAWKER2	I was away. I went to the hinterland to buy vegetables to sell.
HAWKER 1	I told the woman, that is my friend's spot and she is coming back. She [the interloper] did not go away. I told her that when my friend got back, she would have to move.
CHAMLEE-WRIGHT	[To Hawker 2] Did she move when you returned?
HAWKER 2	No. She was there and she refused to move.
CHAMLEE-WRIGHT	What did you do?
GRACE	[Laughing] Ooh, we shouted at her. We told her that this was not her spot. She was so frightened, she ran away. [More laughter]

As this exchange demonstrates, *de facto* property rights are not as efficient as full rights of ownership. Following the Alchian and Demsetz (1973) identification of the essential elements of private ownership, *de facto* property rights fall short of the mark. Specifically, while *de facto* private property rights provide some level of stability and excludability, the element of transferability is significantly stunted. Stability is maintained as long as a trader consistently returns to the same location. As we have seen, neighbors will often exclude would-be interlopers from taking over a selling position in the case of the limited absence of another trader. But the efficient allocation of the resource depends on the ability of a trader to smoothly transfer it to another. While selling positions can be "handed down" from mother to daughter, for example, traders cannot sell the space to the highest bidder.

Transfer of the trading position takes place over an extended period of time. The mother, for instance, will begin by bringing her daughter to the market. The daughter will circulate goods on the street, returning to her mother's position for more supplies when needed. Eventually, the daughter may sit with her mother, establishing a rapport with the other traders. By the time the mother quits the market or moves to a better selling position, the daughter has already established her legitimate claim to her mother's selling space. But, again, the *de facto* right is still relatively tenuous and will be forfeited if the trader does not return to the position consistently.

Many women are fortunate enough to have established a contact with a store-front shop owner, with the agreement that the owner will allow the street vendor to hide in the shop when the city guards pass by. While there is an opportunity for side payments here, most women who have such a position acquired the favor through personal contacts. The lack of payment, however, should not be seen as a sign that such permission does not represent a valuable resource to the street vendors. Such an arrangement enables the trader to engage in more substantial credit relationships because of the decreased flight risk. Further, the stable position enhances profits as the trader is able to establish a regular clientele.

Among the hawkers who secure stable trading positions at the entrance of a store, the group *susu* societies grow from about four to about twelve members. The monthly pot of a four-member group in which each contributes ₵200 per week is ₵3,200 ($7.53) while the monthly pot of a twelve-member group with the same contribution is ₵9,600 ($22.59). The annual return per member does not change as the size of the group grows, but the larger monthly pot will be more helpful in acquiring costly pieces of equipment or a move into selling a more lucrative product. Further, because of the combined effect of the reduced flight risk and the benefits of building a regular clientele, the contributions tend to increase among traders who have

143

established trading positions. Thus, we see that a well-established trading position translates into more substantial levels of capital accumulation when we consider the difference between ₡9,600 ($22.59) per capita annual savings for a *susu* association with contributions of ₡200 per week, and ₡28,800 ($67.76) per capita annual savings where the contributions increase to ₡600 per week.

The market stall traders

Credit, savings, and mutual assistance societies take on a different character once inside the established market stalls. Though the market stalls officially belong to the city council, the *usus fructus* property right in the market stall allows for more complex credit and mutual assistance associations to develop. The number of participants in even the informal arrangements increases significantly, in the range of fifteen to twenty. The level of the contribution also increases, partly because once they establish a fixed trading position, entrepreneurs have more money to save. Further, an entrepreneur with a market stall is unlikely to abandon it in order to avoid reimbursing a group *susu* organization. The market stall fees act as a sort of bond, reducing the risks of large group *susu* contributions (Klein and Leffler 1981).

Trust, however, still plays an extremely important role here, as newcomers are not quickly included in such arrangements. A trader's behavior is carefully observed and her character closely assessed before she is given a chance to prove her trustworthiness. If she drinks too much or comes to the market late, her neighboring traders are likely to conclude that she will not last long in the market, and thus she is a risk to the rest of them if she were to be included in any financial arrangements. But if the new trader establishes a reputation for hard work and honesty, her opportunities to accumulate greater stocks of capital improve dramatically relative to trade on the street.

Within the established markets, a separate trade association exists for almost every type of good sold. Trade associations will serve as a source of business advice to those just starting out in trade or experiencing financial difficulty. Trade associations generally do not provide credit, though informal side arrangements are facilitated by the frequent contact made between members in the associations. Trade associations serve a quasi-political function as grievances to the city council will be made through these organizations. They also carry out a regulatory function by establishing standards of cleanliness and enforcing behavioral norms. Consistently rude or dishonest behavior can be met with termination from the association. In turn, the association provides financial security in the form of mutual assistance benefits for funerals, marriages, and births. Health benefits can also be provided out of the fund of regular contributions. Membership of the association is not required, though membership is particularly advantageous for those far from their home villages and separated from the family support system.

Some associations have attempted to restrict the number of sellers and enforce cartel prices, though these efforts have been largely unsuccessful. The general feeling in the market is that such anti-competitive behavior is not a legitimate role of the associations. As Fariata, a jewelry trader, explains,

> Some think it would be a good idea to fix the price so that no one can steal away their customers. I think it is a bad idea. I am planning a trip to England to buy new supplies. To buy the ticket, I need to sell all that I have very quickly. What business is it of the other traders what price I charge? . . . I would quit any association that had this rule.

The hair stylists' association recently tried to prohibit any non-member from practicing inside the Makola markets in central Accra. The issue was brought before the market queen who ruled in favor of the hair stylists who wished not to be a part of the association.

As discussed in the previous chapter, trade associations provide a reliable system of dispute resolution. Disputes between members of the same association can usually be handled internally. If the dispute involves traders of two different associations, the case can be brought to another association leader and ultimately to the market queen. Officially, disputes among market women could ultimately be appealed to the city council. According to Francis Eshun, the public relations officer of the Accra city council in 1992, these disputes are often simply "petty female squabbles" and the council is reluctant to become involved. If the city council must pass down a judgment, they generally support the decision of the market leaders so as to discourage future requests for intervention by the council. Though it is a misconception that these disputes and their resolution have no real economic consequences, it is on the other hand a fortuitous one. By endorsing a policy of staying out of "petty female squabbles," the integrity of the system of conflict resolution is not undermined by bureaucratic tinkering.

145

A market queen also presides over the collection of the smaller individual markets in the urban areas. In Accra, this position has been held by a woman named Manan Lokko since the early 1950s. Since she is too old to come to the market every day, her role is primarily symbolic. However, she is an extremely important symbol, as is demonstrated by her ability to mobilize opposition against some municipal policies. When the city council announced they were moving the market women away from the Rex Cinema, a central location in Accra, in order to start construction of new office space, the market queen was able to summon thousands of women to the steps of the city council. The administrators in the city council reported many staff problems during this period. Virtually all the workers in the office had some connection, either a sister, a mother, an aunt, or a wife, in the market. The market women pressured their relatives working for the city council to use their influence to stop the policy from being implemented. As argued previously, indigenous structures of authority and conflict resolution still operate, despite the lack of official recognition.

The lock-up shop traders

Alongside the open market stalls are the lock-up shops, concrete structures in which traders can leave their goods overnight. These are the most prestigious locations in the marketplace. Entrepreneurs running lock-up shops frequently have more opportunities for acquiring credit than stall traders. Some cloth importers, for example, put high-volume traders in contact with one another, in hopes that by pooling their resources the traders will be able to purchase even larger quantities. This is also a way for the import firm to share the risk, and thereby grant more cloth on credit. If a member of the cluster is short on her share of a payment, the other members will cover it knowing that they may need the favor returned at some future time. These clusters often form the basis for expanded business ventures, and are a trusted source of business advice.

The capital needed by a trader to secure a lock-up shop is considerable. To be assigned use of the space, she must pay the city council ¢26,000 ($61.18). She is also responsible for the construction of the structure itself, a structure which still officially belongs to the city council even though she pays for its construction. A simple 8 foot by 12 foot concrete structure costs about ¢550,000 ($1,294). In addition to this, she pays an annual rent to the city council of ¢20,000 ($47).[8] If she has this kind of working capital, she is far more likely to be able to secure a loan through one of the official banking institutions. Once she is operating at this level, acquiring a bank loan is generally not a problem. The problem rests in reaching that level. The minimum savings and deposit requirements for starting and maintaining a savings account—the only way to prove one's credit worthiness to the official banking establishment—are a distant possibility for most traders in the market.

IMPEDIMENTS TO INDIGENOUS INSTITUTIONS

We are left to ask why indigenous credit institutions have not yet produced greater advances in economic development. Whereas once it appeared that the elaborate voluntary organizations promised to usher in economic development, such organizations have lost their prominence in recent decades. In her study of Ivorian market women, Barbara Lewis (1976) cites the erosion of tight kinship ties and particularly the individualistic character of the market as the reasons for the decline of the rotating credit associations and indigenous mutual assistance societies. It seems unlikely, however, that after centuries of competitive markets, individualism is the cause of these relatively recent problems. In her analysis, Lewis does not consider the role government policies have played in stunting the effectiveness of indigenous arrangements for credit and mutual assistance, a line of inquiry essential to understanding the Ghanaian experience. More than any other factor, state and municipal control of resources and market mechanisms has inhibited the growth of indigenous credit institutions and the local economy.

Criminalizing market activity

When Rawlings first took power in the 1979 coup, he and his Armed Forces Revolutionary Council (AFRC) identified the rampant corruption of the preceding military regime as the source of Ghana's economic and social decline. Rawlings and the AFRC declared that their role was to clear the way for civilian rule by re-establishing order and by bringing those who had conspired to cheat ordinary Ghanaian citizens to justice. As noted earlier, former dictators Acheampong and Akuffo, and several other members of the Supreme Military Council were executed, and more than fifty corrupt officials and businessmen were imprisoned. Yet in Rawlings' zeal to punish

147

those who plundered Ghana's wealth, the rising prices of corn, cassava, yam, prepared foods like *kenkey*, and other basic items were unfortunately seen as part of the general graft and corruption, rather than the results of perverse incentives introduced by government manipulation within the agricultural sector.

In retaliation against the market women who sold their goods above the state-controlled prices, the major markets of Accra were destroyed. In Central Accra, government soldiers flattened Makola Market No. 1 with dynamite and bulldozers. The military publicly flogged and shaved the heads of market women. Many women were imprisoned where they were again beaten by the prison guards. In Kumasi, a cloth trader was shot for "profiteering," though as Robertson (1983) notes, the soldiers were sensitive enough to have her baby removed from her back before she was killed. The general economic decline of this period was only exacerbated by the destruction of the urban markets. Even produce which grows abundantly in the Ghanaian climate could not be found for sale in Central Accra, at least not in the open. If they did not turn to black market trading, many women abandoned the urban areas to return to their rural villages, as subsistence farming was more lucrative than urban trade under such circumstances.

When Rawlings returned the country to civilian rule and Limann was elected president, the situation for market traders improved relatively little, as Limann maintained price controls on the sale of local foodstuffs. After Rawlings returned to power in 1981, the mayhem and destruction imposed upon the market returned. The main markets in Kumasi, Sekondi, and Koforidua were also destroyed along with Makola Market No. 2 in Accra. The deepening economic crisis and a growing political opposition led Rawlings to reverse his anti-market campaign in 1983, by accepting the conditions of the IMF's Economic Recovery Plan (ERP). As price controls were lifted and trade liberalization progressed, the local economy has slowly improved, but the experience has left deep scars.

Currently, the illegality of trading on the street is still a major barrier facing the most marginal of all traders to accumulate the capital necessary to secure a market stall, cooking equipment, or any other means of expanding a business. While officially trading on the street is illegal, unofficially it is tolerated. This does not mean, however, that the city council simply turns a blind eye. Rather, the ambiguous status of hawkers places them in the precarious position of being hit from both sides. Because hawking is officially illegal, city council guards use their position to extort bribes. Street vendors are under constant threat that they may lose all their savings with a single fine. Because hawking is officially tolerated, however, street vendors pay a daily tax to the city council. The irony that trading on the street is illegal, yet taxable, is not lost on the street vendors. As Benedicta, a street vendor selling vegetables notes,

> All the time the guards are coming by to collect the tax. I pay in the morning but sometimes I lose my ticket, so I have to pay again. If you don't bribe them sometimes, they take your goods and give you a fine. If all the [city council] guards were fired, I would have enough money to buy my own stall.

The ambiguous status of these women is demonstrated by the behavior of the city council guards. At mid-day, guards can be seen carrying on polite conversation and purchasing *kenkey* or small meat pies from the same women to whom they are meant to issue a citation. Yet, once or twice a week, guards can also be seen making their way up a street, violently smashing the stools and tables upon which women will sit or set their wares. During these demonstrations, no fines are issued, no bribes are solicited. There is no purpose here other than to send a clear message that the street traders are in fact criminals.

The most cautious strategy a street vendor can take is always to keep moving, as the general rule is that city council guards will not fine a trader as long as she does not loiter in one spot. This, however, means that she cannot establish a predictable trading position and therefore cannot build a regular clientele. On the other hand, hawkers who establish a consistent trading position run a greater risk of being fined or at least pressured for a bribe. Apparently, the guards are keen enough to price discriminate. The bribes are often a token ₵200 (about $0.50) or a bag of rice or tomatoes every couple of weeks. Yet, bribes are often far more substantial, approximately ₵1,000 to ₵2,000 ($2.35 to $4.71) a week if the city council guard targets a trader he knows is running a profitable enterprise.

In Accra, about 1,500 traders per month have their goods confiscated and must pay at least ₵5,000 to the city. A single ₵5,000 citation can mean the difference between being able to feed a family and economic ruin. Besides the taxes and fines, the city council imposes implicit costs as well. Even if the fine is paid and the goods are returned, perishable supplies are often spoiled as it may take several days to borrow the money from friends and family. Further, once confiscated, the goods are in considerable danger of disappearing into the pockets of city council employees. In turn, the trader is likely to lose a valuable source of credit if, because of the financial burden of the fines and the loss of her goods, she is late or unable to pay her suppliers.

Monthly incomes of full-time street vendors have a wide variance, anywhere from ₵7,000 ($16) to ₵12,000 ($28). The daily tax and two small tributes of ₵250 translate into approximately 23 percent of a ₵7,000 monthly income. Nearly 95 percent of a ₵7,000 monthly income is lost to the city council if in addition the trader is unfortunate enough to be issued a single ₵5,000 fine. As the city guards tend to extract more from successful traders, those at the upper end of the income scale also lose a considerable amount of their income to the city council and the pockets of the city guards. The daily taxes, regular tributes of ₵3,000 per month and one ₵5,000 fine translate into 69 percent of a ₵12,000 monthly income. This percentage increases if a trader's goods are spoiled or stolen while in the custody of the city council. If a trader also loses half of a stock of goods worth ₵4,000, the effective rate rises to just over 86 percent. A trader is not likely to be fined every month, yet two to three fines a year can devastate any savings a trader may have accumulated. This loss of savings dashes any chance of establishing a stationary selling position, a prerequisite for substantial levels of both formal and indigenous credit.

Fortunately, the city council no longer controls prices. However, a considerable amount of waste and inefficiency is still introduced by other restrictions on market activity. As valuable resources are diverted from the productive market sector to the unproductive bureaucratic sector, the potential of the local economy to enhance the financial prospects of the most marginal entrepreneurs is mitigated.

Unintended consequences of bureaucratic intervention

While legal sanctions against street vending have the obvious and intended consequence of frustrating this sort of market activity, bureaucratic maneuvering often erects systematic, though unintended barriers to successful market trading. Finally recognizing the deleterious effects of price controls, all was to be remedied as the city council began to rebuild the markets after the 1983 ERP was under way. Yet all was not remedied. The market traders were compensated with new stalls, but the city council could not rebuild the trust relationships which had developed over decades of face-to-face interaction among neighboring traders. Market women were given new stalls, but not the same neighbors. Rebecca, a batik trader explains why she does not engage in group *susu* any longer.

> I used to save with the other women at Rawlings Park. When they tore it down, many of the women left the market. Some of them still owed money in the group *susu*. I paid, but I did not get my turn. I don't want the same thing to happen again, so I don't do group *susu* anymore.

The potential benefits from forging new relationships have been dampened given the general atmosphere of uncertainty. No trader is sure whether markets will once again be destroyed.

Since the inception of the ERP, other reasons have been found to relocate traders, either to make room for a parking lot—the result of a successful lobbying campaign by the taxi companies—or to thin out the market to help the flow of traffic. No matter what the motivation, the result is the same: the destruction of the credit and mutual assistance societies that had emerged over years of interaction with the same people. Further, such disruptions particularly frustrate elderly traders, such that they do not return to the new locations. This is a devastating blow to the indigenous credit institutions, as a vacuum of experience and trust is left, rather than a gradual transition of authority.[9]

At the time the interview data were collected for this study, the Accra city council was planning to spread the markets out to alleviate traffic problems in the most central part of the city. The criterion by which the city council decides who gets moved to the new location will be according to the size of the delivery trucks involved. For example, yams are delivered in large vehicles which block traffic, thus yam sellers will be removed to the new, more distant location. Tomatoes, on the other hand, are delivered in smaller vehicles, so tomato vendors will be allowed to remain in the central markets. This proposal demonstrates the inherent danger of allowing market decisions to be made solely on the basis of bureaucratic concerns.

This is not to say that traffic congestion is not a problem in Central Accra, but overriding market considerations is not the solution. If the campaign is successful, the move will once again wrench traders from their network of trust and support, and thereby under-mine the evolved system of indigenous credit. If entrepreneurs anticipate the move and shift their behavior in response to such a policy measure (e.g. yam sellers may switch to selling tomatoes), this will in turn increase the costs and risks associated with buying and selling yams, an important dietary staple. It should not go unnoticed that this proposed "solution" reflects the male bias at the bureaucratic level. Only someone who has never shopped for the family meal, after working an eight-to-ten-hour day, would see separating the items needed for the traditional daily meal across distant ends of the city as a solution. The real solution lies not in overriding the market process, but rather, in allowing it to work. The congestion problem will be best addressed by a system of market, not state-set prices for selling space. The issue of privatiza-tion is discussed below.

Lack of scarcity-indicating prices for selling space

On any given day, a market trader could walk into the city council offices and acquire selling space within the market. According to the city council, many spaces are currently vacant. For ¢25,000 ($59), a trader can secure an assignment to a market stall. Yet, many street vendors say that no spaces are available in the market. Others will say that spaces are available, but the prices are too high. When asked how much they would have to pay to acquire space in the market, they quote prices two to sometimes three times higher than the price quoted by the city council. This is particularly puzzling, given that in 1990, the city council provided new market stalls at no cost, to which street traders could move. However, the women stubbornly refused to stay and returned to trading on the street.

Was this a case of the hawkers acting irrationally or at the very least belligerently? Are city council officials lying when they say that spaces are available? Or are the market traders simply confused, not realizing that the stalls are available and less expensive than they think? The answer is "none of the above." The fact is that spaces are available in the market. Further, the city council did (unsuccessfully) attempt to move traders from the street by providing free selling space. Yet, the traders are not confused, nor was their response to the offer of free selling space irrational. The confusion stems solely from the fact that the state-controlled stall prices do not reflect relative scarcity or desirability.

As the state officially owns the market stalls, it is incapable of reflecting their true value in the price structure. The fact that some spaces are available at the prevailing rate should not lead us to conclude that the rent charged by the city council comes close to reflecting scarcity conditions. In charging a single rate, the city council assumes that a homogeneous good, "market stall space," is being offered. But not all market stalls are created equally. The market stalls span a wide heterogeneous array in terms of location, access to facilities, sanitary conditions, and customer appeal.

Some stalls are near the openings of the market and attract a significant amount of traffic. Yet, the same price will be charged for a stall which is tucked away in an obscure part of the market which sees little traffic. Some stalls are on a dirt surface, yet it will cost as much as another stall on concrete. Concrete stalls attract customers even during the rainy season and will not ruin a trader's goods with mud stains. When hawkers were offered stall space at no cost only to return to the street, this was again a situation in which the selling space was inappropriately priced. In fact, the city council placed the "free" selling space in an obscure corner of the city that attracted little traffic. Thus, the zero price charged was simply too high, as the opportunities for profit were more abundant on the street.

Likewise, the differences in perception with regard to prices and availability of selling space reflects not confusion on the part of the traders, but the city council's inability to appropriately price heterogeneous resources. Most street traders know that some stalls are available at the set price of ₵25,000. But they are quick to point out that the only stalls available at this price are in a poor location and will not attract customers. Regarding the stalls that are currently available, one street trader remarked, "The stalls by the latrine are open, but the stink is so bad, no customers ever go there."

The prices that traders quote which are two to three times higher than the official price are the prices in the secondary market. As a trader leaves the market, she will pass on the stall space at a price which reflects the true value of the resource. It is important to note that stall space in a good location is a valuable resource which is often passed from one generation to the next. A well-placed market stall acts as a source of venture capital for a daughter or niece expanding a business, or perhaps a grand-daughter starting out. By the same token, the stall space provides a source of security for the retiring trader. As an older woman makes a gift of the space to a daughter, niece, or grand-daughter, she can expect some form of support (either financial or in kind) from the recipient. However, the secondary market is officially illegal, and therefore ownership cannot be guaranteed if a stall is acquired through a black market or informal transaction.

The argument here is not that the city council officials are just too simple-minded to see the obvious. In fact, on the surface, the market stalls do all seem to look alike. If we look only at their structure and design, they are more alike than different. Their heterogeneity is only manifest as the market process unfolds. In other words, it is only through market activity that we discover what the true value of such resources are. Thus, merely encouraging greater attentiveness on the part of the city council will not produce a price structure which appropriately reflects relative scarcity. As it is absent a mechanism for discovering what the value of these resources are, the bureaucratic process has no means of acquiring this sort of particularized knowledge. Prices which reflect the relative scarcity and desirability of a resource can only be discovered through a market process.

POLICY CONCLUSIONS

Full scale privatization of the marketplace stalls and shops would solve or at least mitigate the most debilitating obstacles facing indigenous trade. By affording the occupants of market stalls private ownership rights, the pricing and allocation of stall space would fully reflect market conditions rather than arbitrary state-set prices. Private ownership would also afford the opportunity to unbundle the resource by allowing owners of stalls to rent to more than one occupant. Traders could then either divide the space, split the selling day or week, or employ a combination of the two. This would reduce the per person cost of acquiring space in the market and thus reduce the crowding on the street.

Privatization would also open the way for private developers to erect new structures which would likewise reduce the level of crowding. A private developer would price the spaces in a new structure according to market conditions and not need to rely on a rigid set price structure as is the case under municipal management. Further, by allowing private developers the opportunity to erect new markets, they would have to compete for occupants, not only by pricing the stall space according to market conditions, but through services as well. The lack of adequate toilet and locker facilities, security, and shelter from the rain were all cited as serious drawbacks to the current market-place environment. Once the monopoly the state holds on rental space is broken, the market will reward those developers who provide services seen as essential to the marketplace.

This is not to say that all developments will necessarily provide these services. Some may offer only the barest elements of a market-place structure. But the prices of such stalls would then reflect the lack of services and would allow those at the lower end of the income scale to establish a fixed location for trading. Such a move is essential for the most marginal of traders, as this is a clear indication of a person's growing credit worthiness to a potential creditor. Thus, an array of quality will allow for an array of prices, such that the move from street vending to a fixed location is not such a cataclysmic jump.

Private rather than municipal management of the marketplace is likely to result in fewer cases of full-scale upheaval, and the resulting loss of valuable credit and mutual support networks. The allocation of stall space and location would be based on market conditions, not polit-ical or bureaucratic considerations. If a marketplace is the most profitable venture, political maneuvering will not override market conditions as they do in the case of municipal management. If market conditions were to shift dramatically, however, at least in the private context, the traders would have the option of establishing themselves in a new space as a block, by renting a row of stalls, for instance. This option is a virtual impossibility under current municipal management. Further, in the private context, opportunities for long-term leasing and purchasing arrangements emerge. In this case, traders would have to be compensated if they were to be enticed to move; again, an option which is clearly not available under municipal management.

Thus, privatization efforts would have both the expected benefits of rational market pricing and allocation of resources, but it would also have some not so obvious benefits as well. Future private devel-opment would supply new market space at prices which reflect scarcity conditions. The array of rental rates or prices which is likely to emerge would provide opportunities for the most marginal of traders to establish a fixed location and therefore access to greater sources of credit. The private context would allow the unbundling of resources, providing even further opportunities for the small-scale entrepreneur. Perhaps most importantly, by fostering stable prop-erty rights, privatization efforts would support and enhance the performance of indigenous credit and mutual assistance networks.

5
TOWARDS AN INTERPRETIVE ECONOMICS
Three profiles of urban market women

Economists should become more like anthropologists, in the sense that they should do more of their empirical work "up close" through participant observation rather than only from the distance required for statistical work. The fact that virtually all the empirical work economists undertake is preoccupied with the application of statistical techniques brings about a corresponding need for large sample sizes . . . . A more interpretive approach to empirical economics would challenge this whole attitude, both about what it means to do empirical research and about what it takes to see general lessons in such research. Indeed, I would argue, the best empirical work in economics has not sought large sample sizes at all but instead has tried to see a few cases "up close." The case study, which pays attention to how individual choices were made under specific circumstances, is able to explicate empirical facts that simply cannot be seen from the distance required for most statistical studies.

(Lavoie 1990: 169)

To render the general patterns of indigenous culture and market institutions more intelligible, it is necessary to pull bits and pieces of experience from the life stories told by entrepreneurs. The danger in this is that we may forget that the general patterns are formed by the actions of individuals, each with a unique and complex history of her own. Street vendors, stall traders, and lock-up shop traders face distinct sets of obstacles, for instance. But even within these categories, an extraordinary diversity still exists. Three profiles are presented here to give a sense of how real human beings interpret their circumstance, make plans for the future, and make sense of their lives.

The choice of profiles is not random. These particular women were extremely cooperative and candid about their personal and professional lives. I have deliberately chosen one entrepreneur from

156

each of the categories analyzed in Chapter 4. Abiba is a street vendor on the verge of financial collapse, Anna is a seamstress who runs a mid-level stall operation, and Mary is a relatively successful cloth trader who operates from a lock-up shop in Central Accra.

The profiles will provide a glimpse into the context within which entrepreneurs make choices and confront obstacles. The profiles will also serve to illustrate the benefits of an anthropological or "up close" approach to economic research advocated by Lavoie. Lavoie (1990) argues that positivist economics has provided an excuse for economists to stray dangerously far from the real world. The over-reliance on the "as if" proposition (economic agents act "as if" they are perfect profit maximizers, for example) ostensibly releases the researcher from having to understand how market participants perceive their own situation. Human beings are reduced to utility functions, mechanically responding to objective constraints. Yet, as we have seen, this approach is not conducive to investigations in which the judgments and interpretations of market participants rather than exogenous forces drive the market process. By talking to people, or in the case of historical analysis, reading what people wrote of their own situation, we see that decisions are not mechanical responses, but rather are complex readings shaped by cultural, political, and historical influences.

As Geertz (1973) cautions, interpretive social science is not abstract and pristine, but is grounded in the world. As interpretive cultural analysis is necessarily tied to its own dictates of thick description—of being in the world—it cannot be disembodied into abstract variables for the sake of showing its inner logic.

> This is the first condition for cultural theory: it is not its own master. As it is unseverable from the immediacies thick description presents, its freedom to shape itself in terms of its internal logic is rather limited. What generality it contrives to achieve grows out of the delicacy of its distinctions, not the sweep of its abstractions.
>
> (Geertz 1973: 24–5)

Particularly when considering questions of culture, abstract economic models will do little to render complex market phenomena more intelligible. As opposed to the abstract economic models of general equilibrium and perfect competition, statistical empirical research takes an important step towards understanding the real world, as it seeks to explain data derived from the real world. Yet a purely statistical approach does not go far enough. The bias on the part of the economics profession to package a social science in the style and method of the natural sciences has distanced the researcher as far from the subject as possible (Hayek 1952). In the name of objectivity, empirical economists assemble large data sets of quantifiable facts which lend themselves to mathematical manipulation. Yet the distance required for such an investigation minimizes the researcher's chances of understanding how economic actors view their own situation. The researcher is fundamentally disconnected from the web of meaning in which the entrepreneurs form judgments and take action.

The point here is not that the construction of large data sets and econometric analysis are useless endeavors. Indeed, broad surveys can address pervasive phenomena which hinder or promote development across time and distance. The argument here is that the kind of information gleaned from participant observation is unique, and cannot be generated by econometric analysis. Only an anthropological approach provides access to the life-world of complex meanings in which people operate. Particularly when grappling with the role culture plays in economic processes, it scarcely seems possible to ascertain which variables would be of interest, without first talking to the participants in that process. Thus, participant observation in empirical research is an essential complement to the generalized pattern approach of standard econometrics.

An interpretive approach to the social sciences makes no pretense of providing a "purely objective" report of the subject's circumstance. First, the subject's own responses will often be shaped by who is asking the questions, as is most likely the case in this study. The fact that I am female probably meant that Abiba and the other informants felt freer to express their distrust for the men in their lives and in the city council, than if the researcher had been male. The fact that I am Caucasian and American more than likely provided a frame for many of Mary's responses, as members of the elite often take pride in their knowledge of Western culture. Thus the very fact that questions are being asked by a particular person will shape the data in particular ways.

Further, the data which is collected still needs interpreting if it is to improve our understanding of the phenomena under study. The researcher's role is not simply to report the objective facts and details, but to offer an interpretation of the significance behind the details. Replication of the subject's own understanding of his or her situation should not be the goal of the social sciences. Practically speaking, such a replication would be impossible. The researcher cannot relate all of the subject's experiences and all their effects. Even more importantly, the experiences the subject conveys will hold different significance for the social scientist than for the subject.

Every interpretation is one made through the eyes of a specific scholar with a specific set of tools. An economist will see things as important that a sociologist or historian would scarcely notice. A macroeconomist will tend to ask a different set of questions than the public choice economist. They all have a different bundle of questions they regard as important, or have a particular advantage in pursuing. In providing an account of the subject's situation, the social scientist is reinterpreting events through a particular disciplinary lens.

Yet this reality is not to be lamented. The best work in the social sciences is not that which comes the closest to replicating the subject's own account of his or her situation. The best work within the social sciences is that which tells us something more than we could have gleaned from reading a transcript of the interviews. In other words, by *reinterpreting* the subject's situation, the social scientist opens up new avenues of knowledge. Precisely because the social scientist has biases, such as working within a theoretical framework, we improve our understanding. In the previous chapter, we saw that traders quoted vastly divergent prices for stall space within the marketplace, for example. However, the theoretical understanding of the "law of one price" keeps us from simply accepting this account. The subjects provide the clues, but it is the theoretical framework which allows the social scientist to piece these clues together to offer a coherent explanation of how government ownership has fostered secondary markets. Thus, even if it were possible to offer a "purely objective" account, it would not be desirable, as we would lose the value of our science, which is to render complex social phenomena more intelligible.

Interpretive social science recognizes the reciprocal influence theory and empirical data have on one another (Lavoie 1986). It is theory which guides us to ask a specific set of questions in the first place. Yet the particular advantage of participant observation is that it allows the researcher to learn more with each interaction. This is not to favor a crude form of empiricism by which we draw general conclusions from isolated occurrences. Rather, this approach takes advantage of the fact that an in-depth understanding of the real world can enhance our theory, just as theory helps us to understand the world. We may find that a theoretical approach previously considered to be of little importance is now highly relevant. We may find an exception to our theory which had not been considered previously. In turn, as experience accumulates, we are better equipped to pursue more relevant lines of questioning. The constant interplay of theory and data enables the social scientist to hone in on the significant phenomena worthy of study. In virtually every interview conducted for this study, something new was revealed. Sometimes it was nothing more than a window into what might be a common attitude. Sometimes it turned out to be a central focus of the analysis. The profiles will illustrate how interacting with real human beings sharpens the analytical focus and improves our understanding.

ABIBA

Abiba is a thirty-four-year-old street vendor. She is thin, but strong, with a demeanor to match. She is Hausa, and speaks little English. My interpreter translates throughout our conversations. During the interview, she bags rice into small sacks. As is usually the case with interviews on the street, it is impossible to have a private dialogue with a single person. The neighboring traders are interested in the break of routine. With almost a protective demeanor, they want to know why I am asking her so many questions. Once they are satisfied that I have no interest in reporting their activities to the city council, they begin to trust me. Although I am interviewing Abiba, often neighboring traders will chime in with a story of their own. Abiba is strong-willed, however, and eventually tells her friends to be quiet. "Madame is here to speak with me!" she insists.

Abiba's experience illustrates some of the obstacles as well as the opportunities West African family structure affords market women. Until recently, Abiba had been selling vegetables. She is the mother of two children; a daughter five years old, and a son three years old. She was married for a short time to the father of her first child, but he left within the first year after her birth. When she became pregnant, the father of her second child offered to formalize their relationship with a legal marriage, but Abiba refused.

> I did not want to marry him. It would just mean more work
> to be married again. Some women think that by getting

married, their lives will be made easier. The exact opposite is
the real truth.

She recalls the day she brought her husband prepared food from the
market for his dinner.

> I was working all day, very hard. I do not like to cook after
> such a long day. I bought *kenkey* in the market for his dinner.
> He began yelling at me and cursing me. He said I was trying
> to poison him.

The connections between cooking, marriage, and sex are so tightly
interwoven, that the term "cooking for" is euphemistically used to
connote sexual intimacy. As Clark notes,

> The symbolic and practical connection between cooking the
> evening meal and marital sexual and financial exchanges make
> it risky for married women to delegate cooking or utilize
> widely available shortcuts. Compromising standards of quality
> and timing for the evening meal threatens the continuance of
> a marriage and of the financial support a husband provides,
> because women have less latitude within marriage than as
> parents. These considerations create pressures to conform
> closely to ideal meal patterns that interfere quite directly with
> market trading.
>
> (Clark 1994: 345)

Thus, by bringing home prepared foods from the market, Abiba
was signaling more than a refusal to cook. Refusing to cook the
evening meal, or significantly to compromise on its quality, often
signals a woman's desire to break off a marriage (Clark 1994).

Although she was sad for a short time after he left, she was also
relieved that she no longer had to care for him. Abiba's husband
represented a drain not only on her physical energy, but also on her
financial resources.

> I had to hide the money I made in the market. Sometimes he
> found my hiding place. Sometimes he didn't. If he really
> wanted the money badly, he would curse me until I gave it to
> him.

Abiba thought that this was unfair since he had never provided any
capital for her business.

She suspected that he sometimes gave the money to other

161

women. This outraged her, given that he had pressured her into having a Christian wedding. Even though she is not Christian, she went along with it to make him happy.

> In a Christian marriage, the man promises to give up all the other women. He wanted to be married in the [Christian] church but he does not keep the promises he made to the priest.

Yet, for every disappointing experience she faced within the nuclear family, her extended family and friends within the trading community offered a valuable opportunity. Abiba's parents live in a village in northern Ghana. She does not receive any assistance from them, yet she still receives support from the extended family. Abiba lives with her great aunt, Halima, who was also a street vendor. Now Halima stays home to look after the children and prepare the meals. Abiba considers this a great help to her, and she is happy to provide for Halima, indicating the crucial role the extended family can play in facilitating market activity. She is afraid, however, that given her current situation, she may not be able to meet her family's needs.

The trading community has also provided an essential system of support. Abiba had a stall once but the marketplace was demolished to make way for a taxicab parking lot. Many of the women were compensated with new stalls, but she could not prove to the city council that she was an established trader in the market. She had "inherited" the space from her mother's cousin, who has since moved back to northern Ghana. This demonstrates the dangers of a poorly defined system of property rights. Abiba could not prove that she had a legitimate claim to the stall in the old market. She is angry that the city council administrators would not believe that she had occupied a stall in the old market.

> I traded in the market [stall] for many years. Everyone knew that it was my stall. I went to the city council for the compensation that they had promised. They promised all of us a stall in the new market. They did not believe me that I owned the stall. My friends told them that I had traded there for many years. They said that my friends were lying to get a new market stall without paying. Many traders lie to get the new stalls, but I was not lying. She [my mother's cousin] gave me that stall.

Abiba had built a good reputation among her customers and neighboring traders, but the city council would not listen to those who spoke of their respect for her. She then had no choice but to sell on the street.

Several months passed before she was able to find a stable trading position on the sidewalk. She says she spent much of the day avoiding the city guards. She was lucky to find a friend, Ama, from the old market who had also lost her space. Ama introduced Abiba to some of her friends and asked if they could make room for her in their area. Another friend of theirs had recently returned to her village. They were holding her space for her, but several weeks had already passed and it appeared that she was not returning. They agreed to admit Abiba and, since that time, she has also become friends with these women. Ama's introduction was crucial in establishing a fixed position, as Abiba says that she would not have imposed herself on strangers.

Abiba demonstrates the keen sense of independence legendary among Ghanaian women. Both her love of the urban environment and her general distrust of men are reflections of this independent spirit. Many accounts of West African entrepreneurs make note of this attitude (Guglar 1981; Brydon 1985). Along with this sense of independence, however, is the crucial network of support received from her aunt and close friends. Again, the cooperative efforts among West African women are well documented (Wipper 1984; Little 1965, 1973). Yet this raises the question as to whether a contradiction exists between the independence afforded by the urban environment, on the one hand, and the interdependence among women in the various networks of support, on the other.

Tannen's (1990a, 1990b) work on gender-specific culture suggests that this does not necessarily represent a contradiction. It is exactly the interdependence among women that allows female entrepreneurs to enjoy a relative independence from men if they so desire. Tannen's argument that women tend to use language to establish connections rings true when Abiba describes the process of acquiring selling space on the sidewalk. If she had demanded the spot on the sidewalk, she would have had little chance of forging friendships. By withholding their friendship, the neighboring traders would also have withheld any offer of mutual economic support. The decisive factor is not "might makes right," as if status were the established norm. Rather, Abiba was successful in acquiring a place on the sidewalk, and most importantly, in the circle of friends, by making the necessary connections through a mutual friend, Ama. This dynamic of connection is precisely what Tannen suggests occurs within female-specific culture.

Gudeman (1986) and Bird-David's (1990, 1992) concept of "primary metaphor" also comes into play here. In Abiba, we see the possible applicability of "rivalry" as a primary metaphor as many of Abiba's responses demonstrated a clear hostility towards the city council guards, a sentiment that was shared by many street vendors. Such hostility is not surprising, given the obstacles the guards place in the way of the traders. What was particularly revealing, however, was that the verbal attacks against the guards tended to be general-ized to all men. As virtually all the city council guards are men, many female street vendors see the conflict as "us vs. them," as Abiba's comments suggest.

> It takes me all day just to make a small profit but the men [the city council guards] walk around doing nothing. They get their money by bribing the market women. They get money to do nothing but make trouble for us.

This is not to say that all men are despised, only that the female street vendors' enemy has a decidedly male face. Thus, it is not so surprising that women feel more comfortable engaging in financial arrangements with other women—arrangements which require a tremendous amount of trust.

The cluster includes Abiba and five other women. They engage in group *susu* when they have enough money to save. Usually they each contribute ₵500 ($1.25) a week, and distribute the lump sum in turn each Saturday. They would rather distribute a larger lump sum on a monthly basis, but their revenues are not consistent enough for this. Recently, one of their friends, Doris, (who generally sells the same produce as Abiba) had a baby and each of her friends contributed to the "outdooring" ceremony. Doris experienced complications late in her pregnancy, so Abiba sold some of her goods for her while she was bedridden. Here is a case in which even direct competitors were able to forge a relationship of mutual support. By being involved in one another's lives, they lay the foundation for mutual financial support, and the trust necessary to engage in credit agreements.

Doris and Abiba generally sell their goods at the same price, yet this does not indicate a collusive agreement. Many produce traders are dispersed throughout the market, rendering any such agreement worthless. Nor do neighboring traders try to control the pricing behavior of their competitors, as this exchange with Abiba and Doris illustrates.

CHAMLEE-WRIGHT   If another woman sells her produce at a cheaper price than you, how do you respond?

ABIBA   Most of us charge the same price. It depends on the prices we pay for the goods. If a trader gets a special price, perhaps she can charge a lower price to her customers.

DORIS   Some traders sell at a lower price to get money fast. They may want to quit the market to return to their village.

CHAMLEE-WRIGHT   How do you compete with other traders who lower their prices?

DORIS   I wait. The market women who sell at these low prices will not be in the market for long.

At the time of our meeting, Abiba had no goods of her own to sell. She was helping her friend Gloria sell rice. Abiba separates and bags the rice in exchange for a small sum at the end of the day. She is not providing any service that Gloria could not easily perform herself. Rather, the real purpose of this arrangement is to provide a support system for Abiba. The support is not only the direct assistance Abiba receives. By coming to the market, Abiba maintains her position in the cluster, even though she does not have any goods to sell. When she is able to resume selling, she will not have lost access to the credit and savings network her friends represent. Further, if she were to abandon the market for any significant amount of time, she would be in danger of losing her selling spot on the sidewalk. Her friends could help her to ward off interlopers if she had only been gone for a few days, but if the absence turns into weeks, the claim to the space is no longer considered legitimate. This demonstrates one of the limitations of a *de facto* property rights system operating for sidewalk selling space, as it only affords limited stability.

Abiba lost her goods and working capital through fines imposed by the city council. She had built up enough savings to purchase vegetables in bulk and she was planning to sell to other hawkers in the market. But before she could sell the produce, the city guards confiscated her goods. Since she had such a large amount of produce, the city council fined her ₵15,000, three times the normal fine. She had to borrow the money from relatives and friends to retrieve the goods, but this took several days. Over half of the vegetables were stolen while in the hands of the city council. When she sold the remaining produce, most of the money went to repay her supplier (who gave half of the produce on credit) and to repay the loans for the fine. Ultimately, nothing remained of her working capital. She did not have enough capital to purchase any more supplies.

She fears that she may be forced into returning to the north where the rest of her extended family lives. She desperately wants to avoid this. "My relations in the hinterland are always wanting to know my business. There is no privacy in the village. In Accra I can decide everything on my own."

She realizes, however, that if her financial situation does not improve, she will have to return to her home village. For now, she relies on the support she receives from her friends, but she cannot burden them indefinitely. As Abiba points out, "My friends have families of their own, and I cannot take food away from their children's mouths."

Abiba hopes that one day she will be able to return to the market stalls. In the market stalls, the frustration of avoiding the city council guards is absent as long as the monthly stall fees are paid on time. Also when selling on the street, the sun can be exhausting. She does not know, however, how she will acquire the capital necessary to return to the established marketplace. Within her Hausa community, the elders will sometimes provide a loan, but they will most likely insist that she secure a market stall for herself first to guarantee that the money will go to expand the business, and not simply for consumption.

She has some hope that things will turn around for her in the coming harvest season, which will bring an abundance of produce at cheap prices. Wholesale traders are anxious to sell all of their supplies, so they are more likely to supply produce on credit. This could be the boost she needs to regain her financial independence. She says, however, that if she is lucky enough to get back on her feet, she will never buy such a vast amount of produce at one time again. "I will only buy what I can put on my tray. If I am caught by the guards again, my fine will not be so large." The fear of being caught for illegal trading demonstrates the most costly consequences of the municipal sanctions against entrepreneurial behavior. We will never know how many profit opportunities are not pursued because of the potential penalties involved.

ANNA

Anna is a twenty-five-year-old seamstress from Madina, a forty-five-minute drive from central Accra. Compared to the teeming streets of Accra, Madina is quiet and relatively small. When I met Anna in 1991, she conducted her business from an open stall, and carted her materials and sewing machine to and from the market every day. A year later, she was operating a closed stall in which she could lock her equipment at night. She considers this a great relief, as she no longer has to carry a heavy sewing machine to and from the market every day. In the summer of 1992, she was eight months pregnant with her second child, and was particularly happy to leave her machine locked up in the stall at night.

Anna's father started her in business by providing her living expenses and materials during her apprenticeship with a woman named Mamma, a skilled seamstress from Kaneshi. In return for her training, Anna worked for Mamma a full year after her training was completed. As Anna set out on her own, she needed a sewing machine and money for a small shop. Her older brother Kojo provided these for her. Anna now employs another young woman, as an assistant. She does not consider this an apprenticeship, as there is no formal agreement to train her, but the assistant reports that she has learned much from her employer.

Anna lives with her husband, their three-year-old daughter, and her infant nephew. Six months prior to our meeting, her brother Kojo asked Anna to take care of his son. The child was born out of wedlock, and the mother had literally left him on Kojo's doorstep. As Anna was grateful to her brother for helping her expand her business, she was more than willing to help him.

> My brother works in the factory all day. He has no way of looking after a baby. I can bring the babies here to the market. My brother requested my help and I could not refuse. He was not selfish when I needed his help, so I must help him now.

Finances are extremely tight, however. The family relies solely on Anna's income. Her husband is a ministry student at Trinity College in Accra. His church is sponsoring his tuition fees, but he draws no income of his own.

Anna belongs to an Akan-based mutual assistance society which provides social benefits, though not credit directly. She is relying on this society to provide the resources necessary for the elaborate "outdooring" ceremony, which takes place on the eighth day after the birth of a child. During the first eight days, the child is traditionally believed to be in a fragile balance between the world of the living and the world of the ancestors. The ceremony symbolizes the entrance of the child into the world of the living.

Like, funerals, outdoorings are a grand social event, in which no expense is spared. Anna explains, however, that if performed correctly, the outdooring ceremony can be a substantial source of financial gain.

> The guests give a gift [usually cash] for the new child. But the guests will not give a lot if the food is poor quality or the schnapps is cheap. It takes a great deal of planning to do it properly.

The other essential element for a (financially) successful outdooring ceremony is a guest list which includes influential and wealthy friends. Except for her mentor in Kaneshi, none of Anna's closest friends are wealthy, but her husband has made ties with some influential members of the ministry. Not only are they likely to contribute themselves, even more importantly, they will encourage some of the wealthier members of the church to attend. She does not know exactly how much money she will receive from the mutual assistance society, but she is sure that most, if not all, of it will be put into the preparations for the ceremony.

CHAMLEE-WRIGHT In America, we have saying, "It takes money to make money." Is this what preparing for the outdooring is like?

ANNA This is exactly the case! If the minister's friends [the wealthy parishioners] are to come, they must know it to be a grand occasion. If the preparations are not the best, the guests will be insulted.

Anna and her husband are both Christian, but they exemplify the manner in which Christianity has been absorbed into the traditional context. The extraordinary popularity of Christian churches in the urban centers does not mean that Christianity has completely replaced traditional belief structures or the values they transmit. For example, in her study of religion in Central Africa, Fields (1985) finds that the Christian ritual of baptism is associated with witchcraft eradication. Most Christian churches include drumming and chanting, drawn from traditional religious practices, as part of the weekly worship ceremony. Thus, Christianity has not replaced but has been integrated into traditional belief and practice. Likewise, Anna and her husband still favor the traditional outdooring ceremony. In the ceremony, libations are poured to the ancestry so that the baby will be brought safely into the world of the living. However, they will also have their minister give the child a Christian name at the same ceremony. Anna is not concerned that the Christian ministers will object to the traditional elements in the celebration.

> The outdooring is a great celebration. Everyone is happy. The ministers teach that alcohol is evil, but I think that schnapps is okay. I saw the ministers drink schnapps at a funeral once. I think it is okay.

Perhaps even more appropriate than Ayittey's (1991) notion of "layering," Christianity has helped to generate a complex mixture of belief and practice. As Middleton notes in his study of church membership in the Ghanaian town of Akuropon, people will seek to identify the ritual, practice, or practitioner who will address their particular concern.

> [M]ost people in the town find out which of these various forces can best help them remove afflictions and then they use the beliefs and rites associated with them in order to remove the troubles. This is, I think, a more accurate way of regarding the situation than the more usual one of defining a person as an adherent of one particular faith who would never have anything to do with others; but many, possibly most, people prefer to go from one to another practitioner seeking cures for their afflictions.
>
> (Middleton 1983: 8)

Thus, to understand the influence of Christianity in the African context adequately, one must go beyond statistics of church membership, as they will not reveal the integrated nature of indigenous and Christian faith and practice.

The interviews I had conducted before speaking with Anna had included a line of questioning regarding the role ancestral spirits played among the living. The questions generally inspired negative responses—that ancestral spirits played no role—indicating that at least on this issue, traditional beliefs had been replaced. But it was

Anna's description of the outdooring/christening ceremony which made me realize that perhaps I was not being subtle enough. My translator suggested the questions begged a negative response, as the informants were aware of Christian teachings that only the Christian God influences the course of people's lives. It is possible that the questions could have been construed as a challenge to their allegiance to Christian principles.

In subsequent interviews, we turned to a more subtle approach, inquiring about outdooring and funeral ceremonies. This revealed a complex mixture of traditional and Christian practices even among those who had originally denied any role to the ancestry. Traditionally, birth and death are seen as journeys between the earthly life and the ancestral realm. Though Christian forms are also observed, customary practices believed to equip the passenger for this journey play a dominant role in these ceremonies. We also asked informants if they would play an active role in guiding the lives of their children or grandchildren after they had died. By placing the issue of ancestral influence on this personal level, even devout Christians often saw themselves as having an important role to play, particularly in protecting the very young.

Anna belongs to the seamstress trade association. One of the main functions of the associations in the Madina market is to ensure that the grounds are kept clean. Anna does not like the rules much because seamstresses have to clean up just as often as the women who sell *banku* and *fufu*, a process which makes a tremendous mess. Anna says that the seamstresses hardly generate any garbage. She abides by the rules, however. She is glad that provisions are made to maintain cleanliness, as she thinks her customers would rather come to see her in this environment than in the unsanitary conditions of the central markets in Accra. The trade association also provides some level of mutual assistance, though there are only about fifteen women in her association and the sums are not as great as within the central markets. This is why she also belongs to the Akan-based mutual assistance society.

Anna would like to expand her business, but she has no money to do so now. All her profits go to providing for the family. She realizes that she could probably get more customers if she were to move into Central Accra, but she cannot afford one of the nice lock-up shops, and would once again have to carry her machine and supplies to and from the market. With another baby on the way, this would make life very difficult. When she is not in school, her daughter comes to the market with Anna. (In actuality, the "school" is religious education provided for several hours a week through their church.) She likes it that her daughter can play around the stall without becoming covered in filth.

> The markets in Accra are so dirty. The children can't even play there. Madina is much cleaner. In Accra, people urinate in the gutters because there is no place else to go. No one would do that here. Here, there is plenty of room to go away from the market. [Anna points to the vast area of grass and low-lying brush just beyond the market area.]

Anna exemplifies the savvy entrepreneurial spirit so common among West African market women, as this exchange illustrates.

CHAMLEE-WRIGHT Do you have any plans for expanding your business?

ANNA Yes. I want to buy the best cloth and make dresses ready to sell. The customers will see that I can make the fancy dresses that wealthy ladies like. [Most customers purchase their own fabric and bring it to a seamstress.] If I had a bigger shop, wealthy ladies would like coming to me.

CHAMLEE-WRIGHT What is your best chance of acquiring the capital necessary to expand in this way?

ANNA Why *you* are, Emily! The next time you come to Ghana, you will bring me an electric sewing machine and I will become a wealthy woman. [Anna's English was usually quite poor, but this declaration came through flawlessly.]

CHAMLEE-WRIGHT Besides me, what is your best chance of expanding your business?

ANNA My teacher from Kaneshi is getting too old to work all the time. She is always complaining that she is too old to come to the market. If she sees that I have many customers, she may give me her business to run.

In return for inheriting Mamma's customers and location, Anna would pay her rent and, if business was good enough, she would give her a percentage of the profits made from Mamma's old customers. Anna knows that Mamma has had many other apprentices, but she thinks Mamma likes her the best. Anna has continued to visit her regularly. Mamma has no daughters of her own, and most of her other apprentices who are still in the area specialize in making school and office uniforms. Anna argues that it takes more skill to make the intricate dresses that Mamma's customers like. She thinks her chances of taking over Mamma's business are good. She will try to broach the subject when she sees Mamma at the outdooring ceremony.

MARY

Mary is a cloth trader. She operates a lock-up shop in Accra. She runs a relatively high-volume operation, as she supplies four other women with cloth. She purchases the cloth from the manufacturer in large quantities at a reduced price and resells to others, securing a profit on the resale.

Many of Mary's remarks coincide with what Oppong (1974) points to as a possible movement away from traditional cultural values among the educated elite in favor of Western ideals. Among others, Oppong cites Jahoda (1959), Little (1966), and Bird (1958) as representative examples of this thesis. Indeed, Mary shuns much of what she considers to be "backward" African beliefs. She demonstrates a strong affinity towards Western styles. Though she exudes all the strength and pride characteristic of Ghanaian women, she speaks of the West in glorified terms. She speaks with what is almost a British accent, though she has never traveled outside of Ghana. She has a telephone in her shop, an anomaly in Makola. Mary is well educated by Ghanaian standards. She correctly asserts that a translator is not needed and that she wishes to converse in English; clearly a point of pride for her. Mary's religious attitudes demonstrate a conscious turn away from the traditional belief system. Mary is a devout Methodist. She renounces all traditional African religious beliefs. She does not believe that ancestral spirits have any power, arguing that only God affects the living. Rather than having outdooring ceremonies, she had her children christened.

Mary exhibits a fierce independence with regard to the other women in the market. She does not belong to the cloth sellers' trade association, and in general does not rely on the network of mutual assistance offered in the market.

CHAMLEE-WRIGHT   Do you belong to the cloth seller's trade association, or belong to any mutual assistance organizations?

MARY   I used to belong to these groups, but the women were always meddling in my affairs. I do not need the advice of illiterate women about how to run my business. I learned bookkeeping at a school. These women just want to look at my books so they can gossip about me.

CHAMLEE-WRIGHT   If you were to fall ill or run into financial difficulties, how would you keep your business afloat?

MARY   My husband would help me. I would not need to rely on the women in the market. Such organizations are more for the uneducated women.

Nor does Mary seem to be interested in the social relationships market trading afford most women.

> When I was a member of the cloth seller's trade association, the women put pressure on me to spend a great deal of time socializing. I simply wanted to finish my business and be done with it. After the meetings, many of the women wanted to stay out drinking and gossiping. I would rather spend the time with my husband and children.

Mary said that she was happy to give advice to any trader who asked for her counsel, but that she would rather not spend her free time with the other women in the market. Mary does get together with several other high-volume traders, however, to buy material in large quantities from time to time. These women could be a source of advice and short-term loans, but generally she relies on her husband if either is needed.

Since the decline of the colonialist era, Ghanaian social critics have lamented the popularity of Western over African culture and beliefs. In his novels on post-colonial Ghana, for instance, Ayi Kwei Armah (1968, 1969) offers a scathing critique of West African affinities towards Western materialism and elitism. But what is most revealing about Mary's responses is that they put in relief the importance credit and mutual assistance associations have for entrepreneurs who are not as affluent as she. Released from the financial constraints faced by most entrepreneurs, Mary has the luxury of choosing not to be a part of a close network of friends, as her husband is her main source of financial capital. This, then, indicates that for most entrepreneurs, the connections they forge in the marketplace play not only a social role, but a significant financial role as well.

After she finished secondary school, Mary trained with the wife of a diplomat for two years to acquire cooking and entertaining skills. She learned to prepare Western dishes and how to entertain in a formal (Western) setting. Mary's parents sent her to apprentice with this woman in hopes that she would later find employment as a cook for a member of the diplomatic corps. Mary never worked for another family, but she says that the training has served her well over the years. Towards the end of her service, the diplomat's wife introduced Mary to her young cousin. The two were married shortly after they met.

Mary considers herself to be an important part of her husband's career. She regularly entertains his colleagues as well as visiting VIPs, including members of the World Bank staff. Mary recalls her training in the service of the diplomat's wife.

I learned to cook Western dishes. When white people come to visit, they do not want to eat *fufu* and other African dishes. Whites will not come to your house if you serve them *fufu* and make them eat with their hands. My husband values my skills at giving parties.

This was not the only reference to what Westerners preferred. Without being obsequious, it seemed important to her to convey that she was acutely aware of what Westerners were accustomed to.

Mary's husband is a civil engineer. She does not know how much money he makes, but it is enough for them to have purchased a large two-story home outside of Accra. This is at least one indication that her husband is among the bureaucratic elite. It also enabled Mary to expand her business, as she could keep extra supplies in the house. Since she was then able to purchase larger quantities, her suppliers gave her an even better price. With the new house, Mary was also able to produce batik cloth and sell it along with the wax print cloth. The batik process takes up a considerable amount of space, so the house provides a great advantage.

Mary's affinity for Western styles carries over to her family life as well. Even though she runs a successful business, Mary considers her primary role as the caretaker of the nuclear family.

> I could sell more if I stayed later. Every day I leave by three o'clock. I could stay longer but I like to get home before my husband. I prepare his dinner every evening, so I do not like to be late.

Her husband helped to establish her in business, and has provided the capital necessary to expand over the years. However, she does not let the business take too much time away from her husband and five children. Except during the holiday rush, she does not come to the market on the weekends.

She and her husband consider their children's welfare to be of paramount importance. Their eldest son is in England studying at Cambridge University. They have plans to send their daughter abroad to study as soon as she is ready for university. As further evidence of their commitment to the nuclear family, they have a written will which designates their children as the sole beneficiaries of the family's inheritance. Mary feels that the written will is important so that her husband's brothers and nephews cannot use tribal custom to take away their children's inheritance. She feels that her husband's relatives are jealous of their social standing and if she and her husband were to die, she cannot trust them to take care of their children.

Yet, as Oppong (1974) observes, the elite still operate well within traditional parameters on many counts, and in fact Mary sees herself as operating within the extended family structure. She says that she does not trade so much because they need the money,[1] but rather because she likes to have her own resources. When Mary's niece moved to Accra, she had no source of credit and no capital of her own. Mary started her business by giving her a few bales of cloth. She continues to sell her niece cloth at cost, which represents a significant saving given the small quantities she sells. Though Mary speaks of the primacy of the nuclear family, she still demonstrates a sense of responsibility for the extended family as well. While she has benefited from her husband's affluent position, she recognizes the need for financial assistance and business contacts among her less affluent relatives. Mary's deliberate efforts to renounce many traditional beliefs have not erased the values inherent in the extended family system.

As for plans to expand in the future, Mary is hoping that her sister will be able to establish some lucrative business contacts for her. Mary's brother-in-law recently moved to England, in hopes of finding a factory job. Mary paid for her sister to travel to England, with the understanding that she would attempt to contact suppliers who would be willing to bypass the middleman. Her sister Joyce has met with several suppliers already. The English wax prints are expensive, thus it would be a profitable business move if she could establish a direct link with the manufacturer and not have to deal through the Ghanaian importer. Other than this, Mary has no plans to expand further. She says that trading already takes up too much of her time and she may decide to retire from the market in the next several years.

CONCLUSION

In general, participant observation techniques provide a view to the functions of indigenous institutions not available with abstract or statistical models. By their nature, indigenous credit and mutual assistance organizations do not lend themselves to systematic quantitative documentation. The government does not keep any statistics on such activities. No impact studies are conducted. No position papers or memos are issued when a market area is closed or destroyed. Thus, while speaking to market participants offers some advantages in all cases, participant observation is particularly advantageous within the context of the indigenous economy. In turn, economic theory provides a deep reservoir from which to draw relevant lines of inquiry. Ethnography consists of a constant interplay between the social scientist's own theoretical tools and the subjects' understanding of their situation.

The interpretive approach is particularly well suited to understanding the role of culture in economic development. If we are to understand how entrepreneurs perceive the obstacles and opportunities before them, we must acquire some comprehension of the complex web of meanings which guides and directs their focus. Understanding the web of meaning in which entrepreneurs form their plans cannot be achieved through arms-length statistical analysis. If there are benefits to be had in conducting such an investigation, however, our results are likely to be far more illuminating if we start with a firm understanding of the important questions to be pursued. Such questions are not formed in the abstract. They are generated by listening to the plans, frustrations, and expectations of market participants themselves.

6

CONCLUSION

Culture and economic development within the subjectivist framework

> The language of economic theory, like any language, provides a framework for thought; but it constrains our thought to remain within that framework. It focuses our attention; determines the way we conceive of things; and even determines what sort of things can be said. A conceptual framework is, therefore, at one and the same time an opportunity and a threat. Its positive side is that it facilitates thought within the framework. But its negative side arises from the fact that thought must be within the framework.
>
> (Coddington 1972, quoted in Addleson 1986: 5)

In his work on the role of subjectivism in economic theory, Mark Addleson (1986) suggests that while it is neither necessary nor possible to replace entirely one theoretical framework with another, it is necessary to work with the most suitable framework given the issues or problems to be addressed. If our task is to understand how equilibrium is achieved, then the neoclassical paradigm is the most suitable framework. But if our task is to understand how individuals make decisions and plans within a specific cultural context, the issues involved require a dramatically different approach. Specifically, the subjectivist framework is more appropriate for an understanding of this process.

> Agents [within the neoclassical framework] are "functions," . . . purely mechanistic abstractions . . . . Clearly, what is lacking is both a notion of a "mind at work" and a logical understanding of the accomplishments (intended as well as unintended) of one or more such "minds." Whether their absence is important depends on the issues economists seek to resolve with their theories. If these considerations are

deemed to be important, it should be recognized that the problem lies in the construction of the theory itself.

(Addleson 1986: 7)

As argued in the previous chapters, we are in a better position to understand economic development if we incorporate the role culture plays in that process. Yet this dramatically alters the theorist's picture of the world. Rather than describing the world as inhabited by cultureless economic agents who calculate maximizing solutions, the subjectivist describes it as being inhabited with "minds at work." The notion of "minds at work" does include the ability to weigh relative costs and benefits, yet the concept is much broader than the pure optimizing agent. Within the subjectivist framework, the individual is a creative being who, through a life of differentiated experience and influence, acquires a unique perspective. This unique perspective allows for an interpretive process through which the individual pieces together profit opportunities, makes production plans, and learns.

This unique interpretive perspective functions like a bundle of tools with which individuals approach problems and decisions. Within the subjectivist framework, choice is the result of individuals interpreting their own position in relation to their expectations of the external environment and the plans of others. Here, the "correct" path is not necessarily a determinate outcome. In seeking profit, prices are not marching orders for action. Different people will "read" different opportunities from the same set of prices, just as two people will glean different messages from the same work of literature.

As we include culture into our analysis of economic development, we start from the position that individuals must interpret market strategies from a particular perspective, and are not just mechanically responding to it. In analyzing a world inhabited by interpretive beings, the issues to be addressed shift dramatically. While equilibrium analysis is central to an optimization framework, it has less relevance within the subjectivist framework. However, other issues do emerge. For example, how do individuals engender the trust necessary to engage in mutual assistance associations? How does an entrepreneur convince a stranger that she is credit worthy? While such questions fall outside of the neoclassical framework, the subjectivist approach can accommodate this line of analysis.

While the basic logic of economics is applicable no matter what the cultural setting, the particular manifestation institutions and entrepreneurship take is culturally dependent. Credit markets in West Africa reflect the unique position women hold relative to their children for whom they must provide, and their husbands, who may pose a potential drain on their resources. Commonly shared notions of credit worthiness, tolerance of risk, and trust, which are all essential to the operations of the credit market, are also culturally dependent and will be responsible for its unique character. Yet, such considerations cannot be accommodated within an acultural construct. If we want to account for the diversity of interpretations within the market, a subjectivist or interpretive economics is required.

Further, radical subjectivism allows us to address the epistemological issues surrounding not only market processes, but cultural processes as well. The fundamentally dispersed nature of economic and cultural knowledge (in the Hayekian sense of the term) takes us a long way in understanding why the Ghanaian state failed to serve in the role of entrepreneur immediately following independence, and why government interventions designed to promote the indigenous market sector often do more harm than good. In addition, it explains why the state fails to anticipate the consequences of development policy, both economic and cultural. The state, either as development planning board or municipal authority, cannot centralize all the tacit rules of operation, subtle distinctions required of good judgments, or the information incorporated in the price system required to engineer or redirect the market process successfully.

Lastly, given the diversity which culture generates in economic processes, we come to understand why institutions grown up in the Western context meet with limited success once transplanted into the African context. The subjectivist framework is the most suitable approach with which to appreciate this point, as it is here that we understand why institutions emerge in the first place. Individual market participants operate in a perpetual state of ignorance. The "unlistability" of all the possible outcomes any one action might generate, and the constant reassessment of plans and expectations in light of new information, means that this state of ignorance is fundamental (O'Driscoll and Rizzo 1996). Out of this pervasive uncertainty emerge social institutions. As individuals are incapable of optimizing in the neoclassical sense, they adopt rules of thumb and behavioral conventions. The more uncertain the environment, the more individuals will engage in rule following behavior (Heiner 1983). By adopting a rule rather than optimizing, an individual limits the scope of possible choices to a relatively narrow set. If the convention is adopted community-wide, it constitutes a social institution. The networks of mutual support which have emerged among West African market women illustrate this point. Establishing a spirit of mutual support among close peers enables them to share risk, and better cope within an atmosphere of uncertainty.

In a world of dispersed knowledge, institutions serve the function of communicating information across individuals. Institutions such as credit organizations augment the price system in establishing a network of information concerning time preference, credit worthiness, and risk aversion. Whereas a maximization framework must treat institutions as forces exogenous to the market process, the subjectivist framework offers an explanation for their existence. The specific nature of the rules adopted will reflect the cultural context from which they emerge. Different communities will adopt specific rules and institutions, as the perspective of the individuals involved has been shaped by their particular cultural and historical context. While general institutional arrangements, such as the enforcement of contracts, private property rights, and free trade, are crucial to the development process in all cases, the particular arrangements by which such institutions are implemented will vary from one culture to another.

The tradition of radical subjectivism within the Austrian school of thought offers an opportunity to go beyond the acultural neoclassical model, not only with regard to development issues, but in all market processes. Regarding market participants as thinking, interpreting human beings requires that cultural forces be taken seriously, as it is culture which provides the framework in which that interpretation takes place. Thus, the arguments made here are both a challenge and an invitation. An interpretive, culturally informed economics represents a challenge to mainstream theorists to consider the limitations of acultural theory, particularly in the investigation of endogenous economic change such as entrepreneurship and economic development. The arguments made here are also an invitation to cultural and economic anthropologists in search of an interpretive alternative within the economics discipline, as it is not necessary to abandon economic theory in the investigation of non-Western economic phenomena. Further, the arguments made here are an invitation to Austrian economists to recognize the radical nature of their own paradigm when it comes to empirical research. The position of radical subjectivism, when taken seriously, suggests that cultural analysis has the potential to play a central role in the future development of Austrian economics. Lastly, as it has made an opening for cultural analysis to enter into economic investigations, Austrian economics stands to expand its influence across the social science disciplines.

NOTES

CHAPTER 1

1 For a detailed description of the wholesale markets in Kumasi, see Clark (1994).

2 Note also that Malinowski's explanation implies that Western economic agents do not display this sort of behavior, but rather are narrow maximizers of material wealth. The difference between the Trobriand Islander and the American who proudly tends his own garden only to give the produce away to neighbors and co-workers is a difference in degree, not in kind.

3 O' Driscoll and Rizzo (1996) argue further that neoclassical search theories which purport to demonstrate how economic agents acquire knowledge over time still fail to explain the process of market discovery, as what is to be discovered in such models is already determined within the starting assumptions of the model.

4 In Chapter 3, suggestions for further research on what may be primary metaphors operating for Ghanaian market women will be offered, but conclusions cannot be drawn here, as the present author does not possess the linguistic expertise required for such analysis.

5 For comparative anthropological work on production, see Halperin (1988). Halperin employs an evolutionary approach to demonstrate how the systematic differences in divisions of labor across gender and age, and political structure affect production methods over time.

CHAPTER 2

1 P.T. Bauer (1954) and Basil Yamey (Bauer and Yamey 1957) represent notable exceptions to the mainstream of development thought in the 1950s. Bauer and Yamey's arguments against the use of interventionist policies to stimulate development were largely dismissed by the mainstream of the discipline at the time.

2 Lewis (1959) advised that government spending ought to focus on public services, particularly on food agriculture, rather than on state-owned factories. Yet, Lewis was still in favor of state protection and

subsidization of industry where possible, for example in the case of beer, cement, bricks, wood products, soap, cigarettes, and prepared foods such as biscuits.

3 The plan was reminiscent of development planning strategy in Stalinist Russia. Evgenie Preobrazhensky provided the Soviets with a socialist model for industrialization, built around the concept he called "primitive socialist accumulation." Under Soviet industrialization, the state apparatus systematically siphoned off surplus from the agricultural sector, redirecting it to the industrial sector. For a detailed account of the similarities among the Soviet and Ghanaian industrialization drives, see Dowse (1969). See also Preobrazhensky (1965).

4 While Nkrumah was indeed a Marxist, he was also heavily influenced by Leninism. As was the case with Lenin, Nkrumah saw his political party as providing the role of socialist educator of the masses, i.e. the vanguard of the proletariat.

5 Such strategies were implemented regardless of the fact that private farmers had already established organizations which would help them to stabilize their income on their own (Coppin and High 1989).

6 For the purpose of this discussion, NGO and PVO programs will refer to programs principally supported by private foundations or voluntary contributions, though it is recognized that such programs often receive support, such as subsidized office space, from government agencies. The key issue is whether the program can establish and enforce its own rules of operation, or if it must answer to a government agency. Also for the purposes of this discussion, the World Bank and IMF are not considered NGOs or PVOs, as they rely on donor funds from governments and are answerable to them.

7 The gender specificity is accurate here. Virtually all of these mobile bankers known within the Makola Markets of Accra are in fact men.

CHAPTER 3

1 Destooling necessitated the severing of direct ties between the chief and the ancestors. This could be accomplished by causing the chief to sit on the ground or walk in bare feet, thereby repealing his sacred status (Busia 1968).

2 Islamic custom in Hausaland in northern Ghana does not allow for women to engage in trade openly, yet, remarkably, women are still a major source of local economic activity by using a network of children to market the goods the women produce (P. Hill 1969; Schildkrout 1983).

3 Formal education is often criticized for eroding apprenticeship arrangements on the one hand, yet not providing a useful education on the other (Robertson 1984a: 161–2, 1984b: 46).

CHAPTER 4

1 A version of this chapter appears in Chamlee (1993).

2 All dollar conversions are according to 1992 exchange rates.

3 Of the twenty-seven women who were asked about their religious affiliation, four were Muslim, two were agnostic, and the rest were Christian. Among the twenty-one Christians, fourteen different churches are represented: four Methodist, two Anglican, two Presbyterian, two Catholic, two Baptist, one Assemblies of God, one Eternal Life Bible Church, one Holy Church of God, one International Full Gospel Ministry, one Amazing Love Ministries, one Nazarene Healing Church, one Praise Chapel, one Central Gospel Church, one Deeper Life Ministries. Only Assemblies of God, Central Gospel Church, and Deeper Life Ministries did not offer mutual assistance for funerals, births, and marriages. All but the Anglican Church and the Central Gospel Church offered regular opportunities to receive business advice.

4 Clark (1994) observed a greater segregation according to tribal affiliation in her study of Kumasi market women. This difference between Accra and Kumasi may be due to the fact that the Ashanti so clearly dominate in Kumasi, whereas in Accra, the Akan had to negotiate their position into the urban environment with the traditionally urban Ga.

5 "Group *susu*" refers to a rotating credit organization which is administered by the women themselves as opposed to an outside agent, such as a *susu*-man.

6 A profile of Mary is presented in Chapter 5.

7 A profile of Abiba is presented in Chapter 5.

8 Note that these figures do not include taxes, the magnitudes of which will depend on the particular goods sold and the volume of trade. The operating taxes range from C40 per day (about $0.10) for small-scale street vendors to C100,000 per year ($235) for larger-scale cloth sellers in lock-up shops.

9 For a description of the effects of state and municipal policies on credit and trade associations in the central market of Kumasi, see Clark (1994).

CHAPTER 5

1 Such reports need to be taken "with a grain of salt," as many elite women consider it a sign of affluence if the family does not rely on the wife's income.

BIBLIOGRAPHY

Abu, Katharine (1983) "The Separateness of Spouses: Conjugal Resources in an Ashanti Town," in C. Oppong (ed.).

Adams, Dale W. and Von Pischke, J.D. (1992) "Microenterprise Credit Programs: Deja Vu," *World Development* 20(10): 1463–70.

Adepoju, Aderanti and Oppong, Christine (eds) (1994) *Gender, Work and Population in Sub-Saharan Africa*. London: James Currey.

Addleson, Mark (1986) "Radical Subjectivism and the Language of Austrian Economics," in I. Kirzner (ed.).

Afshar, H. (ed.) (1985) *Women, Work, and Ideology in the Third World*. New York: Tavistock Publications.

Ahmad, N. (1970) *Deficit Financing, Inflation and Capital Formation: The Ghanaian Experience 1960–1965*. Munich: Weitforum Verlag.

Akerlof, G.A. (1980) "The Theory of Social Custom of Which Unemployment May Be One Consequence," *Quarterly Journal of Economics* 94 (June): 749–75.

Alchian, Armen and Demsetz, Harold (1973) "The Property Rights Paradigm," *Journal of Economic History* 33(1): 17–25.

Althusser, L. (1969) *For Marx*. Harmondsworth: Penguin Books.

Ampofo-Tuffuor, E., DeLorme, C., and Kamerschen, D. (1991) "The Nature, Significance, and Cost of Rent Seeking in Ghana," *Kyklos* 44(1): 537–59.

Anker, Richard (1994) "Measuring Women's Participation in the African Labor Force," in A. Adepoju and C. Oppong (eds).

Arhin, Kwame (1983) "The Political and Military Roles of Akan Women," in C. Oppong (ed.).

—— (1985) *Traditional Rule in Ghana: Past and Present*. Accra: Sedco Publishing Company.

Armah, Ayi Kwei (1968) *The Beautiful Ones Are Not Yet Born*. London: Heinemann Educational Books.

—— (1969) *Fragments*. London: Heinemann Educational Books.

Armstrong, Robert P. (1996) *Ghana Country Assistance Review: A Study in Development Effectiveness*. Washington DC: The World Bank.

Arregui, Mariva and Baez, Clara (1991) "Free Trade Zones and Women Workers," in T. Wallace and C. March (eds).

185

Aryeetey, Ernest (1994) "Private Investment Under Uncertainty in Ghana," *World Development* 22(8): 1211–21.

Aryeetey, E., Baah-Nuakoh, A., Duggleby, T., Hettige, H., and Steel, W.F. (1994) "Supply and Demand for Finance of Small Enterprises in Ghana," *World Bank Discussion Papers: Africa Technical Department Series, Number 251.* Washington DC: The World Bank.

Axelrod, Robert (1981) "The Emergence of Cooperation Among Egoists," *American Political Science Review* 75(2): 306–18.

Ayittey, George (1991) *Indigenous African Institutions.* New York: Transnational Publishers.

Bahl, Roy W. (1972) "A Representative Tax System Approach to Measuring Tax Effort in Developing Countries," *IMF Staff Papers* (March).

Balkenhol, Bernd (1990) "Guaranteeing Bank Loans to Smaller Entrepreneurs in West Africa," *International Labor Review* 129(2): 245–53.

Bates, Robert H. (1981) *Markets and States in Tropical Africa.* Berkeley, CA: University of California Press.

—— (1995) "Social Dilemmas and Rational Individuals: An Assessment of the New Institutionalism" in J. Harris *et al.* (eds).

Bauer, P.T. (1954) *West African Trade: A Study of Competition, Oligopoly, and Monopoly in a Changing Economy.* Cambridge: Cambridge University Press.

—— (1981) *Equality, the Third Word, and Economic Delusion.* Cambridge, MA: Harvard University Press.

Bauer, P.T. and Yamey, Basil (1957) *The Economics of Underdeveloped Countries.* Chicago: University of Chicago Press.

Beckman, Bjorn (1976) *Organizing the Farmers: Cocoa, Politics, and National Development in Ghana.* New York: Holmes and Meier.

Belasco, Bernard (1980) *The Entrepreneur as Cultural Hero: Pre-adaptations in Nigerian Economic Development.* New York: J.F. Bergin.

Berger, Brigitte (1991) *The Culture of Entrepreneurship.* San Francisco: ICS Press.

Berger, Peter L. and Luckmann, Thomas (1966) *The Social Construction of Reality: A Treatise in the Sociology of Knowledge.* New York: Doubleday.

Berger, Marguerite (1989) "Giving Women Credit: The Strengths and Limitations of Credit as a Tool for Alleviating Poverty," *World Development* 17(7): 1017–32.

Bird, M. (1958) *Social Change in Kinship and Marriage Among the Yoruba of Western Nigeria.* Unpublished Ph.D. Dissertation, Edinburgh.

Bird-David, Nurit (1990) "The Giving Environment: Another Perspective on the Economic Systems of Gatherer-Hunters," *Current Anthropology* 31(2): 189–96.

—— (1992) "Beyond 'The Affluent Society': A Culturalist Reformulation," and Discussion, *Current Anthropology* 33 (February): 25–34.

Boserup, E. (1970) *Women's Role in Economic Development.* London: George Allen and Unwin; new edition (1989), London: Earthscan Publications.

Brett, E. A. "Institutional Theory and Social Change in Uganda," in J. Harris *et al.* (eds).

Brydon, Lynn (1985) "The Dimensions of Subordination: A Case Study of Avatime, Ghana," in H. Afshar (ed.).

Busia, K. A. (1968) *The Position of the Chief in the Modern Political System of Ashanti*. London: Frank Cass and Company.

Burling, Robbins (1962) "Maximization Theories and the Study of Economic Anthropology," *American Anthropologist* 64: 802–21.

Chamlee, Emily (1993) "Indigenous African Institutions," *The Cato Journal* 13(1): 79–99.

Chazen, Naomi (1983) *An Anatomy of Ghanaian Politics: Managing Political Recession, 1969–1982*. Boulder: Westview Press.

Chenery, Hollis B. (1959) "The Interdependence of Investment Decisions," in Abramovitz *et al.* (eds) *The Allocation of Economic Resources*. Stanford: Stanford University Press.

—— (1960) "Patterns of Industrial Growth," *American Economic Review* 50(4): 624–54.

Clammer, John, (ed.) (1978) *The New Economic Anthropology*. New York: St. Martin's Press.

—— (ed.) (1987) *Beyond the New Economic Anthropology*. London: Macmillan Press.

Clark, Gracia (1994) *Onions Are My Husband: Survival and Accumulation by West African Market Women*. Chicago: University of Chicago Press.

Clarkson, Kenneth (1975) "Property Rights, Incentives, and Economic Development," *Growth and Change* 6(April): 23–8.

Clegg, Stewart. and Redding, S. Gordon (eds) (1990) *Capitalism in Contrasting Cultures*. New York: Walter de Gruyter.

Coase, Ronald H. (1937) "The Nature of the Firm," *Economica* 4:3, 86–405.

—— (1960) "The Problem of Social Cost," *Journal of Law and Economics* 3: 1–44.

Cockcroft, James D., Frank, A.G., and Johnson D.L. (1972) *Dependence and Underdevelopment: Latin America's Political Economy*. Garden City, NY: Doubleday.

Coddington, Alan (1972) "Positive Economics," *Canadian Journal of Economics* 5(1): 1–15.

Cook, Scott (1966) "The Obsolete Anti-Market Mentality: A Critique of the Substantive Approach to Economic Anthropology," *American Anthropologist* 68: 323–45.

Coppin, Clayton and High, Jack (1989) "Property Rights, Entrepreneurship, and Economic Development: Case Studies of Ghana and Cameroon," *US AID Report* Washington DC.

Cornell, Stephen and Kalt, Joseph (1995) "Constitutional Rule Among the Sioux and Apache," *Economic Inquiry* 33(3): 402–26.

Cutler, A., Hindess, B. Hirst, P., and Hussain, A. (1977) *Marx's Capital and Capitalism Today*. New York: Routledge and Kegan Paul.

Daaku, Kwame (1971) "Trade and Trading Patterns of the Akan in the Seventeenth and Eighteenth Centuries," in C. Meillassoux (ed.).

Dadson, J.A. (1973) "Farm Size and Modernization of Agriculture in Ghana," in I.M. Ofori (ed.) *Factors in Agricultural Growth in West Africa*. Legon: ISSER, University of Ghana.

Dalton, George (1961) "Economic Theory and Primitive Society," *American Anthropologist* 63: 1–25.

Danquah, J.B. (1968) *The Akan Doctrine of God*. London: Frank Cass and Company.

De Marees, Pieter ([1602] 1985) *Chronicles of the Gold Coast of Guinea*. A. Van Dantzig and A. Smith, translators, Oxford: Oxford University Press.

Denzau, Arthur and North, Douglass C. (1994) "Shared Mental Models: Ideologies and Institutions," *Kyklos* 47(1): 3–31.

De Soto, Hernando (1989) *The Other Path: The Invisible Revolution in the Third World*. New York: Harper and Row.

Dinan, Carmel (1983) "Sugar Daddies and Gold Diggers: The White-Collar Single Women in Accra" in C. Oppong (ed.).

Dowse, Robert (1969) *Modernization in Ghana and the USSR: A Comparative Study*. New York: Routledge and Kegan Paul.

Dupre, G. and Rey, P. (1973) "Reflections on the Pertinence of a Theory of the History of Exchange," *Economy and Society* 2(2): 131–63.

Ebeling, Richard (1986) "Toward a Hermeneutical Economics: Expectations, Prices, and the Role of Interpretation in a Theory of the Market Process," in I. Kirzner (ed.).

Economist Intelligence Unit (1995) *Ghana: Country Profile*. London: EIU Press.

Elson, Diane (1991) "Structural Adjustment: Its Effect on Women," in T. Wallace and C. March (eds).

Ensminger, Jean (1991) "The Political Economy of Changing Property Rights: Dismantling a Pastoral Commons," *American Ethnologist* 18 (4) (November): 683–99.

—— (1992) *Making a Market: The Institutional Transformation of an African Society*. Cambridge: Cambridge University Press.

Etienne, Mona (1983) "Gender Relations and the Conjugality Among the Baule," in C. Oppong (ed.).

Field, M.J. (1937) *Religion and Medicine of the Ga People*. Oxford: Oxford University Press.

Fields, Karen E. (1985) *Revival and Rebellion in Colonial Central Africa*. Princeton: Princeton University Press.

Firth, Raymond (1951) *Elements of Social Organization*. London: C.A. Watts and Co.

Fischer-Quinke, Gerhard (1990) "Small Enterprises for the Needs of the People? Ghana's 'Small-Scale Industrial Take-Off'," *African Development Perspectives Yearbook, Volume I*. Berlin: Verlag, Schelzky and Jeep.

Fong, P. E. (1988) "The Distributive Features of Two City-States' Development: Hong Kong and Singapore," in P. Berger (ed.) *In Search of an East Asian Development Model*. New Brunswick: Transaction Books.

Frank, Andre Gunder (1969) *Capitalism and Underdevelopment in Latin America: Historical Studies of Chile and Brazil*. New York: Monthly Review Press.

Frankenberg, R. (1967) "Economic Anthropology: One Anthropologist's View," in R. Firth (ed.) *Themes in Economic Anthropology*. London: Tavistock Publications.

Frimpong-Ansah, Jonathan H. (1991) *The Vampire State in Africa: The Political Economy of Decline in Ghana*. Trenton, NJ: Africa World Press.

Geertz, Clifford (1973) "Thick Description: Towards an Interpretive Theory of Culture," *The Interpretation of Cultures: Selected Essays*. New York: Basic Books.

George, Charles H. and George, Katherine (1958) "Protestantism and Capitalism in Pre-Revolutionary England," *Church History* 27: 351–71.

Godelier, M. (1972) *Rationality and Irrationality in Economics*. London: New Left Books.

Goldschmidt-Clermont, Luisella (1994) "Assessing Women's Economic Contributions in Domestic and Related Activities," in A. Adepoju and C. Oppong (eds).

Goodfellow, D.M. (1939) *Principles of Economic Sociology*. London: Routledge and Kegan Paul.

Grossman, Gregory (1977) "The Second Economy of the USSR," *Problems of Communism* 26(5): 25–40.

—— (1982) "The Shadow Economy in the Socialist Sector of the USSR," *The CMEA Five-Year Plans (1981–1985) in a New Perspective: Planned and Non-Planned Economies*. NATO: Economics and Information Directories.

Gudeman, Stephen (1986) *Economics as Culture: Models and Metaphors of Livelihood*. London: Routledge.

Guglar, Josef (1981) "The Second Sex in Town," in C. Steady (ed.).

Guyer, Jane (1978) *Women's Work in the Food Economy of the Cocoa Belt: A Comparison*. Brookline, MA: African Studies Center, Boston University.

Hafkin, Nancy J. and Bay, Edna G. (eds) (1976) *Women in Africa: Studies in Social and Economic Change*, Stanford: Stanford University Press.

Hagan, George P. (1983) "Marriage, Divorce and Polygyny in Winneba," in C. Oppong (ed.).

Halperin, Rhoda (1988) *Economies Across Cultures: Towards a Comparative Science of the Economy*. New York: St. Martin's Press.

Harris, J., Hunter, J., and Lewis, C.M. (eds) (1995) *The New Institutional Economics and Third World Development*. London: Routledge.

Hay, Jean and Stichter, Sharon (eds) (1984) *African Women South of the Sahara*. New York: Longman Group.

Hayek, F.A. ([1935a] 1948) "Socialist Calculation I: The Nature and History of the Problem," in *Individualism and Economic Order*.

—— ([1935b] 1948) "Socialist Calculation II: The State of the Debate (1935)," in *Individualism and Economic Order*.

—— ([1940] 1948) "Socialist Calculation III: The Competitive 'Solution'," in *Individualism and Economic Order*.

—— ([1945] 1948) "The Use of Knowledge in Society," in *Individualism and Economic Order*.

—— ([1946] 1948) "The Meaning of Competition," in *Individualism and Economic Order*.

189

—— (1948) *Individualism and Economic Order*. Chicago: University of Chicago Press.

—— (1952) *The Counter-Revolution of Science*. Glencoe, IL: Free Press.

—— (1967) *Studies in Philosophy, Politics and Economics*. Chicago: University of Chicago Press.

—— (1973) *Law, Legislation and Liberty, Volume I: Rules and Order*. Chicago: University of Chicago Press.

—— (1978) "Competition as a Discovery Procedure," in *New Studies in Philosophy, Politics, and Economics*. Chicago: University of Chicago Press.

—— (1988) *The Fatal Conceit*. Chicago: University of Chicago Press.

Haynes, Jeffrey (1989) "Ghana: Indebtedness, Recovery, and the IMF, 1977–87," in T. Parfitt and S. Riley (eds).

Heiner, R. (1983) "The Origin of Predictable Behavior," *American Economic Review* 73: 560–95.

Herskovits, Melville J. ([1940] 1952) *Economic Anthropology*. New York: Alfred A. Knopf.

Hiebert, Murray (1993) "Chain Lending: Informal Credit Fills Void Left by Vietnam's Banks," *Far Eastern Economic Review* (March 4).

High, Jack (1982) "Alertness and Judgment: Comment on Kirzner," in I. Kirzner (ed.) *Method, Process, and Austrian Economics*. Lexington: Lexington Books.

Hill, Christopher (1961) "Protestantism and the Rise of Capitalism," in F.J. Fisher (ed.) *Essays in the Economic and Social History of Tudor and Stuart England in Honour of R.H. Tawney*. Cambridge: Cambridge University Press.

—— (1966) *Society and Puritanism in Pre-Revolutionary England*. London: Secker and Warburg.

—— (1969) *Reformation to Industrial Revolution: A Social and Economic History of Britain, 1530–1780*. London: Weidenfeld and Nicolson.

Hill, Polly (1969) "Hidden Trade in Hausaland," *Man* 4: 392–409.

—— (1986) *Development Economics on Trial*. Cambridge: Cambridge University Press.

Hirschman, Albert O. (1958) *The Strategy of Economic Development*. New Haven: Yale University Press.

Ibrahim, Rhoda (1991) "The Changing Lives of Somali Women," in T. Wallace and C. March (eds).

International Labor Organization (1990) *African Employment Report*, Addis Ababa: International Labor Organization.

International Monetary Fund (annual) *International Financial Statistics* Washington DC: International Monetary Fund.

Jahoda, G. (1959) "Love, Marriage, and Social Change: Letters to the Advice Column of a West African Newspaper," *Africa* 29: 177–90.

Jevons, William Stanley ([1879] 1965) *The Theory of Political Economy*, 2nd edition. New York: Kelley Augustus.

Kahn, Joel S. (1978) "Marxist Anthropology and Peasant Economics: A Study of the Social Structures of Underdevelopment," in J. Clammer (ed.).

Katsenelinboigen, A. (1977) "Coloured Markets in the Soviet Union," *Soviet Studies* 29(1): 62–85.

Keesing, Roger M. (1975) *Kin Groups and Social Structure*. New York: Holt, Rinehart, and Winston.

Killick, Tony (1978) *Development Economics in Action: A Study of Economic Policies in Ghana*. New York: St. Martin's Press.

Kilson, Marion (1974) *African Urban Kinsmen: The Ga of Central Accra*. New York: St. Martin's Press.

Kirzner, Israel (1973) *Competition and Entrepreneurship*. Chicago: Chicago University Press.

—— (1979) *Perception, Opportunity and Profit: Studies in the Theory of Entrepreneurship*. Chicago: Chicago University Press.

—— (ed.) (1986) *Subjectivism, Intelligibility and Economic Understanding: Essays in Honor of Ludwig M. Lachmann on his Eightieth Birthday*. New York: New York University Press.

Klein, Benjamin and Leffler, Keith (1981) "The Role of Market Forces in Assuring Contractual Performance," *Journal of Political Economy* 89(4): 615–41.

Knight, Frank (1928) "Historical and Theoretical Issues in the Problem of Modern Capitalism," *Journal of Economic and Business History* 1: 119–36.

Kolakowski, Leszek (1978) *Main Currents of Marxism, Volume I: The Founders*. New York: Oxford University Press.

Konig, Wolfgang and Koch, Michael (1990) "External Financing of Microenterprises in LDCs: Lessons From Colombia," *Savings and Development* 14(3): 233–45.

Kotkin, Joel (1992) *Tribes: How Race, Religion, and Identity Determine Success in the New Global Economy*. New York: Random House.

Kronman, Anthony (1985) "Contract Law and the State of Nature," *Journal of Law, Economics, and Organization* 1(1): 5–32.

Kuhn, A. and Wolpe, A. (eds) (1978) *Feminism and Materialism*. London: Routledge and Kegan Paul.

Kurwijila, R. and Due, J.M. (1991) "Credit for Women's Income Generation: A Tanzanian Case Study," *Canadian Journal of African Studies* 25(1): 90–103.

Lachmann, Ludwig M. (1971) *The Legacy of Max Weber*. Berkeley: Glendessary Press.

—— (1976) "From Mises to Shackle: An Essay on Austrian Economics and the Kaleidic Society," *Journal of Economic Literature* 14: 54–62.

—— (1978) *Capital and Its Structure*. Kansas City: Sheed, Andrews and McMeel.

Landa, Janet (1991) "Culture and Entrepreneurship in Less Developed Countries: Ethnic Trading Networks as Economic Organizations," in B. Berger (ed.).

Lange, Oskar ([1936] 1964) "On the Economic Theory of Socialism," in B.E. Lippincott (ed.) ([1938] 1964) *On the Economic Theory of Socialism*. New York: McGraw-Hill.

—— (1967) "The Computer and the Market," in C.H. Feinstein (ed.) *Socialism, Capitalism, and Economic Growth: Essays Presented to Maurice Dobb*. Cambridge: Cambridge University Press.

Langley, J. Ayo (ed.) (1979) *Ideologies of Liberation in Black Africa, 1856–1970*. London: Rex Collins.

Lavoie, Donald C. (1986) "Euclideanism vs. Hermeneutics: A Reinterpretation of Misesian Apriorism," in I. Kirzner (ed.).

—— (1990) "Hermeneutics, Subjectivity, and the Lester-Machlup Debate: Toward A More Anthropological Approach to Empirical Economics," in W. Samuels (ed.) *Economics As Discourse*. Boston: Kluwer Academic Publishers.

—— (1991) "The Discovery and Interpretation of Profit Opportunities: Culture and the Kirznerian Entrepreneur," in B. Berger (ed.).

Lavoie, Donald C. and Chamlee-Wright, Emily (forthcoming) *Culture and the Spirit of Enterprise*. Washington DC: Cato.

Lawson, Rowena M. (1971) "The Supply Response of Retail Trading Services to Urban Population Growth in Ghana," in C. Meillassoux (ed.).

LeClair, Edward (1962) "Economic Theory and Economic Anthropology," *American Anthropologist* 64: 1179–203.

LeClair, Edward and Schneider, Harold (1968) *Economic Anthropology: Readings in Theory and Analysis*. New York: Holt, Rinehart, and Winston.

Leibenstein, Harvey (1957) *Economic Backwardness and Economic Growth*. New York: Wiley Press.

Levy, B. (1993) "Obstacles in Developing Indigenous Small and Medium Enterprises: An Empirical Assessment," *World Bank Economic Review* 7(1): 65–83.

Lewis, Barbara C. (1976) "The Limitations of Group Action Among Entrepreneurs: The Market Women of Abidjan, Ivory Coast," in J. Hafkin and S. Bay (eds).

—— (1977) "Economic Activity and Marriage Among Ivorian Urban Women," in A. Schlegel (ed.) *Sexual Stratification: A Cross Cultural View*. New York: Columbia University Press.

Lewis, W.A. (1944) *Machinery for Economic Development in the Colonies*. London: Colonial Economic Advisory Committee.

—— (1955) *The Theory of Economic Growth*. London: Allen and Unwin.

—— (1959) "On Assessing a Development Plan," *Economic Bulletin of Ghana* no. 6–7.

—— (1965) *Politics in West Africa*. London: Allen and Unwin.

Little, Kenneth (1965) *West African Urbanization: A Study of Voluntary Associations in Social Change*. Cambridge: Cambridge University Press.

—— (1966) "Attitudes Towards Marriage and the Family Among Educated Young Sierra Leoneans," in P.C. Lloyd (ed.) *The New Elite of Tropical Africa*. London: Oxford University Press.

—— (1973) *African Women in Towns*. Cambridge: Cambridge University Press.

Lycette, Margaret (1985) "Financing Women in the Third World," *International Center for Research on Women Occasional Paper 1*. Washington DC: International Center for Research on Women.

Lycette, Margaret and White, K. (1989) "Improving Women's Access to Credit in Latin America and the Caribbean: Policy and Project Recommendations," in M. Berger and M. Buvinic (eds) *Women's Ventures: Assistance to the Informal Sector in Latin America*. West Hartford, CT: Kumarian Press: 19–44.

Malinowski, Bronislaw ([1922] 1961) *Argonauts of the Western Pacific*. New York: Dutton and Company.

Manoukian, Madeline (1950) *Western Africa: Akan and Ga-Adangme Peoples*. London: International African Institute.

Marshall, Gordon (1982) *In Search of the Spirit of Capitalism: An Essay on Max Weber's Protestant Ethic Thesis*. New York: Columbia University Press.

McClelland, D.C. (1961) *The Achieving Society*. Princeton: D. Van Nostrand.

McCloskey, D. (1994) *Knowledge and Persuasion in Economics*. Cambridge: Cambridge University Press.

McCloskey, D. and Klamer, Arjo (1994) "One Quarter of GDP is Persuasion," Keynote Address for the Southern Economic Association.

McIntosh, S.K. and McIntosh, R.J. (1984) "The Early City in West Africa: Towards an Understanding," *African Archeological Review* 2: 73–98.

—— (1993) "Cities Without Citadels: Understanding Urban Origins Along the Middle Niger," in T. Shaw, *et al.* (eds).

Meillassoux, Claude (ed.) (1971) *The Development of Indigenous Trade and Markets in West Africa*. London: Oxford University Press.

—— (1972) "From Reproduction to Production: A Marxist Approach to Economic Anthropology," *Economy and Society* 1(1).

—— (1976) "The Social Organization of the Peasantry," in D. Seddon (ed.) *Relations and Production: Marxist Approaches to Economic Anthropology*. London: Frank Cass.

Menger, Carl (1976) *The Principles of Economics*. J. Dingwall and B.F. Hoselitz (trans.) New York: New York University Press.

Middleton, John (1983) "One Hundred and Fifty Years of Christianity in a Ghanaian Town," *Africa* 53(3): 2–19.

Mikell, Gwendolyn (1989) *Cocoa and Chaos in Ghana*. New York: Paragon House.

Mises, Ludwig von ([1922] 1932) *Socialism*. Indianapolis: Liberty Press.

—— (1933] 1981) *Epistemological Problems of Economics*. G. Reisman (trans.), New York: New York University Press.

—— ([1949] 1966) *Human Action*. New Haven: Yale University Press.

Morewagae, Boitumelo S., Seemule, Monica, and Rempel, Henry (1995) "Access to Credit for Non-Formal Micro-Enterprises in Botswana," *The Journal of Development Studies* 31(3): 481–504.

Mullings, L. (1976) "Women and Economic Change in Africa," in N. Hafkin and E. Bay (eds).

Myrdal, Gunnar (1953) *The Political Element in the Development of Economic Theory*. London: Routledge and Kegan Paul.

—— (1956) *An International Economy*. New York: Harpers Publishing.

—— (1957) *Economic Theory and Under-Developed Regions*. London: Methuen.

Nabli, Mustapha K. and Jefrey B. Nugent (1989) "The New Institutional Economics and Its Applicability to Development," *World Development* 17(9): 1333–47.

Newbury, Colin W. (1971) "Prices and Profitability in Early Nineteenth Century West African Trade," in C. Meillassoux (ed.).

Nkrumah, Kwame (1964) "The Programme for Work and Happiness," in *The Revolutionary Path*. New York: International Publishers.

North, Douglass C. (1987) "Institutions, Transactions Costs, and Economic Growth," *Economic Inquiry* 25(July): 419–28.

—— (1989) "Institutions and Economic Growth: An Historical Introduction," *World Development* 17(9): 1319–32.

—— (1990) *Institutions, Institutional Change, and Economic Performance*. Cambridge: Cambridge University Press.

—— (1994) "Economic Performance Through Time," *American Economic Review*. 84(3): 359–67.

—— (1995) "The New Institutional Economics and Third World Development," in J. Harris *et al.* (eds).

O'Driscoll, Gerald and Rizzo, Mario (1996) "Subjectivism, Uncertainty, and Rules," in I. Kirzner (ed.).

—— (1996) *The Economics of Time and Ignorance*. Revised edition. London: Routledge.

Olson, Mancur (1965) *The Logic of Collective Action*. Cambridge, MA: Harvard University Press.

—— (1982) *The Rise and Decline of Nations: Economic Growth, Stagflation, and Social Rigidities*. New Haven: Yale University Press.

Oppong, Christine (1974) *Marriage Among a Matrilineal Elite*. London: Cambridge University Press.

—— (ed.) (1983) *Female and Male in West Africa*. London: George Allen and Unwin.

Pala, Achola O. (1981) "Definitions of Women in Development: An African Perspective," in C. Steady (ed.).

Parfitt, Trevor W. and Riley, Stephen P. (1989) *The African Debt Crisis*. New York: Routledge.

Parker, Ronald L., Riopelle, Randall, and Steel, William F. (1995) "Small Enterprises Adjusting to Liberalization in Five African Countries," *World Bank Discussion Papers: African Technical Department Series, Number 271*. Washington DC: International Bank for Reconstruction and Development.

—— (1970) *West African Religion*. New York: Barnes and Noble.

—— (1976) *Africa's Three Religions*. London: Sheldon Press.

Peil, Margaret (1979) "Urban Women in the Labor Force," *Sociology of Work and Occupations* 6: 482–501.

Pellow, Deborah (1977) *Women in Accra: Options for Autonomy*. Algonac: Reference Publications.

Pellow, Deborah and Chazen, Naomi (1986) *Ghana: Coping With Uncertainty*. Boulder: Westview Press.

Phillipson, David W. (1993) *African Archeology*, 2nd edition. Cambridge: Cambridge University Press.

Plattner Stuart (ed.) (1989) *Economic Anthropology*. Stanford: Stanford University Press.

Poggi, Gianfranco (1983) *Calvinism and the Capitalist Spirit: Max Weber's Protestant Ethic*. London: Macmillan Press.

Polanyi, Karl (1944) *The Great Transformation*. New York: Holt, Reinhart, and Winston.

—— (1957) "The Economy as Instituted Process," in Polanyi *et al.*

Polanyi, Karl, Arensberg, C.W. and Pearson, H.W. (eds) (1957) *Trade and Market in the Early Empires*. New York: Free Press.

Preobrazhensky, E. (1965) *The New Economics*. B. Pearce (trans.) London: Oxford University Press.

Putnam, Robert D. (1993) *Making Democracy Work: Civic Traditions in Modern Italy*. Princeton: Princeton University Press.

Putnam, Robert D., Leonardi, R., Nanetti, R., and Pavoncello, F. (1983) "Explaining Institutional Success: The Case of Italian Regional Government," *The American Political Science Review* 77: 55–74.

Rayfield, J.R. (1974) "Theories of Urbanization and the Colonial City in West Africa," *Africa* 44: 163–85.

Rimmer, Douglas (1969) "The Abstraction from Politics," *Journal of Development Studies* 5 (5): 190–204.

—— (1992) *Staying Poor: Ghana's Political Economy 1950–1990*. New York: Pergamon Press.

Robbins, Lionel (1932) "The Subject Matter of Economics," in *An Essay on the Nature and Significance of Economic Science*. London: Macmillan; New York: St. Martin's Press.

Robertson, Claire (1974) "Economic Women in Africa: Profit-making Techniques of Accra Market Women," *Journal of Modern Africa Studies* 12: 657–64.

—— (1976) "Ga Women and Socioeconomic Change in Accra, Ghana," in N. Hafkin and E. Bay (eds).

—— (1983) "The Death of Makola and Other Tragedies," *Canadian Journal of African Studies* 17(1): 469–95.

—— (1984a) *Sharing the Same Bowl: A Socioeconomic History of Women and Class in Accra, Ghana*. Bloomington: Indiana University Press.

——(1984b) "Women in the Urban Economy," in J. Hay and S. Stichter (eds).

Robertson, H.M. (1933) *Aspects of the Rise of Economic Individualism: A Criticism of Max Weber and His School*. Cambridge: Cambridge University Press.

Roemer, Michael (1981) *Economic Development in Africa: Performance Since Independence and a Strategy for the Future*. Cambridge: Harvard University Press.

Rooney, David (1988) *Kwame Nkrumah: The Political Kingdom in the Third World*. New York: St. Martin's Press.

Sahlins, M. (1960) "Political Power and the Economy in Primitive Society," in G. E. Dole and R.L. Careiro (eds) *Essays in the Science of Culture*. New York: Crowell.

—— (1963) "On the Sociology of Primitive Exchange," in *The Relevance of Models for Social Anthropology*. London: Tavistock Publications.

—— (1968) "Notes on the Original Affluent Society," in R.B. Lee and I. De Vore (eds) *Man and Hunter*. Chicago: Aldine: 85–59.

—— (1972) "The Original Affluent Society," in *Stone Age Economics*. London: Tavistock: 1–39.

——(1976) *Culture and Practical Reason*. Chicago: University of Chicago Press.

Samuelson, Kurt (1961) *Religion and Economic Action*. London: Heinemann.

195

Sandesara, J.C. (1991) "Small-Scale Industrialization: The Indian Experience" in H. Thomas, F. Uribe-Echevarria, and H. Romijn (eds) *Small-Scale Production*. London: IT Publications.

Sanjek, R. and Sanjek, L. (1976) "Notes on Women and Work in Adabraka," *African Urban Notes* 2(2): 1–27.

Sarbah, John Mensah (1968) *Fanti Customary Laws*. London: Frank Cass and Company.

Schapera I. (1957) "The Sources of Law in Tswana Tribal Courts: Legislation and Precedent," *Journal of African Law* 1(3): 150–62.

Schildkrout, Enid (1983) "Dependence and Autonomy: the Economic Activities of Secluded Hausa Women in Kano," in C. Oppong (ed.).

Schumpeter, Joseph ([1934] 1983) *The Theory of Economic Development*. New Brunswick: Transaction Books.

Scitovsky, Tibor (1954) "Two Concepts of External Economies," *Journal of Political Economy* 62(2): 143–51.

Seddon, David (1978) "Economic Anthropology or Political Economy?: The Barotse Social Formation—A Case Study," in J. Clammer (ed.).

Seers, D. and Ross, C. (1952) *Report on the Financial and Physical Problems of Development in the Gold Coast*. Government Printer: Accra.

Shanmugam, Bala (1991) "Socio-Economic Development Through the Informal Credit Market," *Modern Asian Studies*. 25(2): 209–25.

Shaw, T., Sinclair, P., Andah, B., and Okpoko, A. (eds) (1993) *The Archeology of Africa: Food, Metals and Towns*. London: Routledge.

Silber, Ilana F. (1993) "Monasticism and the 'Protestant Ethic': Asceticism, Rationality and Wealth in the Medieval West," *The British Journal of Sociology* 44(1): 103–23.

Simis, Konstantin (1982) *USSR—The Corrupt Society: The Secret World of Soviet Capitalism*. New York: Simon and Schuster.

Simms, Ruth (1981) "The African Woman as Entrepreneur: Problems and Perspectives on Their Roles," in C. Steady (ed.).

Smith, Paul (1978) "Domestic Labor and Marx's Theory of Value," in A. Kuhn and A. Wolpe (eds).

Squire, L. (1981) *Employment Policy in Developing Countries : A Survey of Issues and Evidence*. Oxford: Oxford University Press.

Steady, Chioma (ed) (1981) *The Black Woman Cross Culturally*. Cambridge, MA: Schenkman Publishing.

Steel, William and Aryeetey, Ernest (1994) "Informal Savings Collectors in Ghana: Can they Intermediate?" *Finance and Development* 31(March): 36–7.

Steel, William F. and Takagi, Yasuoki (1983) "Small Enterprise Development and the Employment-Output Trade-Off," *Oxford Economic Papers* 35: 423–46.

Steel, William F. and Webster, Leila M. (1991) "Small Enterprises Under Adjustment in Ghana," *World Bank Technical Paper Number 138, Industry and Finance Series*. Washington DC: The World Bank.

Stein, Howard (1995) "Institutional Theories and Structural Adjustment in Africa," in J. Harris *et al.* (eds).

Sudarkasa, Niara (1973) *Where Women Work: A Study of Yoruba Women in the Marketplace and in the Home*. Museum of Anthropology, Anthropological Papers Number 53, Ann Arbor: University of Michigan Press.

—— (1981) "Female Employment and Family Organization in West Africa," in C. Steady (ed.).

Szereszewski, R. (1965) *Structural Changes in the Economy of Ghana 1891–1911*. London: Weidenfeld and Nicolson.

Tannen, Deborah (1982) "Ethnic Style in Male-Female Conversation," in J.J. Gumperz (ed.) *Language and Social Identity*. Cambridge: Cambridge University Press.

—— (1990a) "Gender Differences in Topical Coherence: Creating Involvement in Best Friends' Talk," *Discourse Processes* 13:1.

—— (1990b) *You Just Don't Understand*. New York: Ballantine Books.

Tawney, R.H. ([1926] 1972) *Religion and the Rise of Capitalism*. Harmondsworth: Penguin.

Terray, E. (1972) *Marxism and Primitive Societies*. New York: Monthly Review Press.

—— (1974) "Long Distance Exchange and the Information of the State: the Case of the Abron Kingdom of Gyaman," *Economy and Society* 3(1): 315–45.

Timberg, Thomas A. and Aiyar, C.V. (1984) "Informal Credit Markets in India," *Economic Development and Cultural Change* 33(October): 43–59.

Trevor-Roper, H.R. (1963) "Religion and Reformation, and Social Change," in *Historical Studies 4* (Papers read before the Fifth Irish Conference of Historians). London: Bowes and Bowes.

United Nations (1995) "Issues Concerning SMEs' Access to Finance," in *United Nations Conference on Trade and Development*, 2nd Session (July 3)

Vellenga, Dorothy D. (1983) "Who is a Wife? Legal Expressions of Heterosexual Conflicts in Ghana," in C. Oppong (ed.).

Wahid, Abu N.M. (1994) "The Grameen Bank and Poverty Alleviation in Bangladesh: Theory, Evidence and Limitations" *The American Journal of Economics and Sociology* 53(1): 1–15.

Wallace, Tina and March, Candida (1991) *Changing Perceptions: Writings on Gender and Development*. Oxford: Oxfam Press.

Wallis, John J. and North, Douglass C. (1986) "Measuring the Transaction Sector in the American Economy, 1870–1970," in S.L. Engerman and R.E. Gallman (eds) *Long-Term Factors in American Economic Growth*. Chicago: University of Chicago Press.

Waring, Marilyn (1988) *If Women Counted: A New Feminist Economics*. San Francisco: Harper and Row.

Waters, Alan Rufus (1987) "Economic Growth and the Property Rights Regime," *Cato Journal* 7(1): 99–115.

Weber, Max ([1922] 1958) *The Protestant Ethic and the Spirit of Capitalism*. London: Unwin Paperbacks.

Wipper, Audrey (1984) "Women's Voluntary Associations," in J. Hay and S. Stichter (eds).

Yelpaala, Kojo (1983) "Circular Arguments and Self-Fulfilling Definitions: Statelessness and the Dagaaba," *History of Africa* 10: 49–385.

INDEX